D0788669

Gender Influences in
Classroom Interaction

EDUCATIONAL PSYCHOLOGY

Allen J. Edwards, Series Editor
Department of Psychology
Southwest Missouri State University
Springfield, Missouri

In preparation

Leo H. T. West and A. Leon Pines (eds.). Cognitive Structure and Conceptual Change

Gilbert R. Austin and Herbert Garber (eds.). Research on Exemplary Schools

Published

Louise Cherry Wilkinson and Cora B. Marrett (eds.). Gender Influences in Classroom Interaction

Catherine T. Best (ed.). Hemispheric Function and Collaboration in the Child

Charles D. Holley and Donald F. Dansereau (eds.). Spatial Learning Strategies: Techniques, Applications, and Related Issues

John R. Kirby (ed.). Cognitive Strategies and Educational Performance

Penelope L. Peterson, Louise C. Wilkinson, and Maureen Hallinan (eds.). The Social Context of Instruction: Group Organization and Group Processes

Michael J. A. Howe (ed.). Learning from Television: Psychological and Educational Research

Ursula Kirk (ed.). Neuropsychology of Language, Reading, and Spelling

Judith Worell (ed.). Psychological Development in the Elementary Years

Wayne Otto and Sandra White (eds.). Reading Expository Material

John B. Biggs and Kevin F. Collis. Evaluating the Quality of Learning: The Solo Taxonomy (Structure of the Observed Learning Outcome)

Gilbert R. Austin and Herbert Garber (eds.). The Rise and Fall of National Test Scores

Lynne Feagans and Dale C. Farran (eds.). The Language of Children Reared in Poverty: Implications for Evaluation and Intervention

Patricia A. Schmuck, W. W. Charters, Jr., and Richard O. Carlson (eds.). Educational Policy and Management: Sex Differentials

The list of titles in this series continues at the end of this volume.

Gender Influences in Classroom Interaction

Edited by

Louise Cherry Wilkinson

Wisconsin Center for Education Research
University of Wisconsin, Madison
  and
Doctoral Program in Educational Psychology
City University of New York-Graduate School
New York

Cora B. Marrett

Wisconsin Center for Education Research
University of Wisconsin, Madison

1985

ACADEMIC PRESS, INC.

(Harcourt Brace Jovanovich, Publishers)

Orlando   San Diego   New York   London
Toronto   Montreal   Sydney   Tokyo

This book is based upon work supported by the National Institute of Education under Grant No. NIE-G-81-0009. Any opinions, findings, and conclusions or recommendations expressed in this publication are those of the authors and do not necessarily reflect the views of the Institute or the Department of Education.

ACADEMIC PRESS, INC.
Orlando, Florida 32887

United Kingdom Edition published by
ACADEMIC PRESS INC. (LONDON) LTD.
24/28 Oval Road, London NW1 7DX

Library of Congress Cataloging in Publication Data

Main entry under title:

Gender influences in classroom interaction.

"Derived from papers presented at a conference funded
by the National Institute of Education and held at the
Wisconsin Center for Education Research, University of
Wisconsin-Madison in October 1983"--Pref.
    Includes indexes.
    1. Interaction analysis in education--Congresses.
2. Teacher-student relationships--Congresses.   3. Sex
differences in education--Congresses.   4. Classroom
management--Congresses.   I. Wilkinson, Louise Cherry.
II. Marrett, Cora Bagley.   III. National Institute
of Education (U.S.)   IV. Wisconsin Center for Education
Research.
LB1033.G39   1985   371.1'02   84-24352
ISBN 0-12-752075-9 (alk. paper)

PRINTED IN THE UNITED STATES OF AMERICA

85 86 87 88   9 8 7 6 5 4 3 2 1

Contents

Contents vii

Contents vii

Contents   vii

Contents   vii

*Chapter 7: Gender Differences in Preschool Classrooms: The Effects of
Sex-Typed Activity Choices*
ALETHA C. HUSTON and C. JAN CARPENTER

Contents

vii

**Chapter 11: Gender, Classroom Organization, and Grade Level as
Factors in Pupil Perceptions of Peer Interaction**
GRETA MORINE-DERSHIMER

Contributors

Numbers in parentheses indicate the pages on which the author's contributions begin.

Phyllis Blumenfeld (79), School of Education, University of Michigan, Ann Arbor, Michigan 48109

Jere Brophy (115), Institute for Research on Teaching, College of Education, Michigan State University, East Lansing, Michigan 48824-1034

C. Jan Carpenter (143), Department of Human Development and Family Ecology, University of Illinois, Urbana, Illinois 61801

Chi-Pang Chiang (185), School of Education, University of Wisconsin, Madison, Wisconsin 53706

Jacquelynne S. Eccles (79), Department of Psychology, University of Michigan, Ann Arbor, Michigan 48109-1027

Elizabeth Fennema (17), Department of Curriculum and Instruction, School of Education, University of Wisconsin, Madison, Wisconsin 53706

Linda Grant[1] (57), Department of Sociology, Southern Illinois University, Carbondale, Illinois 62901

Herbert M. Handley (37), Bureau of Educational Research and Evaluation, Mississippi State University, Mississippi State, Mississippi 39762

Aletha C. Huston (143), Department of Human Development and Family Life, The University of Kansas, Lawrence, Kansas 66045

Cathy M. Kenderski (209), Department of Education, University of California, Los Angeles, California 90024

[1] Present address: Department of Sociology, University of Georgia, Athens, Georgia 30602

Janet Lindow (1,185), School of Education, University of Wisconsin, Madison, Wisconsin 53706

Marlaine E. Lockheed (167), Educational Testing Service, Princeton, New Jersey 08541

Cora B. Marrett (1), Wisconsin Center for Education Research, University of Wisconsin, Madison, Wisconsin 53706

Greta Morine-Dershimer (237), Division for Study of Teaching, Syracuse University, Syracuse, New York 13210

Linda Wilson Morse (37), Bureau of Educational Research and Evaluation, Mississippi State University, Mississippi State, Mississippi 39762

Penelope Peterson (17), School of Education, University of Wisconsin, Madison, Wisconsin 53706

Noreen M. Webb (209), Department of Education, University of California, Los Angeles, California 90024

Louise Cherry Wilkinson[2] (1,185), Wisconsin Center for Education Research, University of Wisconsin, Madison, Wisconsin 53706

[2] Present address: Doctoral Program in Educational Psychology, City University of New York–Graduate School, New York, New York 10036

Preface

Researchers have examined gender-related differences in school-age children's attitudes, behavior, and achievement. Yet, the origins, maintenance, and consequences of these differential patterns are not well understood. The contributers to this volume focus on the interactional influences that may be related to differential classroom experiences for females and males. They explore a diversity of issues that have a bearing on gender-related influences, including contextual factors, teacher characteristics, and student characteristics, from both theoretical and empirical perspectives.

The contributors to the book discuss the state of knowledge within given areas and address—both explicitly and implicitly—problems meriting further attention. The book is addressed primarily to researchers, but it should also prove useful to teachers, educational policy makers, and others who want to insure every child, regardless of gender or other status, the opportunity of a rewarding and challenging education.

This volume is derived from papers presented at a conference funded by the National Institute of Education and held at the Wisconsin Center for Education Research, University of Wisconsin—Madison, in October 1983. We gratefully acknowledge the contributions of all the participants at the conference, who include the first authors of the chapters, Herb Handley, Penelope Peterson, and the following people who served as discussants: Marianne Bloch, Phyllis Blumenfeld, B. Bradford Brown, Donna Eder, and Thomas Good. Special thanks go to Chi-Pang Chiang, Janet Lindow, Linda Milosky, and Jean Norman for their assistance during the conference and in the preparation of this volume.

Overview

JANET LINDOW, CORA B. MARRETT, AND LOUISE CHERRY WILKINSON

INTRODUCTION

One presumed goal of education is to maximize each child's chances of academic success and to prepare youth for more schooling or for participating in the occupational structure. Yet, there is evidence that the outcomes of education are not the same for all groups. Male and female students, for example, perform differently from one another in certain subject areas and pursue quite different careers once they have completed their schooling. The stability and persistence of gender differences—in reading and mathematics performance, in entry into technical fields—have given rise to a concern about sex equity in the classroom. It may be that the differences in attainment found between males and females are rooted in gender-based contrasts in interactional experiences in classrooms. The papers in this volume address this possibility.

A voluminous literature covers the general subject of male–female differences, and a sizable body of research exists as well on patterns of interaction in classrooms. Studies that compare the classroom interaction of boys and girls are relatively scarce, but a few of the studies report clear-cut gender-related differences. The chapters in this volume draw together what is

1

known about the kinds of differences that occur and the consistency, prevalence, and influences on those differences.

Students interact with the classroom teacher and with one another. But, as these chapters show, there is less research on student–student or peer interaction than on teacher–student interaction. The phrase *teacher–student interaction* covers a range of behaviors; the chapters describe the dimensions along which these behaviors can vary. We believe this volume should help the research community distinguish the correlates and consequences of peer interaction from those associated with teacher–student interaction and to identify the attributes of teacher–student interaction that deserve systematic analysis.

In reading these chapters, one is struck by the many variables that influence interaction processes. These variables include environmental factors, such as classroom organization, activity structure, and teacher-to-student ratio; teacher attributes such as gender, length of experience, and attitudes toward sex-role stereotypes; and student variables, such as gender, race, ability, grade level, and perceptions of student and teacher characteristics. All these factors interact with each other and with the difficulty and content of the subject matter to affect both students' and teachers' behaviors. The volume is unique in its treatment of and focus on a diversity of variables that shape interaction in the classroom.

Chapter 1 does not present a comprehensive literature review; rather, it highlights recurrent themes in the research on teacher–student interaction and on peer interaction. Although the basic research and theoretical perspectives contained in this volume do not allow us to draw conclusions about the causes, covariates, and consequences of gender-related differences in classroom interaction, they contribute to our understanding of the complex processes that surround these differences, and they offer an agenda for continued research on these processes.

GENDER AND TEACHER–STUDENT INTERACTION

Gender Differences in Achievement

The research on performance in mathematics repeatedly reports that males do better than females on tests of problem-solving skills. No differences appear on tests of computational ability, however. In Chapter 2 of this volume, Fennema and Peterson seek to explain why males surpass females in high-level cognitive skills—the type that the problem-solving tests measure. They contend that to develop the skills an individual must participate in autonomous learning behaviors. These behaviors include choosing to do high-level tasks, working independently on the tasks, persisting on them, and achieving success on such tasks. Fennema and Peterson propose that males have more opportunities than females to pursue autonomous behaviors. Conditions outside of the classroom—in the home, among peers, and through the media, for example—provide males and females with differential opportunities; but in-school experiences also affect chances for independent action. According to the authors, the in-school experiences include the nature of the contact between the student and the classroom teacher. Supposedly, some types of contact enhance autonomous behaviors, but females are not as likely as males to have those contacts.

Fennema and Peterson suggest that gender-related patterns of interaction merit attention because of their consequence for academic achievement. Theirs is a theoretical chapter that leaves two questions for the empirically based chapters that follow. First, are the differences in interaction sizable enough to produce the kinds of achievement discrepancies that Fennema and Peterson describe? Second, what are the conditions that affect the extent and quality of interaction that male and female students have with their teachers? These are the issues addressed in Chapters 3 through 7 of this volume.

Gender Differences in Teacher–Student Interaction

Research conducted in elementary school classrooms shows rather consistently that teachers give more attention to boys than to girls (Berk & Lewis, 1977; Blumenfeld, Hamilton, & Bossert, 1979; Minuchin & Shapiro, 1983, p. 228), although there is also research to the contrary (cf. Field, 1980). However, much of the contact with boys tends to be negative; it is managerial and disciplinary in nature (Bossert, 1981; Huston, 1983, p. 439; Leinhardt, Seewald, & Engel, 1979). There is less consensus regarding teacher instructional contacts. Although several studies found that girls receive more instructional contacts (Biber, Miller, & Dyer, 1972; Fagot, 1973; Fagot & Patterson, 1969), others found the opposite (cf. Sears & Feldman, 1966).

Morse and Handley (Chapter 3), Grant (Chapter 4), and Eccles and Blumenfeld (Chapter 5) may help resolve the apparent inconsistencies in the literature, for these discussions show that the patterns may differ depending on the grade level of the student, his or her background, and the expectations of the teacher. Of the three chapters, only the Morse–Handley discussion stresses sharp gender differences, and even there the patterns are not identical for the two grade levels they studied.

Morse and Handley examine types of teacher questions and feedback to male and female students in a number of junior high school science classes. They selected a group of students, observed them as seventh graders and followed them during their year as eighth graders. At both grade levels, male students had more interaction than females with the teacher; this was true for both student- and teacher-initiated interaction. Nonetheless, the results varied somewhat depending on the particular type of interaction. In both the seventh and the eighth grades, males called out answers to indirect questions more often than did females, but females provided more solicited responses than did males. Nor were the patterns identical from one year to the next: Males initiated more interaction in the eighth grade than they did in the seventh grade, while the reverse was true for females. Although boys received more disciplinary feedback and criticism from teachers in both years than did girls, boys received proportionately more disciplinary contacts in the eighth grade than in the seventh grade.

The Morse–Handley findings caution us that conclusions based on a single time period may be unreliable: The trends found at that time need not persist. Grant (Chapter 4) introduces yet another caveat: Even at a given time the patterns for one racial group may depart from those for another. In her study of interaction in elementary classrooms, Grant discovered that race mattered. She investigated differential teacher communication to four categories of students—black males, black females, while males, white females—in six first-grade classrooms. She examined positive as well as negative feedback on both academic and behavior-related matters. In addition to teacher–student interactions, Grant measured peer contact in these classrooms. Even though there were different relative frequencies across the six classes, white and black females generally had more contacts with teachers than with peers, and the opposite finding occurred with males. Black females showed the largest tendency to engage in more peer and fewer teacher interactions over time. The teachers called on white females more than on black females for assistance and reprimanded black males more than any of the other three race–gender groups.

Eccles and Blumenfeld (Chapter 5) introduce still another variable: teacher expectations for student performance. The authors conclude from their research in junior high school mathematics classes that expectations influence teacher–student interaction; however, they show that the link between expectations and student gender is complicated. Four categories of students were identified: high-expectancy males and females, or those from whom the teacher anticipated good performance, and low-expectancy males and females. Both low- and high-expectancy females received less criticism and asked more questions than did low- and high-expectancy males. Low-expectancy females received more praise than one would have predicted statistically, and high-expectancy females received more public communications regarding incorrect answers than did the other three expectancy–gender groups. Low-expectancy males received more conduct-related criticism and had more private interactions with teachers than the other three groups. Teachers did not, however, praise males and females differentially.

Significantly, high teacher-expectancy females had less confidence in their math ability than high teacher-expectancy males. Furthermore, this difference was greater in the ninth grade than in seventh grade. But overall, the teachers did not appear to cause the gender-different attitudes, perceptions, and achievement; instead they helped maintain the differences.

Brophy (Chapter 6) reinforces the point that the teacher need not cause gender-related differences. His chapter also relates to the preceding chapters in another way: It shows that the gender of the student is not the only attribute researchers should examine as they attempt to understand classroom interaction processes.

Brophy provides an overview of the research on teacher–student interactions and makes the interesting observation that concerns about gender and the classroom have changed over time. Prior to 1974, most of the research focused on the elementary school level and searched for in-class forces to explain the poor reading performance of male students. Since that time, analysts have given more attention to the secondary school classroom and have looked for clues to explain the underparticipation and underachievement in mathematics and science by female students. Brophy indicates that one cannot fully comprehend the research from either period without taking into account such factors as the age of the pupils involved and the nature of the subject matter covered.

Brophy considered the possibility that the gender of the teacher might make a difference. He dispelled this notion, however, after finding that research showed similar reactions to students by male and female teachers. He thought it likely that the subject matter being taught might be a more important variable than the gender of the teacher in producing different reactions to students. Research supports this position. According to Brophy, teacher–student contacts seem to give boys an advantage in mathematics and girls an advantage in reading. His review, then, corroborates the Fennema–Peterson contention that gender differences in mathematics performance might stem from differences in experiences within mathematics classrooms.

Brophy concurs with Eccles and Blumenfeld that the disparities in student experience are not caused by the teacher–student interactional experiences but instead are maintained by them. He calls for more "thick descriptions" of ongoing classroom experiences as well as more precise measurement and delineation of teacher and student characteristics that influence interaction patterns, for example, teachers' expectations and students' degree of adherence to traditional gender roles. In order for the classroom to become more equitable, Brophy suggests that teachers may have to treat boys and girls differently, rather than the same.

Gender Differences in Behavior and Predispositions

The Brophy discussion calls attention to the possibility that student characteristics and expectations as well as teacher attributes may shape teacher–student interaction. Male and female students enter the classroom with different behavioral, social, and cognitive propensities. The Huston and Carpenter discussion (Chapter 7) indicates that generalized gender differences may in fact be present by the time children enter elementary school.

Huston and Carpenter found from their research with preschool children that girls spend more time in highly structured activities than boys. The researchers meant by structure (1) the amount of feedback given by adults, and (2) the extent to which the child could observe adults performing activities similar to those in which the child was engaged. They found that children who were engaged in highly structured activities were more likely to seek approval from adults than those engaged in less structured activities. Quite possibly the gender differences in responsiveness to adults that appear during the preschool years continue into the later years, stimulating teachers to react differently to male than to female students.

The Huston–Carpenter analysis underscores the argument of Fennema–Peterson (Chapter 2) that females tend to be less independent of others than males. This chapter corroborates as well the theme from other research that gender differences appear quite early. Block (1979) noted, for example, that the play experiences of young girls differ from those of young boys. Girls are given toys that encourage imitation, rule-learning, and help-seeking behaviors, while boys are given toys that stress exploration, problem solving, and creativity. The type of toy, then, can influence the type of social and cognitive skills that develop (Liss, 1983; Serbin & Conner, 1979) and the cues for behavior given to others.

The teacher is not a passive force, however. The teacher responds to cues from students and gives cues as well. Some teachers attempt to socialize children into the student role, a role to which the behavior of girls is likely to correspond. By structuring classroom activities and reacting to the behavior of students, teachers reveal their own ideas about appropriate and inappropriate behavior. In summary, the first seven chapters suggest that patterns of teacher–student interaction depend on many more variables than the gender of the student. At a minimum, the age and background of the student as well as the subject matter of the classroom must be considered. Although the expectations of the teachers clearly are important, those expectations and reactions may be influenced by the predispositions the student brings into the classroom. The teacher is not the only force producing differences in achievement outcomes between male and female students.

GENDER AND PEER INTERACTION

The research on peer interaction, although not as extensive as that on teacher–student interaction, reinforces the point that outcomes depend on more than the contact between an individual teacher and a particular student. Students interact with their peers, sometimes because the classroom is structured to foster interaction, other times because students regard the contact as crucial for understanding and completing the assigned tasks. The remaining chapters summarize research on patterns of peer interaction.

Much of the research on peer interaction proceeds from the assumption that gender inequities and sex-role stereotypes are likely to persist in the absence of substantial cross-sex interaction. If females interact primarily with one another, they are not likely to develop the independence that, according to Fennema and Peterson (Chapter 2), facilitates higher level mathematics skills. If males limit their interaction to other males, they are not likely to develop accurate assessments of the abilities and interests of females. Given the long-term significance of cross-sex interaction, it is perhaps not surprising that studies of peer interaction center especially on the extent of sex segregation and the conditions under which it might be discouraged.

Peer Interaction and Sex Segregation

Some settings do not enhance peer interaction, whether that interaction occurs among same-sex or cross-sex peers. The frequency of cross-sex interaction, then, is conditioned by the opportunities that are available for any type of peer interaction. Studies at the preschool level suggest that frequent and sustained interaction is most likely where the teacher–child ratio is low (Reuter & Yunik, 1973), the curriculum stresses free play (Miller & Dyer, 1975), and the teacher issues few directives (Fagot, 1973), and gives verbal feedback (Huston-Stein, Friedrich-Cofer, & Susman, 1977).

Similar variables affect peer interaction beyond the preschool setting. The

Huston–Carpenter (Chapter 7) study of children between the ages of 7 and 11 indicates that the degree of activity structure influenced peer contacts, that is, the higher the level of structure, the lower the level of contacts. Similarly, Grant (Chapter 4) determined that task structure, or the way in which the instructional activities were organized, differently affected peer interactions. Interaction was more frequent when students worked on a variety of assignments during a period than when students worked on a single task at a time.

When students have the opportunity to associate with one another, they are more likely to choose associates from their own gender. There is a wealth of evidence that in social relationships boys and girls prefer same-sex contacts to cross-sex ones. As Lockheed (Chapter 8) shows in her review of the research on sex segregation, whether one analyzes playmate choices, voluntary seating arrangements, or helping behavior, male–female separation is common.

The tendency of children to affiliate with their same-sex counterparts may result from and reflect gender differences in behavior. Rather substantial literature indicates that boys are more active and aggressive, whereas girls are more passive and compliant. Studies of preschool children at play document the differences: Girls engage in more constructive and less dramatic play than do boys (Rubin, Maioni, & Hornung, 1976; Sanders & Harper, 1976). In addition, girls are more likely to play in dyads and engage in imitative fantasy than are boys, who play in larger groups and engage in creative fantasy (Liss, 1983).

There is less evidence that sex segregation prevails in the academic context. Goetz (1981) observed that proximity shaped interaction patterns more than did gender in a group of first graders. When asked the names of classmates from whom they would seek help, the respondents selected children who were near them. When asked to identify preferred playmates, however, the subjects chose classmates of their gender. Other researchers maintain that sex segregation occurs in academic as well as social contacts (Berk & Lewis, 1977; Day & Hunt, 1974; Grant, 1982). But it appears that, in general, cross-sex interaction takes place somewhat more frequently in academic settings than in purely social ones.

Influences on Cross-Sex Interaction

Children may have well-established preferences and gender-specific play styles, but cross-sex interaction does take place. Certain features in the classroom may in fact foster the interaction. Berk and Lewis (1977) conclude that the educational philosophy in the school can be important. They studied four schools guided by different philosophies, which they identified as "traditional," "transitional," "progressive," and "romantic." The greatest volume of cross-sex interchanges emerged in the progressive school; in the other three types, same-sex interactions outdistanced the cross-sex one.

The probability of choosing a same-sex versus a cross-sex partner may be influenced by the kind of activity being undertaken. Day and Hunt (1974) found that same-sex interaction prevailed among 5-year-olds in an open classroom; however, when they examined interaction at each learning center, they found instances of expected proportions of cross-sex interaction. Specifically, at the science and mathematics learning centers boys engaged in equal proportions of same- and cross-sex interaction, and at the dramatic arts learning center girls engaged in equal proportions of same- and cross-sex interaction. The overall pattern of sex-segregated interaction may have emerged due to a prevalence of same-sex interaction during play activities in which the children probably spent the majority of their time.

The argument appears in the literature that teachers shape cross-sex interaction by providing opportunities for it to take place. The Lockheed research (Chapter 8) challenges that argument. Despite the fact that teachers rarely structured their classrooms to facilitate peer interaction, a relatively high percentage of cross-sex interaction occurred during academic activities. The sociometric choices that the student made were only minimally related to the use of cross-sex groupings by the teacher. In other words, participation in cross-sex groups did not lead invariably to cross-sex sociometric patterns; however, less sex segregation was found in classrooms where the most cross-sex interaction occurred. Student attitudes, on the other hand, were quite important. The greater the expressed willingness to cooperate with classmates of the opposite gender, the greater the amount of cross-sex contacts.

Lockheed argues that cross-sex interaction is likely to occur if it can enhance academic performance. Wilkinson, Lindow, and Chiang (Chapter 9) examine same-sex and cross-sex communication in an academic context, that is, in elementary school mathematics work groups. Each of the six groups in the study comprised equal numbers of males and females. The researchers determined that males were more likely to request information from other males than from females, however, the females were not likely to direct their requests to one gender. When disagreements took place within the group, males' answers prevailed more often than did those of the females.

Brophy (Chapter 6) argues that if gender inequities are to be eliminated, different, rather than identical, treatment of males and females may be necessary. The Wilkinson et al. research lends support to the argument. The presence of equal numbers of males and females did not result in equal numbers of requests to males and females from the male students. Nor were differences in the ability of the male and female students explanatory; the groups consisted of students with similar ability profiles. Apparently the males carried with them into the work groups communication styles that resulted in the differences in request patterns.

Webb and Kenderski (Chapter 10) bear as well on the issue of communication differences between male and female students. The authors examined eighth- and ninth-graders' requests for help and receipts of explanations. Specifically, they analyzed the relationship between selected communication variables and consequent achievement in both low-achieving and high-achieving mathematics classes. They found that in high-achieving classes, males were more successful than females in obtaining the requested help, partly because females were more responsive than males to requests for help. Males also achieved higher than females in these high-achieving classes. In contrast, there were no sex differences in achievement or in interaction patterns in the low-achieving classes.

The Webb and Kenderski findings suggest that when females and males interact in cross-sex encounters, females are not as successful as males in getting information and in getting their needs met. Apparently, the differences that males and females bring to the classroom from different informal interaction experiences hurt females more than males. We need to encourage cross-sex interaction; however, in so doing we need to take into account differences that already exist in male and female experiences.

The final chapter approaches the classroom and interaction within it more from a social than from an academic perspective. Morine-Dershimer (Chapter 11) examines gender and grade-level differences in students' perceptions of salient interactional characteristics that determine friendship choices. The perceptions of student characteristics and friendship groups were examined in fourth grade and again in fifth grade in relation to the management structure and frequency of peer interaction within each of three classrooms. The author found that across all three classrooms, pupils emphasized social aspects of classroom interaction when asked what would be "important to know" when telling a new student about their classmates; for example, characteristics that determined membership in friendship groups, such as reading-group membership, shared interest in sports, and so on. The characteristics that students identified were different within each classroom; however, in all classrooms there was sex segregation in friendship choices, and both boys and girls rated the other gender as less friendly than the same gender.

Cross-sex interaction can have positive benefits for both males and females, but such benefits are most probable if deliberate efforts are made to prevent earlier experiences from intruding. If males and females are simply put together in academic contexts, there can be no guarantee that the results will reverberate in the social context as well. Nor can we be certain that the views of the females on the academic issues will be respected and requested by the males. The structuring of cross-sex interaction, then, may be more important for later outcomes than the frequency of and opportunity for male–female contact.

RESEARCH ON GENDER AND CLASSROOMS: THE UNFINISHED AGENDA

If knowledge about gender effects is to accumulate and guide practice, researchers will have to attend to certain conceptual and methodological limitations evident in the extant literature. In this final section we offer some recommendations for research that spring from the papers. Three categories of issues can be placed on the agenda for research regarding the nature, antecedents, and consequences of gender differences in teacher–student and peer interaction. First, certain topics warrant more attention than they have been given thus far. Second, the research on gender differences needs to be more theoretically grounded. Finally, the various methods that have been used should be interwoven and certain sampling problems considered as well.

Topics for Further Research

As indicated by Morine-Dershimer (Chapter 11) and Webb and Kenderski (Chapter 10), the organization of the classroom shapes and constrains interactional processes. A growing literature on classroom structure exists, but the research from that tradition has proceeded rather independently from analyses on gender and interaction. Clearly, then, one topic deserving further scrutiny is the effect of classroom organization on patterns of interaction. As M. Hallinan (personal communication, October, 1984) points out, researchers need to make greater effort in measuring the organizational characteristics—of the classroom and indeed of the school—that may impinge on teacher–student and student–student dynamics.

Most of the papers in this volume emphasize the thesis that student gender alone cannot explain fully the interaction that takes place between the student and the teacher, or among students. Grant (Chapter 4) found that race made a difference, but attributes other than demographics may be important as well. The work from Eder and Hallinan (1978) shows that students vary in their popularity; the chapter by Morine-Dershimer (11) outlines some of the traits that make some students more popular than others. Future research might consider how traits such as popularity, ability, and academic achievement interact with one another and with gender to produce particular communication and contact patterns.

The work on teacher–student interaction has advanced somewhat separately from that on student–student interaction. Consequently, we do not understand fully how and if peer interaction modifies teacher–student interchange. Nor are we certain of the effects of teacher–student contact on peer relationships. Students sometimes bring into the classroom an agenda that differs from the one the teacher stresses; most often, the student agenda is social in nature. The teacher, who alters peer interaction patterns to achieve some intellectual benefit, may in the process disrupt the social agenda of the students. Research on the teacher's awareness of peer dynamics and on the difference that awareness makes for teacher behaviors, and on the consequences of the behaviors for peer interaction is needed (B. Brown, personal communication, October, 1984).

Conceptual Issues

It would not be difficult for us to develop a long list of understudied topics. But it seems that the serious weakness of the research is a theoretical one: The studies do not proceed from or lead to well-integrated theories. This was a theme that Bloch stressed: The variables in existing analyses rarely are chosen according to some integrated perspective (M. Bloch, personal communication, October, 1984). M. Hallinan (personal communication, October, 1984) also laments the tendency for explanations to be post hoc in nature: She recommends that researchers draw on particular bodies of literature, such as teacher expectations or expectation states theory, to predict the dynamics of the interaction process. For theories on the dynamics of gender and classroom to evolve, the research must first be drawn together and assessed. We regard this volume as a first step; we anticipate that the conceptual and theoretical issues will rank at the top of future plans for research on gender and classrooms.

Methodological Issues

Interactions have been studied through survey techniques, observational strategies and experimental studies. Hallinan (personal communication, October, 1984) proposes that greater attention be given to combining techniques, especially survey and observational ones. Survey studies alone cannot ferret out the subtle images, expectations, and behaviors that take place; but neither do the small-scale observational studies provide enough data to justify broad generalizations. The answer may lie in the interweaving of various data collection strategies.

To M. Bloch (personal communication, October, 1984), ethnographic research is essential for identifying the unobtrusive dimensions of interaction; but research is needed as well that can generate measures for the many variables that influence behavior in the classroom. T. Good (personal communication, October, 1984) stresses that qualitative strategies are needed if we hope to understand the thoughts, impulses, and beliefs that lie behind the pen-and-paper reports and the measures of interaction. In addition, he recommends that laboratory-based studies be undertaken more often. In his view, certain constructs, such as autonomous learning behaviors, could perhaps be tested best in the laboratory. Only in a setting where there are few social cues for the student can the research determine whether persistence is internally derived rather than externally induced.

In designing future studies, researchers should pay close attention to the age, demographic, and cultural characteristics of their samples as well as to the types of materials and content being covered. According to M. Bloch (personal communication, October, 1984), middle-class American children, as compared with children from some other cultures, work hard to get attention and recognition. Studies based only on a middle-class sample, then, may offer generalizations about interaction that are in fact culturally limited. B. Brown (personal communication, October, 1984) notes that some variables chosen for analysis may be inappropriate for certain age groups. In particular, friendship choices are relatively unstable among young children. Thus, the questions asked must be appropriate to the sample used if knowledge is to be advanced.

Studies that differentiate classrooms by content area—mathematics classrooms versus reading classrooms, for example—represent an advance over those that combine various classrooms. Yet, even within a subject area further specification may be necessary (P. Blumenfeld, personal communication, October, 1984). The kinds of materials used can vary from one context to another, and the kinds of materials shape interaction patterns in important ways. In other words, researchers need to look quite systematically at the settings they propose to study.

Gender Effects: Outcomes and Antecedents

We began this Introduction with the argument that gender differences in the classroom deserve attention because potentially they influence the academic and the social lives of students. We have not demonstrated a link between classroom processes and long-term academic or other outcomes; nor do we expect the link to be made in the immediate future. Only when the limitations we have identified have been overcome will the research be able to address the long-term consequences of gender-related patterns.

The research agenda must include the consequences and the effect of changes—in schools and in the larger society—on classroom processes. Changes in male–female patterns within classrooms can undoubtedly reverberate beyond the school, but it is also the case that changes outside the boundaries of the school modify expectations for patterns of interaction.

REFERENCES

Berk, L. E., & Lewis, N. G. (1977). Sex role and social behavior in four school environments. *Elementary School Journal, 77*, 205–217.

Biber, H., Miller, L., & Dyer, J. (1972). Feminization in preschool. *Developmental Psychology, 7*, 86.

Block, J. H. (1979). Socialization influences on personality development in males and females. In M. M. Parks (Ed.), *APA master lecture series on issues of sex and gender in psychology.* Washington, DC: American Psychological Association.

Blumenfeld, P., Hamilton, V., & Bossert, S. (1979, October). *Teacher talk and student thought: Socialization into the student role.* Paper presented at the Learning Research and Development Center Conference on Student Motivation, Pittsburgh, PA.

Bossert, S. T. (1981). Understanding sex differences in children's classroom experiences. *Elementary School Journal, 81*, 255–266.

Day, B. D., & Hunt, G. H. (1974, July). *Verbal interaction across age, race, and sex in a variety of learning centers in an open classroom setting.* Final Report submitted to the North Carolina State Department of Public Instruction, Division of Research.

Eder, D., & Hallinan, M. T. (1978). Sex differences in children's friendships. *American Sociological Review, 43*, 237–250.

Fagot, B. I. (1973). Influence of teacher behavior in the preschool. *Developmental Psychology, 9*, 198–206.

Fagot, B. I., & Patterson, G. R. (1969). An in vivo analysis of reinforcing contingencies for sex-role behaviors in the preschool child. *Developmental Psychology, 1*, 563–568.

Field, T. M. (1980). Preschool play: Effects of teacher–child ratios and organization of classroom space. *Child Study Journal, 10*, 191–205.

Goetz, J. P. (1981). Children's sex role knowledge and behavior: An ethnographic study of first graders in the rural South. *Theory and Research in Social Education, 8*, 31–54.

Grant, L. (1982, March). *Sex roles and statuses in peer interactions in elementary schools* (pp. 11). Paper presented at the meeting of the American Educational Research Association, New York.

Huston, A. C. (1983). Sex typing. In P. H. Mussen & E. M. Hetherington (Eds.), *Handbook of child psychology* (Vol. 4, 4th ed.). New York: Wiley.

Huston-Stein, A., Friedrich-Cofer, L., & Susman, E. J. (1977). The relation of classroom structure to social behavior, imaginative play, and self-regulation of economically disadvantaged children. *Child Development, 48*, 908–916.

Leinhardt, G., Seewald, A. M., & Engel, M. (1979). Learning what's taught: Sex differences in instruction. *Journal of Educational Psychology, 71,* 432–439.

Liss, M. (1983). Learning gender-related skills through play. In M. Liss (Ed.), *Social and cognitive skills: Sex roles and children's play.* New York: Academic Press.

Miller, L. B., & Dyer, J. L. (1975). Four preschool programs: Their dimension and effects. *Monographs of the Society for Research in Child Development, 40* (Serial No. 162).

Minuchin, P. P., & Shapiro, E. K. (1983). The school as a context for social development. In P. Mussen & E. M. Hetherington (Eds.), *Handbook of child psychology* (Vol. 4, 4th ed.). New York: Wiley.

Reuter, J., & Yunik, G. (1973). Social interaction in nursery schools. *Developmental Psychology 9,* 319–325.

Rubin, K. H., Maioni, T. L., & Hornung, M. (1976). Free play behaviors in middle- and lower-class preschoolers: Parten and Piaget revisited. *Child Development, 47,* 414–419.

Sanders, K. M., & Harper, L. V. (1976). Free-play fantasy behavior in preschool children: Relations among gender, age, season, and location. *Child Development, 47,* 1182–1185.

Sears, P., & Feldman, D. (1966). Teacher interactions with boys and girls. *National Elementary Principal, 46,* 30–35.

Serbin, L. A., & Conner, J. M. (1979). Sex-typing of children's play preferences and patterns of cognitive performance. *Journal of Genetic Psychology, 134,* 315–316.

Autonomous Learning Behavior: A Possible Explanation of Gender-Related Differences in Mathematics

ELIZABETH FENNEMA AND PENELOPE PETERSON

INTRODUCTION

Gender-related differences in the learning of mathematics are some of the most pervasive and persistent educational inequities that exists. In this paper, we briefly discuss where such differences exist, propose a model that may help in understanding why such differences develop, describe the characteristics of each component in the model, and give a theoretical rationale for the model and its components. Some data are presented that support the validity of the model.

GENDER INFLUENCES
IN CLASSROOM INTERACTION
ISBN: 0-12-752075-9

17

THE MODEL

In Figure 2.1 a model is shown that indicates causative factors that influence the development of gender-related differences in mathematics achievement, its end point. These differences, which indicate male superiority, are found especially in performance in tasks of high cognitive complexity, such as true problem solving where a person has no ready strategy for reaching a solution. It is mathematics of this complex type that enables one to learn more mathematics, to use mathematics in other disciplines, or to solve mathematical problems throughout life. It is in mathematical learning of this type where females are falling behind males.

In order to learn to do tasks of high cognitive complexity, we hypothesize that one must participate in autonomous learning behavior (ALB) that enables the development of high-level cognitive skills. These ALBs serve as the mediators between internal and external influences and performance on high-level cognitive tasks themselves. Internal influences consist of internal motivational beliefs about oneself that have a direct influence on participation in ALB. This belief system includes attributional style, confidence in one's ability to learn mathematics, and perceived usefulness of mathematics. Also included are perceived congruency between one's sex-role identity and participation in ALB.

Many external and/or societal factors influence the participation in ALB, including family, peers, and media. We have chosen to emphasize classroom processes as significant determiners of whether or not one participates in ALBs. We are particularly interested in teacher–pupil interactions and classroom activities in which boys and girls participate.

To explicate the model, we present the known facts about gender-related differences in mathematics that are accepted as reasonably accurate by most scholars. Then we discuss the theoretical rationale for the remaining portions of the model and present relevant literature.

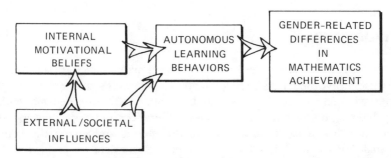

Figure 2.1 Development of gender-related differences in mathematics achievement.

Gender-Related Differences in Mathematics

The existence of differences between females and males in learning mathematics has long been accepted. Early reviews by noted mathematics educators reported differences that existed by kindergarten (Glennon & Callahan, 1968; Aiken, 1971) with boys performing at higher levels than girls. A deeper understanding of where such differences lie emerged during the modern mathematics movement of the 1960s. The National Longitudinal Study of Mathematical Abilities (NLSMA) reported that although young girls sometimes performed at higher levels than boys on routine computational tasks, by adolescence boys showed superior performance on tasks which involved higher cognitive skills, such as applications and problem solving (Wilson, 1972).

During the 1970s, as more and more people were questioning the traditional role of women in our society, the importance of mathematics for career development of women as well as of men was recognized. In addition, many questioned the results of prior research by arguing that sample selection, performance measures, and interpretation of results were suspect because the research was done from the dominant male perspective. This questioning certainly had some basis in truth. Many of the conclusions cited previously had been drawn from the study of large, national samples. In these studies, the number of mathematics courses taken by female and male students was not controlled. Since it appeared that many more males than females enrolled in advanced mathematics classes in high school, it was reasonable to assume that males learned more mathematics than females, partially because of the time spent with mathematics. It was hypothesized then that the main causative factor of gender-related differences in mathematics was differential course taking. Some support for this hypothesis was provided by the results of studies by Fennema and Sherman (1976) who found no gender-related differences in mathematics learning in two of four high schools when the number of mathematics courses enrolled in was held constant. A reanalysis of the NLSMA data reported similar findings (Perl, 1979).

Data collected since that time have often shown somewhat different results. The second and third mathematics portion of the National Assessment of Education (NAEP II and III) collected data about course enrollment by sex and did many analyses controlling for number of mathematics courses taken. Both assessments showed clearly that female students tend to take fewer advanced mathematics courses (Fennema & Carpenter, 1981). However, when analyses of performance were done with the number of mathematics courses held constant, at age 17 males performed significantly higher, both statistically and educationally, on all cognitive levels of tasks that were measured. The more mathematics courses the subjects reported they had taken, the greater were the differences. The differences were also greatest where the cognitive complexity of the task was the highest. Confirming this finding are the results reported by Benbow and Stanley (1980) who found many more young males than females who perform at very high levels on the SAT-M, which includes high-level tasks.

Other studies do not consistently report the same gender-related differences. Dees (1982) found no gender differences in performance on a geometry test on a nationwide sample. No gender differences in performance were found in the 1977–1978 Wisconsin statewide assessment of mathematics learning (Chambers, 1983). The results are even less clear when one looks at individual schools. For example, Marrett and Gates (1983) reported that female and male enrollment differential in six predominantly black high schools varied from 15% more males enrolled to 7% more females enrolled. Peterson and Fennema (in press), in a study of 36 fourth-grade classes, found few differences between the sexes' performance on either complex or simple mathematical items.

One fact is known. Mathematics-related postsecondary school educational options and mathematics-related careers are chosen less often by women than by men (Vetter, 1980). This fact and the knowledge that fewer high school females than males elect advanced mathematics courses, and with NAEP results showing there are gender-related differences in performance on high cognitive levels of mathematics, leads to the conclusion that a pervasive problem remains in the achievement of equity for females in learning mathematics.

It is known that females' enrollment in advanced high school mathematics courses can be increased by an intervention program focused on changing the attitude of females and significant others towards females as learners of mathematics (Fennema, Wolleat, Pedro & Becker, 1981). However, the factors that cause females to perform lower on high-level cognitive tasks in mathematics have not been clearly identified. The ALB model attempts to identify those factors.

Autonomous Learning Behaviors

What are these ALBs which enable one to learn to do high cognitive level tasks in mathematics? Autonomous learning behaviors include working independently on high-level tasks, persisting at such tasks, choosing to do and achieving success in such tasks. These traits do not develop when one becomes an adult. Instead, they develop over a period of years as the person grows and develops. These traits are learned as one is allowed, or forced, or expected to exhibit them. An assumption behind this model is that greater participation in autonomous learning activities leads to greater development of ALB, which, in turn leads to greater performance on high cognitive level tasks.

Some research indicates that participating in these behaviors is important in learning. Gustin (1982), reported that 23 exceptionally talented mathematicians described themselves as independent learners. According to Gustin, the opportunity to work independently during early school years was extremely important to these mathematicians. Having teachers who did not supply answers appeared to facilitate their development. Grieb and Easley (1984) argue strongly that independence in learning is essential to learning the conceptual framework of mathematics that enables one to continue to use mathematics or to do high-level cognitive tasks. According to them memorization and independent thinking typically are forced to be exclusive of one another. An inspection of biographies of outstanding mathematicians shows clearly that they have traits of independence, persistence, and chose to do those mathematical activities that were mentally stimulating (Helson, 1980).

It has long been believed that females are more dependent than males. Maccoby and Jacklin (1974) report that dependency is "one of the two most extensively studied behaviors that are assumed to be sex-linked" (p. 191). Although there is some conflicting evidence (e.g., Hollinger, 1978), most authors conclude that females exhibit more dependent behaviors than do males, and this difference appears at a very young age (Bardwick, 1971; Garai and Scheinfeld, 1968; Kagan, 1964; Mischel, 1970; Sherman, 1971). Dependence is usually defined as a need for reward, help, and/or attention from another person. The actual behaviors that constitute dependency in many studies include seeking physical contact, seeking proximity and attention, seeking praise and approval, and resisting separation (Maccoby & Masters, 1970). An independent person is self-reliant, while a dependent person relies on others. Although Maccoby and Jacklin (1974) question global definitions of dependency and overgeneralization of results from limited studies, it appears that females more than males exhibit behaviors that suggest they need interaction, attention, and reinforcement. Dependence measures also show remarkable stability for females from age 3–14 (Kagan & Moss, 1962).

Dependent–independent behaviors are believed to develop as part of the socialization process, mainly through social interactions. Young girls, more so than boys, are encouraged to be dependent. Girls receive more protection and less pressure for establishing themselves as individuals separate from parents. Therefore, girls are less likely to engage in independent exploration of their worlds (Hoffman, 1975). Because of the sex-typed social reinforcement of dependent–independent behaviors, when children enter school girls tend to be more dependent on others and boys tend to be more self-reliant.

There are few data (or even theories) within educational literature that relate directly to how independence in learning is achieved. It is assumed almost without question that a major goal of education is to develop individuals who are independent thinkers and problem solvers. However, what appears to happen is that schools merely reinforce and further encourage the dependent–independent behaviors that girls and boys bring to school.

Students learn from the learning activities in which they participate. Such an obvious truism seems to need little support, but support can be readily found. Begle (1979) reported that when a textbook used by learners emphasizes understanding of mathematical ideas, learners perform at higher levels on tasks that measure understanding. Good, Grouws, and Ebmeier (1983) report that when more time is spent in classroom activities that develop the reasons for mathematical ideas, children perform at higher levels on tests that measure concepts.

On the other hand, when students spend time on low-level mathematics tasks, they learn and are able to perform mathematics at a low level. For example, in the study of 36 fourth-grade classes in Wisconsin, Peterson and Fennema (in press) found that over 80% of engaged time in mathematics classes was spent doing low-level tasks. Reyes and Fennema (1982) reported about the same amount of time spent in low-level tasks in mathematics classes at Grades 6, 7, and 8. Not surprisingly, the Wisconsin statewide assessment (Chambers, 1983) showed that 90% of the students tested were able to do computational tasks with whole numbers.

Because children learn what they do, and because gender-related differences exist in high-level cognitive tasks, perhaps girls and boys participate in somewhat different ALBs in mathematics. Some evidence supports this position. Grieb and Easley (1984) addressed the question of whether differential behavior of girls and boys (as well as minorities) in classrooms from kindergarten through university years results in gender-related differences. Although only qualitative data are reported, the conclusions are based on systematic observation over a period of years. Grieb and Easley concluded that "We have been able to identify the mathematical difficulties of hundreds of young women . . . in specific patterns of behavior such as dependence on memorizing specific algorithms for specific problem types" (p. 319). They argue strongly that some young white boys maintain their independence by rebelling against the authoritarian restrictions of the typical elementary school classrooms. These young white boys reject performing typical algorithms and instead develop their own procedures for solving problems. They become students "successful in university level mathematics . . . because they have developed some kind of insulation in primary school years against the dogmatism of most mathematics instruction and the moral order it represents" (p. 322). In other words, some boys learn to be independent in mathematics by choosing to do high-level tasks independently and persisting at this independence and persistence over a long period of time.

In summary, in order to perform high-level mathematical tasks, one must be independent. One must choose to work on such tasks and persist until the task is satisfactorily completed. These autonomous learning behaviors are developed over a period of years by participating in them. This somewhat circular definition, however, leaves a major question unanswered: Why do some children participate in activities that lead to the development of ALB while others do not? To find a partial answer, we must look at a person's internal motivational beliefs.

Internal Motivational Beliefs

What motivates a person to participate in behaviors that lead to development of ALB? Certainly, something beyond general intelligence contributes to this motivation and learning. Weiner (1974) argued that general intelligence accounts for only 25% of the observed variance in grades. We argue that an internal belief system about mathematics and oneself plays a highly important role. What one believes about oneself in relation to the learning of mathematics influences what one does as one learns mathematics. Since mathematics is learned over a period of years and is cumulative, internal motivating variables that influence one to persist, to choose high-level tasks, and to work independently are important to consider. We are concerned not so much about overall motivation but about gender-related differences in internal beliefs that might help explain differential participation in and development of ALB.

Several interrelated factors seem important. Self-esteem or confidence in one's ability to use and to learn new mathematics is one internal belief that probably influences choice of activity, persistence, and independence. It seems reasonable to assume that if one feels confident that success is possible, then one is more apt to participate in ALB. Gender-related differences in confidence in learning mathematics appear at least by fourth grade and exist throughout high school (Fox, 1980; Fennema, 1984). Females often feel less confidence in learning mathematics even when no gender-related differences in mathematics performance are evident. Another factor is perceived usefulness of mathematics. Gender-related differences in perception of usefulness of mathematics is found starting as early as sixth grade and lasting through adulthood (Fennema, 1981).

Both confidence in learning mathematics and perceived usefulness of mathematics are related to and perhaps a part of one's causal attributions for successes and failures in mathematics. Causal attribution concerns the perception of causation for various events in one's life. The concern here is with perception of causation of successes and failures, particularly in mathematics. The theoretical model of Weiner (1974) that appears to be most helpful consists of a 2 × 2 matrix with the dimensions being locus of control (internal–external) and stability (stable–unstable). Briefly, the theory predicts that if success is attributed to an internal, stable cause (such as ability) one would expect success in the future and would, therefore, choose to participate and persist in similar activities. If one attributes failure to an unstable cause (such as effort), then failure can be avoided in the future, and one would not hesitate to choose to participate in such activities again. This attributional style indicates personal control of learning (i.e., I am smart enough to learn and if I don't learn, it is because I didn't try) and is believed by many to be the attributional style that most encourages achievement behavior (Bar-Tal, 1978). According to Bar-Tal, an attributional style that influences one's avoiding achievement behavior is one where successes are attributed to external, unstable causes and failures are attributed to internal, stable causes. The latter attribution style has been characterized as learned helplessness and the former as mastery orientation.

Stipek and Weisz (1981) specifically discuss the relation between attributional style and achievement behavior on what they call difficult tasks. Persons who attribute success to ability or effort (internally) are more likely to approach a similar task situation in the future. In particular, if one attributes the causes for success on a difficult task internally, then one will approach subsequent difficult tasks. Thus, if one attributes success in high cognitive tasks to oneself, one will attempt similar tasks more often than if one attributed success externally. The more one practices such tasks, the better one becomes at doing them, and the more one attributes success internally. Achievement behavior leads to greater achievement.

Some researchers have found gender-related differences in attributional style with males more than females exhibiting a mastery orientation, and females tending to exhibit learned helplessness (Deaux, 1976). These differences have also been found when the achievement domain was mathematics (Wolleat, Pedro, Becker, & Fennema, 1980). Most of the available data indicate that males, more than females, exhibit the desirable behavior patterns of mastery orientation. Females, more than males, tend to exhibit attributional styles that lead to avoidance of difficult tasks that in turn lead to lower performance, and so on (learned helplessness).

The relationship of attributional styles and the ALB of persistence, choice, and independence has been demonstrated in the laboratory setting (Dweck & Reppucci, 1973). The theory of causal attribution has an intuitive reasonableness that encourages belief in its usefulness in helping to understand differential participation in ALB of choice, persistence, and independence in mathematical tasks of high cognitive complexity.

Confidence, usefulness, and attributional style are not unrelated. If one attributes success to stable, internal factors, then one can expect success in the future and is more confident that success can be achieved. On the other hand, attribution of failure to an internal, unstable factor (i.e., effort) does not diminish one's feeling of personal control of learning, so failure can be avoided if more effort is put forth. Such a belief would not diminish one's confidence in future mathematical performance. Perceived usefulness also interacts with attributional style to motivate achievement behavior. In order to work to achieve, not only must the learner believe she or he is in personal control of the outcome, but she or he must also value the outcome (Stipek & Weisz, 1981).

These three interrelated beliefs (confidence, perceived usefulness, and attributional style) clearly influence participation in ALB. Gender-related differences exist in all three beliefs. What then influences the development of gender-related differences in these internal motivational beliefs? Perhaps the most important influence is another pervasive internal motivational belief: the congruency seen between one's sex-role identity and achievement in mathematics.

Sex-role identity serves as a mediator of cognitive functioning (see Nash, 1979, for a thorough discussion). Sex-role identity is important to everyone. A portion of that sex-role identity is achievement in domains viewed as appropriate for one's sex. Mathematics is not seen as an appropriate domain for females. Therefore, achievement by a female in the mathematical domain results in her not fulfilling her sex-role identity adequately. She perceives that teachers and peers have lowered expectations of her mathematical success because she is a female. She also perceives that others see her as somewhat less feminine when she achieves in mathematics, and she becomes increasingly uncomfortable with her achievement. Success is not valued because she thinks others have negative feelings about her success.

There is support that congruency with sex-role identity is important. Fennema and Koehler (1983) report decreasing expectations of females in mathematics and increasing negative feelings about female achievements from Grades 6–8. Frieze and Hanusa (1984) develop the argument that science is perceived as difficult, requiring sacrifice and persistence. Scientists are perceived as objective, logical, emotionally neutral, and working alone. These perceptions are in conflict with the sex role of females. Frieze and Hanusa state that "A young woman who is considering a career in science must choose between being 'feminine' or being 'scientific'" (p. 13). "Each of the cultural beliefs about science and the scientist . . . implies a mismatch between a young woman's beliefs about herself as a person and the possibility of herself as a scientist" (p. 14).

External and/or Societal Influences

External and/or societal factors influence the development of internal motivational beliefs and through these beliefs influence participation in ALB. Some of the same external factors also directly influence participation in ALB. Although we are aware that there are many important external factors, we have chosen to restrict our focus for three reasons. We are concerned with (1) those influences that we are most qualified to deal with; (2) those that have the greatest potential for change; and (3) those that have the most direct influence on the learning of mathematics. For these reasons, we focus on schools. Since learners spend most of their school time within classrooms, it is in the classrooms where children participate in ALBs. At least two major variables within classrooms are important to consider: teacher–pupil interactions and learning activities in which girls and boys participate.

TEACHER–PUPIL INTERACTIONS

Most of the relevant research studies in the area of gender-related differences in classroom interactions have explored the notion of equality of treatment of girls and boys. Numerous studies have shown that teachers do not treat girls and boys the same in classrooms. Boys interact much more with teachers than do girls (Brophy & Good, 1974; Fennema et al., 1980; Becker, 1979), and girls have many more days in which they do not interact at all with the teacher (Reyes & Fennema, 1982). Boys initiate more contacts with teachers than do girls (Good & Brophy, 1972; Brophy & Good, 1970; Lippitt & Gold, 1959; Fennema et al., 1980) and teachers initiate more contacts with boys (Brophy & Good, 1974; Fennema et al., 1980). Boys receive more discipline contacts (Serbin, O'Leary, Kent, & Tonick, 1973; Jackson & Lahaderne, 1967; Felsenthal, 1970) as well as more praise (Brophy & Good, 1970). Teachers accept wrong or poor answers more often from boys (Good & Brophy, 1972). Serbin et al. found that teachers respond more frequently to requests for help from boys than from girls. Teachers tend to criticize girls more than boys for the academic quality of their work (Dweck, Davidson, Nelson, & Enna, 1978).

When one looks at specific subgroups of boys and girls, some other interesting differences emerge. Teachers interact more with high-achieving boys than with high-achieving girls (Good, Sikes, & Brophy, 1973). Teachers interact less with girls who have high confidence in learning mathematics than with high-confidence boys. High-confidence boys interact at higher cognitive levels with their teachers more often than high-confidence girls (Reyes & Fennema, 1982).

Although gender-related differences in teacher–pupil interactions clearly exist, do such differences result in differential participation in ALB or in differential performance on high-level cognitive tasks? It seems reasonable to assume that some types of teacher–pupil interactions influence the development of one's internal motivational beliefs and/or directly influence the participation in ALB.

Grieb and Easley (1984) addressed the problem directly. They hypothesized that teachers allow some boys to exert their independence overtly and refuse to learn specific algorithms. This can lead to development of mathematical capabilities of problem solving. In turn, teachers control girls, more so than boys, and impose mathematics as a set of rules or computational devices. This imposition of rules is more apt to lead to dissipated interest in or to lack of development of skills to do high-level tasks than is the tolerance for independent behavior accorded some boys.

Although the negative relationship between high teacher control and motivation has been studied, there are few studies that have reported on within-class gender-related differences in control. Eccles, Midgley, and Adler (in press) reviewed the studies dealing with classroom control and concluded that there were positive relationships found between student control and intrinsic academic motivation (p. 23). However, Grieb and Easley's hypothesis about gender-related within-classroom differences which develop independence has not been empirically tested.

What influences children to participate differently in classroom processes? Although not addressing gender differences, Maehr (1976) has a model of continuing motivation that is similar to the ALB model. Continuing motivation (CM) is "the tendency to return to and continue working on tasks away from the instructional context in which they were initially encountered" (p. 443). Two components of CM are choice of alternative behavior and persistence. Antecedents for the development of CM are self-regard, perception of self as cause in achievement, and self-identity. He also discusses external influences on CM, such as teachers.

Dweck et al. (1978) studied teachers' use of evaluative feedback as a direct cause of learned helplessness or mastery orientation of girls and boys. They reported that less than one-third of the criticism given to boys concerned intellectual aspects of their work, while most of the remainder was for nonacademic matters (neatness, conduct, etc.). Girls received two-thirds of their criticism in relation to the academic components of their work. Boys received praise more for the quality of their work than did girls. They concluded that this pattern of evaluative feedback tends to lead to learned helplessness in girls and mastery orientation in boys. However, this rather dramatic finding was not replicated by Heller and Parsons (1981). They concluded that "there was no evidence supporting the hypothesis that teachers use evaluative feedback differentially . . . for boys and girls" (p. 19). Although the Heller and Parsons study is with older children (junior high vs. fourth and fifth grade), it seems that teachers' evaluative feedback is not as powerful a developer of attributional style as was once thought.

At best, the results from these studies indicate that while the number of interactions of teachers with boys and girls differs, the impact of this differential number of interactions on learning is unknown. Even when there have been results suggesting a strong impact on learning of differential teacher behavior toward girls and boys (as in the case of Dweck's work), later investigations have questioned the conclusions. As a matter of fact, there are few direct data suggesting that differential teacher treatment is the cause of gender-related differences in achievement. This lack of data can be explained in at least two ways: (1) There really is no effect of differential teacher treatment, or (2) We have not been observing the correct types of teacher–pupil interactions. The latter explanation led to a National Science Foundation (NSF) sponsored study. In this study researchers and teachers collaborated and combined expertise to generate hypotheses about teacher–student interaction patterns that have an important influence on girls' and boys' growth in ALB in mathematics.

Two researchers (both female), 2 advanced doctoral students (one female and one male), and 13 fourth- and fifth-grade teachers (4 male and 9 female) participated in the NSF study. The teachers had been selected as exceptionally capable. Teaching experience varied from 2–21 years with a mean of 12.62 years of experience. Five participants had master's degrees while 8 had bachelor's degrees. Although the range of grade level experience for the entire group was K–8, the participants had most of their experience at the fourth- and fifth-grade levels. Almost everyone had some human relations course experience. Two participants had some work with sexism in schools and school materials. Eleven of the participants were classroom teachers. Two of the participants directed a teachers' center and were actively involved in in-service education.

Table 2.1

Teacher-Reported Interactions with High- and Low-Confidence Girls and Boys

	High-confidence		Low-confidence		Total	
Category	Boy	Girl	Boy	Girl	Boy	Girl
Praising	20	23	10	17	30	37
Initiating concern	6	2	5	1	11	3
Prompting	32	21	32	15	64	36
Encouraging	12	8	14	13	26	21
Nonjudging	14	14	8	16	22	30
Social	4	11	0	0	4	11
Showing displeasure with student	10	2	2	5	12	7

The group of teachers, researchers, and doctoral students met 10 times over a 5-month period. Each meeting lasted about 2 hours, involved general discussions about the topic and directed activities, and were audio-recorded. During the study, teachers were asked to generate behaviors that they hypothesized would lead to the development of ALB in children. Each teacher-identified behavior was placed on a 3 × 5 card and the cards placed into categories by 4 advanced doctoral students. Four distinct categories appeared: (1) encouraging independence and responsibility; (2) building problem-solving strategies; (3) building self-image of child; and (4) providing problem-solving role models.

Participants were also asked to characterize their own interactions with selected target students. They were asked to identify high- and low-confidence girls and boys by administering the Cognitive Level Mathematics Attitude (Fennema & Peterson, 1984) scale. Participants were asked to select four children (a high-confidence girl and boy and a low-confidence girl and boy) and to keep logs for 2 weeks. During a later session, two small groups were formed, and teachers were asked to summarize teacher behaviors as they interacted with girls and boys of different confidence levels. These logs were collected and coded by staff members, using categories defined by the teachers. Seven categories yielded interesting results and they are listed in Table 2.1. Teachers reported initiating concern more with boys, prompting boys more, encouraging boys more, had more social interactions with boys, particularly low-confidence boys. Teachers reported being more nonjudgmental with girls than they were with boys. Teachers said they praised low-confidence children, particularly boys, less than high-confidence children.

Thus, reports of the kinds of interactions teachers thought were important and teachers' reports of their actual interactions with children were available. The teachers were emphatic about the importance of building the self-image of children. Most felt that praise built the child's self-image, and indeed they reported that they praised quite a bit. However, the children they reported praising most were high-confidence children. Teachers indicated during the sessions that a variety of teacher behaviors, which were categorized as prompting, would lead to success that in turn would lead to improved self-image and independence. The teachers reported many instances of prompting. Boys were prompted many more times than girls. Overall, it was difficult to generate important teaching behaviors during the study. However, certain themes emerged that are worth discussing.

1. *It is not easy for teachers to identify, or at least to verbalize, teaching behaviors. It is much easier for teachers to focus on children's behaviors.* From the very first session, it was apparent that teachers could describe quite accurately how various children behaved in relation to ALB. The construct of ALB seemed easy to understand and the participants recognized the importance of the construct. Teachers felt that boys, much more than girls, demonstrated ALB and were able to provide many specific examples of girls' and boys' ALBs or lack of ALBs. In particular, examples of girls' avoidance of problem-solving activities were often cited. Girls' dependent behaviors were described (e.g., when a problem-solving assignment is given, girls more often request help. Girls do not take risks. Girls are not active learners. Girls often ask for more directions than do boys). Another easily identified child behavior was the separation of the sexes when free choice was involved. When children could choose where to sit, single-sex grouping resulted. During free play, boys play with boys and girls play with girls.

When the discussion was directed toward what teachers do, participants had difficulty identifying behavior. Categories from the observational study that explicitly identified and described teaching behavior were presented and discussed twice before participants were asked to bring back examples of their own behavior. However, most of behaviors brought back were descriptions of children's behavior. After more discussion and work, participants were able to identify teaching behaviors, but were continually more apt to discuss child behavior than teacher behavior.

2. *Teachers were very reluctant to look at their behavior towards boys and girls as opposed to their behavior towards individuals.* Although all participants were initially concerned about the learning of girls and accepted the idea that educational outcomes for girls and boys were inequitable, the concern diminished during the study. The concern for ALBs and developing positive attitudes toward learning by all children remained high.

Was this a reflection of a deep-seated belief that girls and boys are inherently different? One lengthy (and one could say heated) discussion between researcher and participant on this theme occurred during a session near the end of the year. One point of view was that while girls and boys often do exhibit different behaviors in fourth grade, the differences are due to environmental and educational factors and are not due to inherited tendencies. The other point of view was that the differences in girls' and boys' behavior are due to inherited tendencies that cannot be changed.

Another interpretation of participants' reluctance to look at their behavior in relation to girls and boys is that they honestly were unable to see any differences in their treatment of boys and girls. Participants seemed very aware of individual differences and needs in their students and, as the study progressed, talked increasingly about specific children.

3. *Praise and encouragement are very important for all students but especially for low-confidence students.* Participants felt that teacher praise and encouragement were highly necessary for building students' self-images. They reported that praise was given almost nondiscriminately and in many situations. The praise was given to build the child's self-image. Some participants felt that indiscriminate praise was harmful to children and their development of ALB, but the most often reported teacher behavior was praise.

4. *Teachers often react to a student's behavior as opposed to initiating interactions. As nonschool life is different for girls than boys, does this mean girls start different types of interactions with teachers and thus have different interactions than boys?* Although teachers are no doubt in control of the content covered in the classroom, they do not report being in control of how they interact with children. They respond to, not direct, children.

CONCLUSIONS

Gender-related differences exist in mathematics. While not all males are better able than all females to successfully complete high-level mathematics tasks, mean differences in performance between the sexes are often found. In addition, females participate much less in mathematics-related occupations than do males. The ALB model proposed here attempts to explain why such differences exist.

The learning of mathematics, particularly the skills required to perform high-level tasks, does not occur quickly and at one time. Rather, these skills are developed over a period of years by participating many times in the activities necessary for performing the high-level tasks. Indeed, a very circular path is required. One learns to do high-level tasks by choosing, persisting, and succeeding at high-level tasks.

The autonomous learning behaviors serve as the mediators between classroom processes, internal motivational beliefs, and achievement in mathematics. A learner chooses to participate in ALB by having internal motivational beliefs that encourage such participation and by participating in certain kinds of classroom interactions. However, the identification of these important classroom interactions is difficult and much research needs to be done to ensure their identification.

The model as proposed seems to be cohesive and is supported by some literature. However, there are some questions not yet empirically answered.

1. Do girls and boys actually participate differently in ALB? If so, does this differential participation occur at all ages, in all (or most) classrooms, in all ability levels?
2. Do girls and boys with similar internal motivational beliefs participate similarly in ALB?
3. Do teachers differentially encourage girls and boys to participate in ALB? Do teachers allow or encourage more choice of mathematical learning activities by boys or girls? Are boys encouraged or allowed, to participate in more high-level activities than girls? Is dependence encouraged more for girls than for boys?
4. Does more participation in ALB result in higher achievement?

REFERENCES

Aiken, L. R. (1971). Intellective variables and mathematics achievement: Directions for research. *Journal of School Psychology, 9,* 201–209.
Bardwick, J. M. (1971). *Psychology of women.* New York: Harper & Row.
Bar-Tal, D. (1978). Attributional analysis of achievement-related behavior. *Review of Educational Research, 48*(2), 259–271.
Becker, J. (1979). *A study of differential treatment of females and males in mathematics classes.* Doctoral dissertation, University of Maryland.
Begle, E. G. (1979). *Critical variables in mathematics education.* Washington, DC: Mathematical Association of America and National Council of Teachers of Mathematics.
Benbow, C. P., & Stanley, J. C. (1980). Sex differences in mathematical ability: Fact or artifact? *Science, 210,* 1262–1264.
Brophy, J. E., & Good, T. L. (1970). Brophy–Good system (Teacher–child dyadic interaction). In A. Simon & E. Boyer (Eds.), *Mirrors for behavior: An anthology of observation instruments continued, 1970 supplement* (Vol. A). Philadelphia: Research for Better Schools.

Brophy, J. E., & Good, T. L. (1974). *Teacher–student relationships: Causes and consequences.* New York: Holt, Rinehart & Winston.

Chambers, D. L. (1983). Wisconsin mathematics assessment results, 1982. *Wisconsin Teachers of Mathematics, 34*(1). 3–5.

Deaux, K. (1976). Sex: A perspective on the attribution process. In J. Harvey, W. Ickes, & R. Kidd (Eds.), *New directions in attributional research* (Vol. 1). Hillsdale, NJ: Erlbaum.

Dees, R. L. (1982). *Sex differences in geometry achievement.* Paper presented at the annual meeting of the American Educational Research Association, New York.

Dweck, C. S., Davidson, W., Nelson, S., & Enna, B. (1978). Sex differences in learned helplessness: II. The contingencies of evaluative feedback in the classroom and III. An experimental analysis. *Developmental Psychology, 14,* 268–276.

Dweck, C. S., & Repucci, N. D. (1973). Learned helplessness and reinforcement responsibility in children. *Journal of Personality and Social Psychology, 25,* 109–116.

Eccles, J., Midgley, C., & Adler, T. (in press). Age-related changes in the school environment: Effects on achievement motivation. In J. H. Nicholls (Ed.), *The development of achievement motivation.* Greenwich, CT: JAI Press.

Felsenthal, H. (1970). *Sex differences in teacher–pupil interaction in first-grade reading instruction.* Paper presented at the annual meeting of the American Educational Research Association.

Fennema, E. (1984). Girls, women and mathematics. In E. Fennema & M. J. Ayer (Eds.), *Women and mathematics: Equity or equality* (pp. 137–164). Berkeley: CA: McCutchan Publishing Corporation.

Fennema, E., & Carpenter, T. (1981). The second national assessment and sex-related differences in mathematics. *Mathematics Teacher, 74*(7), 554–559.

Fennema, E., & Koehler, M. S. (1983). Expectations and feelings about females' and males' achievement in mathematics. In E. Fennema (Ed.), *Research on relationship of spatial visualization and confidence to male/female mathematics achievement in grades 6-8.* (Final Report, National Science Foundation Project SED78-17330). Washington, DC: U. S. Government Printing Office.

Fennema, E., & Peterson, P. L. (1984). Classroom processes and autonomous learning behavior in mathematics (Final Report, National Science Foundation, SE8-8109077). Washington, DC: U.S. Government Printing Office.

Fennema, E., Reyes, L. H., Perl, T. H., Konsin, M. A., & Drakenberg, M. (1980, April). *Cognitive and affective influences on the development of sex-related differences in mathematics.* Symposium presented at the annual meeting of the American Educational Research Association, Boston.

Fennema, E., & Sherman, J. (1976). Fennema–Sherman mathematics attitude scales: Instruments designed to measure attitudes toward the learning of mathematics by females and males. JSAS *Catalog of Selected Documents in Psychology, 6,* 31. (Ms. No. 1225)

Fennema, E., Wolleat, P., Pedro, J., & Becker, A. (1981). Increasing women's participation in mathematics: An intervention study. *Journal for Research in Mathematics Education, 12,* 3–14.

Fox, L. H. (1980). *The problem of women and mathematics.* Unpublished paper prepared for the Ford Foundation.

Frieze, I. H. & Hanusa, I. H. (1984). Women scientists: Overcoming barriers. In M. Steinkamp & M. L. Maehr (Eds.), *Women in science.* (pp. 139–164). Greenwich, CT: JAI Press.

Garai, J. E., & Scheinfeld, A. (1968). Sex differences in mental and behavioral traits. *Genetic Psychology Monographs, 77,* 169–299.

Glennon, V. J., & Callahan, L. G. (1968). *A guide to current research: Elementary school mathematics.* Washington, DC: Association for Supervision and Curriculum Development.

Good, T., & Brophy, J. (1972). *Changing teacher behavior: An empirical investigation.* Unpublished manuscript, University of Missouri.

Good, T. L., Grouws, D. A., & Edmeier, H. (1983). *Active mathematics teaching.* New York: Longman.

Good, T. L., Sikes, J. N., & Brophy, J. E. (1973). Effects of teacher sex and student sex on classroom interaction. *Journal of Educational Psychology, 65*(1), 74–87.

Grieb, H., & Easley, J. (1984). A primary school impediment to mathematical equity: Case studies in role-dependent socialization. In M. Steinkamp & M. L. Maehr, *Women in science.* Greenwich, CT: JAI Press. 317–362.

Gustin, W. (1982). *Learning to become a mathematician: The development of independence.* Paper presented at the annual meeting of the American Educational Research Association, New York.

Helson, R. (1980). The creative woman mathematician. In L. H. Fox, L. Brody, & D. Tobin (Eds.), *Women and the mathematical mystique.* Baltimore: Johns Hopkins University Press.

Heller, K. A., & Parsons, J. E. (1981). Sex differences in teachers' evaluative feedback and students' expectancies for success in mathematics. *Child Development, 52,* 1015–1019.

Hoffman, L. W. (1975). Early childhood experiences and women's achievement motives. In M. T. Mednick, S. S. Tangri, & L. W. Hoffman (Eds.), *Women and achievement* (pp. 129–150). New York: Wiley.

Hollinger, C. (1978). *The effects of student dependency, sex, birth order, and teacher control ideology on teacher–student interaction.* Unpublished doctoral dissertation, Case Western Reserve University.

Jackson, P., & Lahaderne, H. (1967). Inequalities of teacher–pupil contacts. *Psychology in the Schools, 4*(3), 204–211.

Kagan, J. (1964). Acquisition and significance of sex typing and sex role identity. In M. L. Hoffman & L. W. Hoffman (Eds.), *Review of child development research.* New York: Russell Sage Foundation.

Kagan, J., & Moss, H. A. (1962). *Birth to maturity.* New York: Wiley.

Lippitt, R., & Gold, M. (1959). Classroom social structure as a mental health problem. *Journal of Social Issues, 15,* 40–49.

Maccoby, E. E., & Jacklin, C. N. (1974). *The psychology of sex differences.* Stanford: Stanford University Press.

Maccoby, E., & Masters, J. (1970). Attachment and dependency. In Mussen, P. H. (Ed.), *Carmichael's manual of child psychology* (Vol. 2, pp. 73–158). New York: Wiley.

Maehr, M. L. (1976). Continuing motivation: An analysis of a seldom considered educational outcome. *Review of Educational Research, 46*(3), 443–462.

Marrett, C. B., & Gates, H. (1983). Male-female enrollment across mathematics tracks in predominantly black high schools. *Journal for Research in Mathematics Education, 14*(2), 113–118.

Mischel, W. (1970). Sex-typing and socialization. In P. H. Mussen (Ed.), *Carmichael's manual of child psychology.* New York: Wiley.

Nash, S. C. (1979). Sex role as a mediator of intellectual functioning (pp. 263–302). In M. A. Wittig & A. C. Petersen (Eds.), *Sex-related differences in cognitive functioning.* New York: Academic Press.

Perl, T. H. (1979). *Discriminating factors and sex differences in electing mathematics.* Unpublished doctoral dissertation, Stanford University.

Peterson, P. L., & Fennema, E. (in press). Effective teaching, student engagement in classroom activities, and sex-related differences in learning mathematics. *American Educational Research Journal.*

Reyes, L. H., & Fennema, E. (1982). *Sex and confidence level differences in participation in mathematics classroom processes.* Paper presented at the annual meeting of the American Educational Research Association, New York.

Serbin, L., O'Leary, K., Kent, R., & Tonick, I. (1973). A comparison of teacher response to the pre-academic and problem behavior of boys and girls. *Child Development, 44*(4), 796–804.

Sherman, J. A. (1971). *On the psychology of women.* Springfield, IL: Charles C. Thomas.

Stipek, D. J. & Weisz, J. R. (1981). Perceived personal control and academic achievement. *Review of Educational Research, 51*(1), 101–137.

Vetter, B. (1980). *Opportunities in science and engineering.* Washington, DC. Scientific Manpower Commission.

Weiner, B. (1974). *Achievement motivation and attribution theory.* Morristown, NJ: General Learning Press.

Wilson, J. W. (1972). *Patterns in mathematics achievement in grade 11: Z population* (National Longitudinal Study of Mathematical Abilities, No. 17). Stanford: Stanford University Press.

Wolleat, P., Pedro, J., Becker, A., & Fennema, E. (1980). Sex differences in high school students' causal attributions of performance in mathematics. *Journal for Research in Mathematics Education, 11*(5), 356–366.

3

Listening to Adolescents: Gender Differences in Science Classroom Interaction*

LINDA WILSON MORSE and HERBERT M. HANDLEY

INTRODUCTION

Traditionally, men and women have not been equally represented in the career areas of science and technology. One major reason for this phenomenon may be that science appears to be incongruent with the gender-role perceptions held by adolescent girls. Current literature suggests that girls self-select themselves out of courses in science and mathematics at the high school level (Haven, 1970; Sells, 1976).

---

* Please note that authorship of this paper is jointly shared and the order of names does not indicate unequal contributions.

GENDER INFLUENCES
IN CLASSROOM INTERACTION
ISBN: 0-12-752075-9

37

The junior high school years appear to be the critical era for emergence of gender-role interests and differences in achievement between boys and girls in science and mathematics (Hilton, 1971; Hardin & Dede, 1973; Fox, 1976a; DeBoer, 1984). Lagging interest in science among adolescent females has been credited in the past to innate sex differences in their aptitude for science and mathematics compared to their male counterparts (Fox, 1976a, 1976b; Benbow & Stanley, 1980). Astin (1974) and Fox (1976b), however, presented a rival hypothesis that gender differences in mathematical aptitude in adolescents result from social factors. The social factor theory also appears feasible for explaining the lag of adolescent girls' interests in science, since mathematics appears to be a major stumbling block for developing women's interests in science (Fox, 1976b). According to Fox, the classroom itself serves as one area in which social roles in science and mathematics are learned through interactions with teachers and peers.

Although the factors affecting gender-related differences in mathematics participation have been fairly well established by investigators such as Fennema and Sherman (1976, 1977), Armstrong (1980), Coleman (1961), and Hawley (1971), such careful study has not yet been given to the study of why girls fail to pursue science. The present study, which is one part of a large investigation of the factors affecting science participation by adolescents (Morse & Handley, 1982), examines classroom interactions within a traditional, teacher-directed science classroom. One major purpose of this study was to determine what gender differences in classroom interaction exist within this type of setting and how these differences change as the adolescents continue through a critical period for pursuing science.

Two major assumptions of this study are that the teacher provides the structure and guidance of the instruction within a traditional setting and that science is an inquiry, question-asking, and question-answering content (Rigdon, 1983). As Huston and Carpenter (see Chapter 7, this volume) point out, it is structure or learning guidance that the teacher can bring to the instructional setting. Within a traditional setting, the teacher provides the guidance through texts and by giving information and questioning the students. This type of structure sets the communication pattern that controls the instructional process and in which both teacher and student play vital roles in the instructional communication. The subject area of science is particularly appropriate for examining the communication–interaction process since science involves learning how to ask questions. Thus, the teacher's role is to carefully structure and control the step-by-step prerequisite skill development that leads to the acquisition of problem-solving skills in science (Rigdon, 1983).

Gender-Related Differences in
Classroom Interaction

A fair amount of literature has been published in the past 10 years that documents gender-related differences in classroom interaction (Brophy, see Chapter 6, this volume.). Boys, in general, receive more attention than girls when interacting with the teacher (Etaugh & Hughes, 1975; Leinhardt, Seewald, & Engel, 1979). Girls are often viewed as the invisible members of the classroom (Sadker & Sadker, 1982). Good, Sikes, and Brophy (1973) compared the behavior of male and female teachers with adolescent male and female students. Boys interacted more frequently and aggressively with teachers than did girls. Teachers were more apt to ask boys process questions and to ask girls product and choice questions. Additionally, studies of teacher–student interactions in science also show that teachers interact more with male than female students (Bean, 1976; Parsons, 1979). Teacher–pupil interactions in instructional settings have been shown to be related to affective outcomes (Rowe, 1974; Santiesteban, 1976) and cognitive learning (Siegel & Rosenshine, 1973) in science.

Observation in Science Classrooms

To study teacher–student interactions, Shymansky (1976) developed an observation scheme classifying students' interactions with peers and teachers in terms of 10 categories designating different degrees of involvement for student subjects. Shymansky and Penick (1979) also reported a classification of teachers' behaviors in classroom interactions utilizing 15 different categories. These classifications categorize teacher interactions ranging from passive observation to asking extended thought questions. According to these authors, these instruments discriminate modestly between behaviors of male and female teachers and, to a lesser degree, between male and female students in the classroom. Such observed behaviors, however, have not yet been linked successfully to students' achievement in science. Possibly the reason for this lack is that the teacher and student behaviors have been described for groups as a whole rather than in terms of individual students, that is, the data were coded as total number of teacher and student behaviors displayed in the group and not as the number of times that the teacher talked to Mary or to John and, subsequently, what social interactions were observed for John and Mary.

Baird (1976) summarized the literature related to sex differences in group communication in terms of gender-role theory of behavior. These differences appear to reflect traits of males that are characteristics of science-oriented students (Handley & Bledsoe, 1968). Baird (1976) described males as being encouraged to be independent, aggressive, problem-oriented, and willing to take risks in social interactions. Females, in contrast, are more willing to self-disclose, more expressive of emotions and perceptive of their emotional states, more sensitive to nonverbal cues, less interested in problem solving, relatively unwilling to assume risks, and more yielding to social pressures. Baird noted that in the current *zeitgeist* of liberality in reinterpreting women's roles, these behavior patterns are rapidly changing. Whether or not Baird's summarization of social traits for the two sexes are stereotypes, he identified several traits in the sex groups that can be observed in classroom behaviors.

Other Teacher Influences

As reviewed by Fennema and Sherman (1976), many studies show that students' attitudes toward mathematics are highly related to their experience with teachers. Students' perceptions of what teachers think of them and their ability in mathematics relate to students' interest and participation in math-related subjects. Teacher expectation, as postulated by Rosenthal and Jacobson (1968), has been demonstrated to have a large effect upon student achievement (Dusek, 1975; Lockheed, 1975). Anderson (1963) also demonstrated the positive relationship between nonsexist and enthusiastic teacher behavior and the intellectual development of girls in science. Parsons (1979) found a direct relationship between teacher expectancies and students' expectancies for success in mathematics.

Ricks and Pyke (1973) observed teachers of both sexes to report that boys and girls behave differently. Male students were more preferred than female students by teachers as a whole and especially by female teachers. Brandt and Hayden (1975), however, observed that teachers of both sexes tended to rate the work of boys and girls to be of equal quality.

The Research Problem

The research problem investigated in this study was whether differential treatment was observed for male and female adolescents in science classroom interactions over a 2-year interval. Although other studies have investigated whether there are gender differences in classroom interaction, none have collected interaction data on a group of students in a longitudinal study in the science classroom.

Answers were sought to the following specific questions: (1) Are there differences in observed classroom interactions between teachers and students when the variable of student sex is considered at the seventh- and eighth-grade levels, respectively, and (2) Do these differences in teacher and student classroom interactions change from the seventh to the eighth grade?

METHODOLOGY

The Setting of the Study

Subjects of the study consisted of students enrolled in general science in a rural middle school in south central Mississippi. This school contains most of the students of middle-school age taught in an entire separate school district serving the county. Students from the cooperating school were nearly equally balanced according to race (44% white and 56% black). While nearly 60% of the students at the seventh-grade level were eligible for full federal lunch program assistance, a mixture of middle income and lower upper-level income families were also represented in the student body.

Relative to the science curriculum at this middle school, major emphasis is placed on biological science during the seventh grade and earth science during the eighth grade. Science classes are generally taught in a traditional lecture and discussion approach with minimum emphasis placed on laboratory work. During the time of the study, science in the seventh grade was taught by two female and one male instructors. Eighth-grade instruction was conducted by one male and one female teacher. Due to the small number of teachers, teacher gender was not examined as a variable.

Subjects

Subjects for the first and second years of the study consisted of 155 early adolescents enrolled in the seventh grade and then the eighth grade for the second year. This group was composed of 46.3% females and 53.7% males. The racial composition of the group was 41.1% white and 58.9% black. More than half the group (62.9%) were eligible for full free-lunch programs. At the beginning of the study, students ranged in age from 12 to 15 years; 78.3% of the group was 12 years old and 19.4% was 13 years old.

The Classroom Interaction/Observation Plan

The observation system was designed by the authors to be used in a structured, traditional classroom setting. The only equipment required was two cassette tape recorders, two watch-timers, and seating charts with the students' identification numbers. Each student was assigned a four-digit identification number that was used throughout the six observations (three for the first year, three for the second year). Each observation session, which lasted 30 minutes, was taped and later transcribed. When an interaction occurred, the observer indicated on the seating chart which student was involved and at what minute and second the interaction happened. The seating charts with the resulting interaction record were then used to identify the interaction on the transcript made of the session. Therefore, for each student, a set of interactions could be identified.

For the purposes of this study, an interaction was defined as any verbal response uttered by the student to the teacher or another student or any call for a response by the teacher directed to the student.

Each interaction was then analyzed using eight descriptive categories. For each interaction, the following questions were asked:

1. Who was the source of this interaction, teacher or student?
2. How can this interaction be described?
3. What type of feedback followed the interaction?
4. Was this an instructional question?
5. If it was an instructional question, what domain of learning would best describe it?
6. If it was a question, was it correctly answered?
7. How much wait-time occurred? (Wait-time was defined as the amount of time that lapsed between interacting sources.) In this study, two wait-times were measured: The first was student response time, which was the length of time it takes for the student to respond to the teacher. The second, called teacher wait-time, is the length of time it takes for the teacher to give feedback to the student's response.

These categories are summarized in Table 3.1.

For the purposes of this study, the variable used was the total number of instances of each category for each student in each year. The interaction was calculated by summing across the three observation occasions for each year for each student, so that each of the participants had a total summed frequency of occurrence for each interaction category. The only exceptions were for student-response time and teacher wait-time, which were calculated by averaging the observed values across the three occasions for each

Table 3.1

Summary of Information Coded on Each Interaction

Category	Levels within category
Source of interaction	Teacher to student
	Student to teacher
	Student to student
Type of interaction	Direct question
	Class business
	Disciplinary
	Social
	Call out to indirect question
	Unsolicited response
	Solicited response
Feedback	None
	Simple acknowledgment
	Restate answer or question
	Prompt
	Praise
	Clarification
	Correction
	Criticism or disciplinary
	Elaboration
	Teacher's answer to student's question
Instructional question	Yes or no
Domain of question	Information
	Intellectual skills
	Cognitive strategies
	Attitudes
	Psychomotor
Student response time	Recorded in seconds and hundredths of seconds
Teacher wait-time	Recorded in seconds and hundredths of seconds

year. For example, the interaction record for Student 4129 is illustrated by Table 3.2. Therefore, the summed total for each variable was calculated. The analysis involved using the summed frequencies for each year. Although each interaction was classified seven times, no sequential analysis was carried out in this study. It is important to note that once an interaction was identified, it was classified by each of the categories listed in Table 3.1. However, for each category, only one decision was made about how to classify that part of the interaction. Interactions were not grouped into more than one type of category. For example, for the category "feedback," an interaction would be classified once based on how it best described that instance of feedback.

Table 3.2

Student 4129: A Sample Partial Analysis

	Observation			Summed for
Variables	1	2	3	Grade 7
Source				
Teacher–student interaction	12	10	2	24
Student–teacher interaction	1	2	2	5
Type				
Direct question	4	9	1	14
Class business	5	0	1	6

RESULTS

Seventh Grade

During the seventh grade, 1802 interactions were identified. Of these, 637 teacher-to-student interactions were observed for the females and 860 teacher-to-student interactions were observed for the males (43% vs. 57%). Many fewer student-to-teacher interactions were recorded for either gender. The seventh-grade females initiated 120 interactions with the teacher and the seventh-grade males had 176 student-to-teacher interactions (41% vs. 59%). Only nine student-to-student interactions were identified for the seventh graders (three for the females and six for the males). On the average, however, males received significantly more interactions than did females (13.03 vs. 10.13, see Table 3.3). In addition to total number of interactions, the seventh-grade males also received significantly more instructional questions than did the females (13.00 vs. 9.93, see Table 3.3).

As previously described, each interaction was classified by the type of interaction that it best represented and the type of feedback that followed it. Comparisons between the genders on type of interaction are presented in Table 3.4. With the exception of solicited responses, males dominated every type of interaction. Although some of these differences in percentages were slight (5.01% for females and 5.47% for males on class business), others were more pronounced (10.67% for females and 16.99% for males on call-outs).

Table 3.5 presents the results of the interactions for type of feedback received. With the exception of praise, the males again dominated the females in the frequency of each type of feedback received. Relative to the distribution of feedback within gender, the seventh-grade females received a greater percentage of feedback that included restating the question,

Table 3.3

Comparison of Overall Interactions and Wait-Time Variables for Males and Females in the Two Grade Levels

| | Grade 7 | | | | | Grade 8 | | | | |
| | Males | | Females | | | Males | | Females | | |
	$\bar{X}$	SD	$\bar{X}$	SD	t	$\bar{X}$	SD	$\bar{X}$	SD	t
Total no. of interactions	13.03	9.52	10.13	7.72	2.07*	15.19	10.24	11.72	6.63	2.48*
Total no. instructional questions	13.00	9.52	9.93	7.73	2.19*	14.68	9.80	11.19	6.16	2.63*
Student response time (sec)	1.79	0.91	1.89	1.12	0.60	1.22	0.50	1.44	0.86	1.99*
Teacher wait-time (sec)	1.87	0.99	1.91	1.57	0.71	1.39	1.15	1.45	1.29	0.34

* $p < .05$.

Table 3.4

Types of Classroom Interaction for Females and Males at Two Grade Levels

Type of interaction	Grade 7				Grade 8				Difference (%) Grades 7 & 8[a]	
	Females		Males		Females		Males		Fe-males	Males
	Frequency	%	Frequency	%	Frequency	%	Frequency	%		
Direct questions	455	59.95	669	64.20	544	62.96	756	62.22	3.01	-1.98
Class business	38	5.01	57	5.47	5	0.58	50	4.12	-4.42	-1.35
Disciplinary	4	0.53	5	0.48	2	0.23	5	0.41	-0.30	-0.07
Social	12	1.58	15	1.44	0	0.00	4	0.33	-1.58	-1.11
Call-out to indirect questions	81	10.67	177	16.99	89	10.30	168	13.83	-0.40	-3.16
Unsolicited responses	7	0.92	9	0.86	22	2.55	79	6.50	1.63	5.64
Solicited responses	162	21.34	110	10.56	202	23.38	153	12.59	2.04	2.03
Total number of interactions	759		1042		864		1215			

[a] Chi-square values calculated by comparing eighth-grade frequencies with those expected from the seventh-grade percentages for each type of interaction. For females $\chi^2(6) = 76.91, p < .001$. For males $\chi^2(6) = 453.85, p < .001$.

Table 3.5

Types of Teacher Feedback for Females and Males at Two Grade Levels

| | Grade 7 | | | | Grade 8 | | | | Difference (%) Grades 7 & 8 [a] | |
| | Females | | Males | | Females | | Males | | | |
Type of feedback	Frequency	%	Frequency	%	Frequency	%	Frequency	%	Females	Males
No feedback	105	14.56	164	16.61	102	12.58	165	14.92	−1.98	−1.69
Simple acknowledgment	128	17.75	180	18.24	108	13.32	205	18.54	−4.43	0.30
Restate answer or question	227	31.48	301	30.49	402	49.57	469	42.41	18.09	11.92
Prompt	107	14.84	159	16.11	140	17.26	156	14.11	2.42	−2.00
Praise	9	1.25	7	0.71	10	1.23	10	0.90	−0.02	0.19
Corrections	41	5.69	54	5.47	30	3.70	35	3.16	−1.99	−2.31
Criticism or discipline	17	2.36	19	1.93	5	0.62	32	2.89	−1.74	0.96
Clarification	77	10.68	80	8.11	10	1.23	23	2.08	−9.45	−6.03
Elaboration	10	1.39	23	2.33	4	0.49	11	0.99	−0.90	−1.34
Total feedback	721		987		811		1106			

[a] Chi-square values calculated by comparing eighth-grade frequencies with those expected from the seventh-grade percentages for each type of feedback. For females $\chi^2(8) = 187.23$, $p < .001$. For males $\chi^2(8) = 130.93$, $p < .001$.

47

praise, corrections-criticism, and clarification than did the males, even though these differences were not large.

One further analysis involved evaluating each instructional question (a subcategory of type of interaction) as to which domain of learning it represented. Only two of the domains were represented by the questions asked: attitudes and information. No instances of questions reflecting intellectual skills, cognitive strategies, or psychomotor skills were recorded from any of the interactions. For the seventh graders, eight attitude questions were recorded, all of them directed to the males. From the domain representing information, 1343 questions were identified. Of these, 540 were directed at the females and 803 were directed at the males.

Student response time and teacher wait-time were similar for both genders for the seventh grade (see Table 3.3). Females and males responded very quickly, and teachers waited less than 2 seconds for either gender to respond. No significant differences were noted for the seventh-grade students on these variables.

Eighth Grade

Eighth-grade males received significantly more interactions than did the eighth-grade females (15.19 vs. 11.72, see Table 3.3). Similar to the findings for the seventh grade, the eighth-grade males received more teacher-to-student interactions (1017 to 790; 56% vs. 44%) and initiated more student-to-teacher interactions (194 to 84; 70% vs. 30%). Only for student-to-student initiated interactions did females outnumber males, but this was for a very small number of instances (five to four). This low number of student-to-student contacts is not surprising due to the traditional structure of the classrooms observed.

For type of interaction (see Table 3.4), male eighth graders dominated every type of interaction except solicited responses. These interactions were followed through with more instances of every kind of feedback for the males (see Table 3.5). As was true for the seventh-grade females, the eighth-grade females received a greater percentage of feedback that involved restatement. They also received a greater percentage of prompting, a reversal from the previous year. Another reversal over the previous year was that males received more criticism-discipline during the eighth grade.

The results of the eighth graders response time and teacher wait-times are given in Table 3.3. Males responded significantly faster than the females during the eighth-grade year. However, teacher wait-time, while still very short, was similar for both genders.

On the average, eighth-grade males were asked significantly more instructional questions than were the females (14.68 vs. 11.19, see Table 3.3). Of these instructional questions, males were asked fewer attitude questions (83 for females vs. 17 for males) than were the females and more information questions (871 for males and 614 for females).

Comparison of Interactions over the 2-Year Span

Differences in the sources of interactions for males and females were observed for both years. In the seventh grade 41% of the student-to-teacher interactions were initiated by girls, whereas as eighth graders these same girls initiated only 30% of the interactions. The girls appeared to become less assertive in the initiation of ideas in the science classes as they matured. In contrast, the males' initiation of interactions in the classrooms increased from 57 to 70% over the 2 years. Females, then, generated fewer student-to-teacher interactions than did males and this difference became more pronounced as they progressed in their science studies.

Over the 2 years, male students, came to participate more in class business. In the seventh grade, the difference was modest (60% vs. 40%), whereas in the eighth grade the boys accounted for 91% of class business interactions.

Teachers also differed in the amount of feedback given to boys and girls in science classes over the 2 years. Boys received more criticism or disciplinary feedback from the teachers. In the seventh grade, the difference was minimal (53% for males vs. 47% for females), but was marked for the eighth grade (86% vs. 14%). When the frequencies of teacher feedback to a student's remarks and questions were collectively tabulated across specific types for the 2 years, the boys received 57% of the teachers' comments while the girls received only 43%. In brief, the boys received more attention from teachers than did the girls in all types of feedback offered and this difference increased as the students matured, though the only significant change was for criticism or disciplinary feedback.

No differences were observed in the domains of instructional questions asked boys and girls over the 2 years, except that of attitudes. As eighth graders, the girls were asked more attitudinal questions, whereas in the seventh grade the boys were asked more attitudinal questions. However, the small number of attitudinal questions asked over the 2 years suggests that this finding be interpreted with caution.

The female students, when in the eighth grade, had a smaller percentage of their interaction in the types of class business, discipline, social, and call-outs than were observed during the seventh grade. In contrast, the relative percentages of direct questions and unsolicited and solicited response interactions increased from Grade 7 to Grade 8.

For the eighth-grade male students, the relative percentage of all types of interaction except unsolicited response decreased in comparison with seventh-grade observations.

For differences in types of feedback received from the seventh to the eighth grades, the females had fewer percentages of all types of feedback except restatement and prompting. The eighth-grade males had greater percentages of simple acknowledgment, restatement, praise, and criticism. In contrast, they had fewer percentages of no feedback, prompting, correction, clarification, and elaboration in the eighth grade.

In order to compare these patterns of classroom interaction by type of interaction and type of feedback across grades, chi-square goodness-of-fit tests were calculated for female and for male students. In each case, eighth-grade observed frequencies in each type of interaction category (e.g., direct question, class business) were compared with the observed proportions from the seventh-grade observations.

For types of interaction, Table 3.4 presents the results of the chi-square goodness-of-fit tests for the female and for the male students. The derived chi-square statistics for both genders were found to be statistically significant at the traditional alpha levels ($p < .001$). Table 3.5 presents the results of the same tests using the types of feedback. These were also statistically significant for both genders.

When comparing differences from year to year, the reader should note that there were only a few teachers at each of the grade levels (three at Grade 7, two at Grade 8). Some of the observed differences across grade level might be attributable to teacher or instructor variation. Due to the small number of teachers, no statistical comparisons were attempted.

DISCUSSION AND SUMMARY

This study confirmed the finding of many other researchers that boys and girls are differentially treated in classroom interactions. While this alone is not an astonishing discovery, it is interesting to note that this was observed by using nearly an entire seventh-grade population followed up in the eighth grade within a school. Students were not randomly selected; rather, an interaction record on each student was tabulated. Moreover, these observations were taken on six occasions during two school years.

These observations took place within science classes. This is important for several reasons. First, pursuit of science at the middle and high school level is a prerequisite for later participation in science and math courses that permit career opportunities. Second, science is a discipline which demands an inquiring approach to problem solving. Success in science is often more a matter of identifying which questions to ask and investigate than in the sheer grasping of factual information; that is, deciding what questions to ask and participating in question-and-answer behavior is an important activity in science. Although it was beyond the scope of this study to gauge the quality of questions posed by the teacher or students, the simple fact that the boys asked and answered more questions has important implications for science learning.

Using the seventh grade as a base, what do the findings suggest about gender differences in classroom interactions in science? The most obvious finding is that the males were the initiates of or reactors to more interactions than were females. In a content area where inquiry and questioning are crucial to learning new concepts, males held the advantage over the females. When these interactions were grouped into descriptive categories, males again dominated and controlled the classroom discussion. This was true for all categories except solicited response, an area in which females outdistanced the males. However, this is to be expected since females are taught from kindergarten days to be prepared. A written report represents conforming to standards and is much "safer" than being exposed to having to think quickly when responding to a question. Although a written report may have required quite a lot of work and thought, it is done on one's own time; it does not present the same kinds of quick mental processing that a question requires. If questioning strategies are one way the teacher structures the learning guidance, then feedback is simply another way of fine tuning this guidance. Feedback is essential in learning new information and concepts, which in turn are critical in learning science. With the exception of praise in which few instances were noted, the males again dominated in feedback and correctness of response.

Why would teachers allow the male students to control the classroom discussion through call-outs? Apparently, the expectation of male aggressiveness coupled with the frequency of such behaviors led to this phenonenon being considered acceptable. An alternative explanation was that the higher frequency of response or participation of males was perceived by teachers as indicative of greater interest in science. The more expansive forms of feedback, elaboration and clarification, lead to longer teacher–student engagement and provide more opportunities for cognitive processing (whether or not the student actually does this or not is unknown, but the availability of the opportunity is present). The immediate implication of these behaviors is that elaboration and clarification are techniques for enhancing transfer of new learning. Again, this type of activity is vital in the learning of science if ideas are to "click" and new discoveries are to be made.

What were the differences observed during the eighth grade? The trend towards male dominance becomes even greater in the eighth grade. Males again received and initiated more interactions, particularly student-to-teacher interactions. Control of the classroom conversations as well as increased opportunities for inquiry into the content gave the males the advantage. But what were the female students doing? They were sitting at their desks ready to give their solicited responses, that is, their previously prepared reports. They chose to participate less, and when they did, they relied on very structured activities, that is, the prepared report (Huston & Carpenter, see Chapter 7, this volume). Why these females initiated fewer interactions and thus allowed the males to control the discussion is a matter for speculation. Not only did males dominate on academic topics, they also conducted more class business, more social interactions, and received more disciplinary responses. In general these males seemed to be more involved in the normal daily classroom life. Males also were recipients of more types of feedback. Thus, both the structure of the classroom interactions and the control of the classroom become more male-dominated. While the females waited for their turn to speak, males were actively involved in the classroom discussions. These structure and control themes are the main differences in how the interactions changed over time. Boys asked significantly more questions during eighth grade then during the seventh. They also became more agressive in their control of the classroom talk other than the instruction. These differences are critical in a science classroom. Asking the right questions is essential in learning science. While it is unknown if they were asking critical questions leading to new understanding, at least the males were asking questions. These questions were given more attention through increased feedback. Other controlling behaviors, such as class business, lead to independence and organization, which are skills essential to the processes involved in the doing of science.

Several interesting findings in the study seemed to be contradictory to the way one might believe that science is best learned. First, nearly all of the questions asked of either gender were information, fact-type questions. The learning of science is not facilitated through this domain but rather through problem-solving skills. This is related to Fennema and Peterson's (see Chapter 2, this volume) discussion of the importance of the development of autonomous learning behaviors. Thus students who are not introduced to such approaches may become bored and resort to other non-school-based activites in which problem-solving inquiry skills are used. Boys are far more likely to experience such outside activities than girls. Thus, it appears that even this situation might lead to boys having the advantage.

Another contradictory finding was in the student and teacher response times. In general, these were very quick. During both years, males responded more quickly than females. This may not be a male advantage. In a science classroom, appropriate questioning to foster inquiry requires time for thinking. Similarly, it has been suggested by Tobin and Capie (1980) that teachers should wait about 3 seconds for promoting students' attending and generalizing. This is nearly twice as long as the eighth-grade teachers were waiting.

Additionally, these teachers did not consciously seem to treat the students differently nor were they willing to admit they might be treating the students inequitably. All the teachers used some type of management strategy for getting students involved in the questioning even if it was a simple method such as going up and down the rows where the students were seated. This inability to identify differences in behaviors on the part of teachers is noted by other researchers (see Chapter 2, this volume by Fennema & Peterson).

Conclusions and Summary

The purpose of this study was to examine what gender differences existed in classroom interactions for adolescents in science class. Six observations across two school years yielded over 4000 interactions. It was found that teachers interacted significantly more with males than females in classrooms. They asked males more questions than they asked females. Teachers spent more time reinforcing or rewording questions for males than for females. Teachers interacted more with boys than with girls relative to social issues and classroom business. Boys gave more unsolicited responses in class than did girls. In general, boys received more teacher feedback that served to prolong the amount of interaction between teacher and student. This prolongation appeared to provide the boys with intermediate support for their responses, giving them more opportunity to answer questions correctly. These observations appeared to reflect higher teacher expectations for boys than for girls in science.

These results held despite the condition that the male and female students did not differ significantly in achievement and aptitude for doing science (Morse & Handley, 1982). Thus, the old stereotype of science as a male domain seemed to exist.

Within a science classroom that is taught in a traditional, large group, lecture method, learning guidance is structured in two general ways: through questioning and through feedback. Both of these represent structure. Questioning provides opportunities and variations for thinking about new concepts. Feedback fine tunes ideas. In both areas, boys received more attention and were also allowed to control other instructional and noninstructional interactions. This opportunity for becoming involved with science even in a very limited extent gave boys the immediate advantage over girls. Couple this idea to the stereotype of science as a male domain and other external pressures that limit participation in science by girls, and it is easy to see why girls do not later pursue science and engineering careers.

Several suggestions can be made for future research. (1) If differences in classroom interaction between the genders widen between seventh and eighth grades, which is a relatively short length of time, at what age level do these differences actually begin? Do they continue to widen throughout the school years? (2) What differences can be detected in the quality of the questioning styles? For example, what types of interaction chains occurred? Would these be qualitatively different for boys and girls? (3) Given a set of observations on the same students over intervals, how would differences emerge over time? Although these types of analysis were beyond the scope of the present study, attention given to the detection of emerging differences might yield a valuable insight into discovering how interaction patterns affect an instructional setting. Last, although learning to ask questions and participating in questioning is important in learning science, such factors are not the only variables that may have causal relationships for explaining observed differences in science participation (Morse & Handley, 1982). As Fennema and Peterson (see Chapter 2, this volume) point out in their discussion of factors influencing participation in mathematics, many such internal, external, and societal influences may affect why gender-related differences may be seen in mathematics. Careful study of these factors, as well as further scrutiny into the quality and subtle nature of verbal interactions and the structure of the learning guidance, should be undertaken if gender-related differences in science are to be fully understood.

REFERENCES

Anderson, K. E. (1963). A comparative study of student self-ratings on the influence of inspirational teachers in science and mathematics in the development of intellectual curiosity, persistence, and a questioning attitude. *Science Education, 47*(5), 429–437.

Armstrong, J. M. (1980). *Achievement and participation of women in mathematics: An overview.* Denver, CO.: Education Commission of the States.

Astin, H. S. (1974). Overview of the findings. In C. H. Austin, H. Suniewick, & A. S. Dweck (Eds.), *Women: A bibliography on their education and careers.* New York: Behavioral Publications.

Baird, J. E. (1976). Sex differences in group communications: A review of relevant research. *Quarterly Journal of Speech, 62*(3), 179–192.

Bean, J. P. (1976). *What is happening in mathematics and science classrooms: Student–teacher interaction.* Paper presented at the annual meeting of the American Educational Research Association, San Francisco.

Benbow, C., & Stanley, J. (1980). Sex differences in mathematical ability: Fact or artifact? *Science, 210,* 1962.

Brandt, L. J., & Hayden, M. E. (1975). Teachers' attitudes and ascription of causation. *Journal of Educational Psychology, 67*(5), 677–682.

Coleman, J. S. (1961). *The adolescent society, the social life of the teenager and its impact on education.* New York: Free Press of Glencoe.

DeBoer, G. E. (1984). A study of gender-effects in the science and mathematics taking behavior of a group of students who graduated from college in the late 1970s. *Journal of Research in Science Teaching, 21*(1), 95–103.

Dusek, J. P. (1975). Do teachers bias learning? *Review of Educational Research, 45*(4), 661–684.

Etaugh, C., & Hughes, V. (1975). Teacher evaluations of sex-typed behaviors in children: The role of teacher, sex, and school setting. *Developmental Psychology, 11,* 394–395.

Fennema, E., & Sherman, J. (1976, February). *Sex-related differences in mathematics learning: Myths, realities and related factors.* Paper presented at the annual meeting of the American Association for the Advancement of Science, Boston, MA.

Fennema, E., & Sherman, J. (1977). Sex-related differences in mathematics achievement, spatial visualization and affective factors. *American Educational Research Journal, 14,* 51–77.

Fox, L. H. (1976a, October). *Gifted girls: Scientists and mathematicians of the future.* Paper presented at the meeting of the National Association for Gifted Children, Kansas City, MO.

Fox, L. H. (1976b). *The effects of sex role socialization on mathematics participation and achievement.* Washington, DC: Career Awareness Division, National Institute of Education, U.S. Department of Health, Education and Welfare.

Good, T., Sikes, J. N., & Brophy, J. (1973). Effect of teacher sex and student sex on classroom interactions. *Journal of Educational Psychology, 65*(1), 74–87.

Handley, H. M., & Bledsoe, J. C. (1968). The personality profiles of influential science teachers. *Journal of Research in Science Teaching, 5*(1), 95–103.

Hardin, J., & Dede, C. J. (1973). Discrimination against women in science education. *Science Teacher, 40*(9), 239–241.

Haven, E. W. (1970). Current innovations and practice in the American high school. *School and Society, 98*(8), 239–241.

Hawley, P. (1971). What women think men think: Does it affect their career choices? *Journal of Counseling Psychology, 18,* 84–89.

Hilton, T. L. (1971). *Intellectual growth and vocational development report.* Princeton, NJ: Educational Testing Service.

Leinhardt, G., Seewald, A., & Engel, M. (1979). Learning what's taught: Sex differences in instruction. *Journal of Educational Psychology, 71,* 432–439.

Lockheed, M. (1975). *Some determinants and consequences of teacher expectations concerning pupil performance: Beginning teacher evaluation study.* Princeton, NJ: Educational Testing Service.

Morse, L. W., & Handley, H. M. (1982). *Relationship of significant others, parental and teacher influences to the development of self concept, science attitudes and achievement among adolescent girls* (Final Report, NIE-G-79-0159). Mississippi State, MS: Bureau of Educational Research.

Parsons, J. (1979). *The effects of teachers' expectancies and attributions on students' expectancies for success in mathematics.* Paper presented at the annual meeting of the American Educational Research Association, San Francisco, CA.

Ricks, F., & Pyke, S. (1973). Teacher perceptions and attitudes that foster or maintain sex-role differences. *Interchange, 4*(1), 26–33.

Rigdon, J. S. (1983). The art of great science. *Phi Delta Kappan, 64*(9), 613–617.

Rosenthal, R., & Jacobson, L. (1968). *Pygmalion in the classroom.* New York: Holt, Rinehart & Winston.

Rowe, M. B. (1974). Wait-time and rewards as instructional variables: Their influence on language, logic, and fate control (Part one). *Journal of Research in Science Teaching, 11*(2), 81–94.

Sadker, M. P., & Sadker, D. M. (1982). *Sex equity handbook for schools.* New York: Longman.

Santiesban, A. J. (1976). Teacher questioning performance and student affective outcomes. *Journal of Research in Science Teaching, 13*(6) 533–577.

Sells, L. (1976, February). *The mathematics filter and the education of women and minorities.* Paper presented at the meeting of the American Association for the Advancement of Science, Boston, MA.

Shymansky, J. A. (1976). How is student performance affected by the one to one teacher-student interactions occurring in an activity-centered classroom? *Journal of Research in Science Teaching, 13*(3), 253–258.

Shymansky, J. A., & Penick, J. C. (1979). Do laboratory teaching assistants exhibit bias? *Journal of Science Teaching, 8*(4), 223–225.

Siegel, M., & Rosenshine, B. (1973). *Teacher behavior and student achievement in the Bereiter-Engleman follow-through program.* Paper presented at the annual meeting of the American Educational Research Association, New Orleans.

Tobin, K., & Capie, W. (1980). *Relationships of selected dimensions of teacher performance with student engagement.* Paper presented at the annual meeting of the Mid-South Education Research Association, New Orleans.

Race–Gender Status, Classroom Interaction, and Children's Socialization in Elementary School*

LINDA GRANT

INTRODUCTION

Research on classroom interaction suggests that children's everyday experiences in public schools differ systematically by their race and by their gender (for summaries, see Brophy, Chapter 6, this volume; Brophy & Good, 1974; Grant, 1981; Lockheed, Chapter 8, this volume; Patchen, 1982; Sadker & Frazier, 1973; Schofield, 1982). Typically, however, research on race effects and on gender effects has proceeded as separate lines of inquiry,

* Portions of this research were supported by a National Institute of Mental Health Predoctoral Fellowship in Sociology and Social Policy. The author wishes to thank the following persons for comments on earlier drafts by Marianne Block, Phyllis Blumenfeld, Steven Bossert, Mark Chesler, Jacquelynne Eccles, Donna Eder, Cora Bagley Marrett, James Rothenberg, and Louise Cherry Wilkinson.

despite increasing evidence that the two ascribed statuses are inseparable in their bearing and their effects (e.g., Leggon, 1980; Rodgers–Rose, 1980).

Studies have documented persistent differences in achievement and attainment in public schools based on students' combined race–gender status (e.g., Chesler & Cave, 1981; Crain & Mahard, 1978a, 1978b; Epstein & McPartland, 1977; Persell, 1977; Thomas, Alexander & Eckland, 1979). Less well documented, however, are variations in classroom processes which might contribute to divergent outcomes. Although the few studies which have examined combined race–gender effects on children's experiences in classroom interaction suggest differences in the experiences of each group, research has varied so widely in major foci, setting, age and grade level of students, and methods that it is difficult to synthesize (see Grant, 1981, for a review and critique.)

GOALS OF THIS STUDY

Longitudinal ethnographic observations of 139 first-grade students in six classrooms were used to explore classroom interaction experiences of four groups: white males, white females, black males, and black females. Over a 5- to 6-month period regularities and variations in each group's interactions with teachers and with peers were examined. Implications of observed patterns for student's academic and social behaviors in classrooms and for their socialization to adult roles are considered. Finally, directions for future research on classroom interaction are suggested.

Some assumptions will be clarified at the outset. First, in this study classrooms are visualized as complex social systems, created and maintained at multiple levels of reality. Actors can experience social life in the same classroom in widely divergent ways (Clement, Eisenhart, & Harding, 1979; Feldman, 1979; Lancy, 1978; Gordon, 1957). Classrooms are also seen as dynamic systems that change over time.

Second, students are viewed as active creators of their own schooling environments, not simply passive responders to influences encountered in these settings (Anyon, 1983; Apple, 1979; Giroux, 1981). Students are the primary actors in peer networks that powerfully affect classroom life and support, mediate, or contradict influences emanating from teachers and other school personnel. Although classroom interaction research in the past focused heavily on teacher–student interactions, researchers in recent years have paid increasing attention to peer interchanges as they affect learning and classroom social life (see Eccles & Blumenfeld, Chapter 5, this volume; Fennema & Peterson, Chapter 2, this volume; Huston & Carpenter, Chapter 7, this volume; Morine-Dershimer, Chapter 11, this volume; Patchen, 1982; Fennema & Peterson, (Chapter 2, this volume); Schofield, 1982; Schmuck, 1978; Webb & Kenderski, Chapter 10, this volume; Wilkinson, Lindow, & Chiang, Chapter 9, this volume). As Schmuck (1978) has observed, for many pupils interactions with peers are much more frequent and meaningful than contacts with teachers.

Finally, public school classrooms are viewed as social units with penetrable boundaries embedded in larger social units such as schools and communities (Boocock, 1980). It is assumed that through the process of status generalization, cultural elements with strong social valuations, such as race and gender, filter into classrooms and affect their internal social life (Berger, Rosenholtz, & Zelditch, 1980). The infiltration, probably largely nonconscious, occurs despite schools' and teachers' adherence to the rhetoric of equal opportunity. One route by which such infiltration occurs is through teacher expectations about performances of different race–gender students that teachers are apt to hold as a result of exposure to prevailing cultural norms, their professional training, or early socialization into the teacher role (see Becker, 1953; Bidwell, 1965; Chesler & Cave, 1981). Although teachers commonly justify their expectations as responses to particular characteristics of individual children, research has shown that expectations vary systematically with children's race and gender as well as with other nonacademic criteria, such as social class, family background, or performance of older siblings (Brophy & Good, 1974; Persell, 1977; Rist, 1970).

External cultural elements also enter the classroom through students. Children of differing race–gender configurations hold varying expectations about teachers (Lightfoot, 1978; Ogbu, 1978) and about other race–gender peers. Peer networks are difficult to regulate and function as transmitters of cultural elements into school settings that can thwart teachers' and school officials' goals for achieving race and/or gender equity in classrooms (e.g., Clement et al., 1979; Gordon, 1957; Grant, 1983, 1984; Guttentag & Bray, 1976; Morine-Dershimer, Chapter 11, this volume; Paley, 1979).

Differentiation in school experience by race–gender status possibly derives from two bases. First, students of each race–gender group may be differentially attuned to certain aspects of classroom life, such as degree of involvement with teachers and with peers. Second, within each of these two domains each group of students may have distinctive experiences that channel members of these student subgroups toward divergent outcomes.

Lee and Gropper (1974) suggest that female elementary school students are more "system dependent" than male classmates. System dependence is a phenomenological concept that was not measured. It connotes high levels of psychic identification with teachers and school systems, high interaction rates with teachers, and strong conformity to classroom rules. System-dependent behaviors are reinforced by teacher praise for conformity. Males are less dependent, more involved with peers, less involved with teachers, less conforming, and less frequently praised by teachers. Lee and Gropper argue that system dependence brings girls rewards early in school but inhibits their development of autonomous learning styles that are necessary to excel at higher levels of education (see also Fennema & Peterson, Chapter 2, this volume; Scrupski, 1975). Boys become more autonomous.

Lee and Gropper (1974) do not consider the effects of race on students' degree of system dependence, but it is possible to extend their formulation and to envision that race–gender status, in combination, affects children's relative balance of attention to teachers and to peers.

Second, within each domain of classroom life (teacher–student interactions and peer interactions), children of differing race–gender status may have qualitatively different experiences. Brophy's (see Chapter 6, this volume) review of the literature suggests variability in gender effects on teacher–student interaction. However, studies of peer interactions suggest that female in comparison to male students are apt to be disadvantaged (Lockheed, Chapter 8, this volume; Wilkinson et al., Chapter 9, this volume), although this effect might be more pronounced among white than among black boys and girls (Grant, 1983).

This paper first explores effects of race–gender status on students' proportions of interactions with teachers and with peers. It then examines qualitative aspects of each group's interactions with teachers and with peers that have the potential for producing divergent academic and social outcomes.

DATA SOURCE AND METHODS

The author completed from 20 to 30 hours of ethnographic observations of six desegregated first-grade classrooms. Observations took place in 20- to 90-minute sessions, with notes from each session expanded into detailed, time-sequential, ethnographic notes within 24 hours. Observations began in September or October in each room and extended into April or May.

Table 4.1 shows characteristics of the six classrooms. (All teacher, student, and district names are fictitious.) Each classroom was located in a district serving a working-class community near a large Midwestern city. Each community had a black population of approximately 15% with no other ethnic groups except whites constituting greater than 1% of the school population. Classrooms in this study enrolled larger proportions of black students than their district-wide averages, with minority students ranging from 21 to 96% in each class (Table 4.2). Three teachers were white and three were black (Table 4.1). All were female. Black teachers

Table 4.1

Characteristics of Six Observed Classrooms

Teacher–classroom[a]	Teacher race	School	District	School year observed
Maxwell	White	Bass	Glendon	1979–1980
Avery	White	Bass	Glendon	1979–1980
Delby	White	Dawson	Ridgeley	1980–1981
Todd	Black	Dawson	Ridgeley	1980–1981
Horton	Black	Dawson	Ridgeley	1980–1981
Douglas	Black	Crescent	Ridgeley	1980–1981

[a] All teacher, school, and district names are fictitious.

taught classes with the highest proportions of minority students, although one (Horton) taught a majority-white class.

Two classrooms (Avery's and Maxwell's) were observed during the 1979–1980 school year; the remainder were observed during 1980–1981.[1] Observations covered all regularly scheduled classroom activities and all parts of the school day.

Because only a few studies have explored race–gender effects on schooling experience, it was not possible a priori to identify a set of indicators useful for examining possible differences. Hence the technique of "theoretical sampling" described by Glaser and Strauss (1967) was employed in the study. Each room was observed until regular patterns of interaction could be discerned. Then greater attention was given to times and events promising the greatest return in understanding these interactions. (See Grant, 1984, for a fuller discussion of the advantages and limitations of such tech-

Table 4.2

Race–Gender Configurations of Children in Six Classrooms[a]

Teacher–classroom[b]	Black females	Black males	White males	White females	Totals (100%)
Maxwell	3 (11%)	3 (11%)	10 (37%)	11 (41%)	27
Avery	3 (13%)	2 (8%)	12 (50%)	7 (29%)	24
Delby	2 (11%)	2 (11%)	5 (26%)	10 (52%)	19
Todd	9 (38%)	5 (21%)	4 (17%)	6 (25%)	24
Horton	2 (10%)	4 (19%)	9 (42%)	6 (29%)	21
Douglas	10 (42%)	13 (54%)	1 (4%)	0 (0%)	24
	29 (21%)	29 (21%)	41 (29%)	40 (29%)	139

[a] Table includes only those children present 80% or greater of the observation times.
[b] All teacher names are fictitious.

niques). Codes for categorizing recurrent behaviors were derived inductively from the data. Portions of the author's coding were coded by two graduate students uninvolved in the original research, yielding reliability scores ranging from .82 to .93, depending on the classroom and the particular behavior.[2]

Intensive interviews with teachers clarified meanings of some classroom activities. Teachers were interviewed toward the end of the observation phase in each room and commented on children's academic skills and social relationships. Only students who were present 80% or more of the observation period were included in the analyses reported here.

Frequency counts of recurrent, straightforward behaviors have been derived from field notes. These constitute what Becker (1958) terms "quasi-statistics." Although not the equivalent of sample data, and hence not appropriate for significance tests, the counts are useful for portraying classroom environments. Counts reported here have been normed to 20 hours, to adjust for actual observation times ranging from 20 to 30 hours in the six rooms.

Comparisons of frequency counts across classrooms are problematic. Each room constituted a distinctive social setting, with meanings of events created in part by members. Some teachers, for example, used instructional activities requiring group work, while others discouraged peer interaction during work (see Bossert, 1979). A peer contact in the first room likely had a different meaning and implication than a similar contact in the second. It is useful, however, to examine relative distributions of behaviors across race–gender groups in each classroom and to compare each race-gender group's ordinal rankings on certain measures across classrooms. Whatever the absolute rate of occurrence of a particular behavior (e.g., teacher praise for work), one group could consistently receive more and another group less. Such a pattern suggests consistencies in differential treatment of children of different race–gender groups. It is also possible that relative distributions of teacher and student behaviors, rather than absolute amounts, are critical in producing varying coutcomes, although this possibility has rarely been examined in classroom interaction studies.

RESULTS

Proportions of Teacher–Student and Peer Interactions

To examine whether children display different levels of attentiveness to teachers and to peers, counts were made of numbers of teacher contacts and peer contacts for each child. All teacher and peer contacts, regardless of

Table 4.3

Proportion of Teacher–Student to Peer Interactions per Child for Each Race–Gender Group in Six Classrooms in 20 Hours

Class[a]	White females	White males	Black females	Black males	All students
Maxwell	1.25	0.761	0.940	0.317	0.963
Avery	1.43	0.863	1.03	0.328	0.884
Delby	0.93	0.411	0.481	0.447	0.562
Todd	1.22	0.836	1.11	0.678	0.992
Horton	1.05	0.831	0.677	0.382	0.834
Douglas	0.00[b]	0.992	0.872	0.657	0.739

[a] Teacher names are fictitious.

[b] Douglas' classroom contained no white females and only one white male.

type or instigator, were included. A ratio of teacher-to-peer contacts for each child was computed by dividing teacher contacts by peer contacts. Then the average number of teacher–student and of peer contacts for children of each race–gender group in each room was tabulated. Ratios of teacher-to-peer contacts for each race–gender group were calculated in the same way as for individual children. Averages were normed to 20 observational hours.

Table 4.3 presents ratios of teacher–student to peer interactions for each race–gender group in each class. The extreme right-hand column of the table shows the ratio for all students in each class, regardless of race–gender status. For each cell of Table 4.3, a number greater than 1 indicates that children of this student subgroup averaged more contacts with teachers than with peers; a number less than 1 indicates the reverse.

There are also classroom-by-classroom variations in patterns shown in Table 4.3. For example, ratios were lower overall, indicating a greater proportion of peer than of teacher interactions, in Delby's class compared to Maxwell's class. Delby used more group-based instructional activities, while Maxwell preferred whole-group activities and individual work. These structural factors affected the relative attention given teachers and peers by all students.

Nevertheless, close examination of Table 4.3 reveals variations by students' race–gender status in proportions of interaction with teachers and with peers. In the five classrooms where white females were enrolled (all but the Douglas classroom) the white girls obtained the highest ratios, indicating their greatest propensity than other race-gender peers to interact with teachers. In fact, in all but one of the five rooms (Delby's), white girls had ratios greater than 1, indicating more contacts with teachers than with peers. Black girls in Maxwell's and Todd's rooms also averaged more contacts with teachers than with peers, but neither white boys nor black boys in any classroom had more contacts with teachers than peers.

Black girls were the group ranking next in proportion of teacher contacts in all but one classroom (Horton's), where white boys had slightly greater proportions of contacts with teachers than did the black girls. Nevertheless, for black girls peer contacts were more common than teacher contacts in all but two rooms.

White boys, on the whole, spent less time with teachers and more with peers than girls of either race (with the exception of Horton's room, noted above). Black boys, however, had the lowest ratios of any group in any room, indicating the most extremely skewed balance of peer contacts as compared with teacher contacts.

The data suggest that race–gender status does have an impact on students' devotion of attention to teachers and to peers. However, the amount of attention devoted to each domain of classroom life is skewed toward more peer interactions for most students, with the exception of white girls in most rooms. Also, for all children in a class the skews appear to be affected by characteristics of classrooms or teachers which have not been examined systematically in this analysis, such as task organization (Bossert, 1979).

As Schofield (1982) noted in her study of desegregated junior high school classrooms, the search for patterns in experiences of student subgroups necessarily deemphasizes variations in experiences of individual children within a group. There also are overlaps, rather than crisp distinctions, in typical experiences of children in each race–gender group. Two notable exceptions to the above-reported patterns deserve mention. First, although teachers generally had the most extensive contacts with white girls, the three teachers in Dawson School (Delby, Horton, and Todd) each had one high-achieving black male student with whom they interacted as heavily as they did, on the average, with white female students. These students, however, typically had higher rates of interactions with peers than did the white girls, making their ratios less than 1. Nevertheless, these *individual* children stood out from other black boys in their classrooms as having more (and on the whole far more positive) interactions with teachers.

Similarly, all the classrooms except one (Todd's) had white girls who acquired a "bad girl" label. This phenomenon is discussed more fully in Grant (1983). Teachers made strongly negative attributions about abilities and personal qualities of these bad girls, especially in contrast to their evaluations of most other white females, and were apt to treat them more harshly than most students. The seven bad girls, who appeared in four classrooms, as individuals had far lower interaction rates with teachers, and far more contacts with peers, than the average white girls in their respective rooms.

Thus, race–gender status seemingly inclines students towards particular balances of teacher–student as compared to peer interaction. Despite overall classroom differences in these balances, with only a few exceptions we find white girls with the highest ratios of teacher interactions, black girls with the next highest ratios, white boys ranking next, and black boys with the lowest proportion of teacher interactions in comparison to peer interactions. However, the fit is not absolute; within each race–gender group there are nonconforming cases, as examplified by the "superstar" black males and the bad girl white females.[3]

Attempts were made to discern patterns of change in children's ratios of interaction with teachers and with peers over time. This proved difficult because of variability in observation time and small numbers of children in each race–gender group in some rooms. Nevertheless, analyses not reported in detail here suggest that over time most students move toward fewer teacher interactions and more peer interactions. The trend is most dramatic for black female students, who seem to be rebuffed more frequently than other children in bids for teacher attention and turn instead to peer interactions (see Grant, 1984).

The ratios reported in Table 4.3 reveal nothing about the qualitative dimensions of students' experiences in interactions with teachers and with peers. These are analyzed in the next section.

Teacher–Student Interactions

It is useful to examine two types of teacher–student interaction in exploring experiences of various race–gender groups. The first are teacher behaviors initiated toward the student. The second are student behaviors initiated toward the teachers. Field notes provided data on each type.

Patterns of teacher feedback were examined by coding four types of teacher-to-student behaviors: praise for academic work, work criticism, behavioral praise, and behavioral reprimands. Praise for academic work included positive remarks made by teachers about work quality, pace, or achievement. Examples included: "Good, you got all those [math] problems right" and "That's a very fine printing paper." Work criticism consisted of negative comments about work quality, pace, or achievement, such as "That paper doesn't look like you had your mind on what you were doing" or "Those are wrong; you didn't listen to my directions." Behavioral praise consisted of comments on nonacademic behaviors of students, such as "I like the way [student's name] is sitting quietly, all ready to begin [a lesson]."

Behavioral reprimands were comments directed at students' nonacademic behaviors, for example, "Be quiet and get back to work." Only feedback which was publicly discernible to the observer was recorded in field notes. Nonverbal feedback was included when its intent was clear and recognized by at least two coders (e.g., pointing a finger and shaking a head at a student who talked out-of-turn during a lesson). Feedback to groups of three or fewer children was coded as if it consisted of individual interactions with each child in the group. Feedback to larger groups, infrequent in these rooms, was not included in tabulations.

Mean instances of the four types of feedback for children of each race–gender group were tabulated for each classroom. Means for each race–gender group were compared to overall means for all children in the class, regardless of race–gender characteristics. Although statistical analyses are not appropriate, standard deviations were also tabulated to describe variations. An arbitrary criterion of 0.5 or greater standard deviation from the mean for all children in a class was used to determine whether a particular race–gender group ranked high, average, or low on a particular behavior.

According to these criteria, there were few systematic variations in teachers' offering of work praise or criticism to certain race–gender groups in the six rooms. Some more subtle differences appeared, however. Occasionally students were singled out for "trusted lieutenant" duties, that is, special assignments such as tutoring peers, orienting a newcomer, or having one's work used as a model for other students. Of 14 assignments of this sort, 10 went to white females. I have argued elsewhere (Grant, 1983) that such special assignments, though not frequent, might have overridden the everyday praise and criticism patterns and marked these students as particularly competent in the eyes of their peers. Children's spontaneous comments recorded in field notes revealed a tendency for students nominated as trusted lieutenants to be identified by peers as bright or smart.

Second, black students, and especially black males, were overrepresented as recipients of control-directed or qualified praise. Depending on classroom they received from four to ten times the proportions of praise in contexts suggestion monitoring or qualification as compared to other students. An example of monitoring was Todd's interchange with Dave (black male):

> Keep on working [on math problems] . . . You know how to do them. Use your counting blocks if you need them. Good, you did that one right. Now don't talk [to another student] and bother her. You have to keep those numbers in a straight line . . . Yes, good, you managed to fix that one.

Qualification was exemplified by Maxwell's comment to Felix that he had turned in a good paper, "almost good enough to be put up on the board [where she displayed good work]."

Table 4.4

Mean Instances of Teacher Praise for Behavior to Each Race–Gender Group, per Child per 20 Observation Hours

Class[a]	Mean per white female	Mean per white male	Mean per black female	Mean per black male	All students	
					$\bar{X}$	SD
Maxwell	1.26	2.11	3.52[c]	0.44	1.73	2.97
Avery	0.20	0.22	0.53[c]	0	0.223	0.43
Delby	0.99	0.20[c]	0.99	0.50	0.73	0.93
Todd	1.43[c]	0.24[c]	1.06	0.20[c]	0.83	1.02
Horton	0.33	1.34	2.01[c]	0.50	0.96	1.47
Douglas	0.00[b]	0	0.98	0	0.43	1.45

[a] All teacher names are fictitious.

[b] Douglas' classroom contained no white females and only one white male.

[c] Mean for this group differs 0.5 or greater standard deviations from the mean for all students in the classroom.

More marked variations by race–gender status appeared for behavioral praise and reprimands (Tables 4.4 and 4.5). These tables again reveal substantial variation by classroom in teachers' propensities to praise or reprimand behavior, but some consistencies in students' experiences by their race–gender status are observed. Table 4.4 shows that black females stand out as the students most likely to be praised for behavior and are above classroom means in receipt of praise in all six rooms (although, notably, teacher Douglas gave little behavioral praise to any students). White females

Table 4.5

Mean Instances of Teacher Reprimands for Behavior to Each Race–Gender Group, per Child per 20 Observation Hours

Class[a]	Mean per white female	Mean per white male	Mean per black female	Mean per black male	All students	
					$\bar{X}$	SD
Maxwell	8.27	12.07	9.01	14.94[b]	10.50	8.77
Avery	8.74	9.54	11.13	7.55	9.31	3.96
Delby	9.92	14.88	3.47[b]	24.79[b]	12.47	6.98
Todd	0.952[b]	5.71	6.14	11.43[b]	5.87	5.18
Horton	15.06	11.50	13.05	14.06	13.15	7.07
Douglas	0.00[c]	33.44[b]	4.23[b]	13.77	10.48	11.61

[a] Teacher names are fictitious.

[b] Mean for this group differs 0.5 or greater standard deviations from the mean for all students in the classroom.

[c] Douglas' classroom contained no white females and only one white male.

tend to be above the mean, although they exceed the criterion noted earlier only in Todd's room. White males are slightly more apt to be below than above the mean in most rooms, while black males are below means in receipt of praise in all rooms. The ordinal rankings of the race–gender groups on receipt of behavioral praise in most rooms are consistent with their rankings on ratio of teacher-to-peer contacts reported in Table 4.3. That is, those groups interacting relatively more heavily with teachers than with peers were also most apt to receive teacher praise for behavior.

Table 4.5, reporting reprimands for behavior, shows male students the most heavily reprimanded in most classrooms, although patterns are not entirely consistent. Black males are the most heavily reprimanded group in four classrooms, but the least often reprimanded in Avery's room, which had only two black males. Although black males were above the mean for reprimands in Horton's room, white females in that class were reprimanded most often. With this exception, however, white females were less apt to be reprimanded than most students in their respective classrooms. Patterns for black females were more variable, although this group tended to be above rather than below the mean in most rooms. While in most rooms black boys were the most heavily reprimanded group and white girls the least heavily reprimanded group, the relative positions in the middle of white boys and black girls fluctuated across the six classrooms.

The data give some support to the existence of consistent variations by race–gender status in students' receipt of feedback from teachers. Although in many ways teachers did not respond differently to children by race–gender status (e.g., day-to-day praise and criticism), there is some indication that girls, and in particular white girls, had warmer, more positive contacts with teachers than did other students. On measures of feedback for classroom behavior boys had fewer positive interactions than girls. Black boys, in particular, stood out from the other race–gender groups as having largely negative interactions with teachers around such issues.

Student-to-Teacher Interactions

An equally important component of teacher–student interactions were behaviors initiated toward teachers by students. Four types were examined. First, tabulations were made of each race–gender group's total number of approaches to teachers, regardless of the reason for the approach. Table 4.6 shows that there was substantial variability by classroom in each group's propensity to approach the teacher. White girls were above the mean compared to that of most students in most rooms, although not above the 0.5 or greater standard deviation criterion level previously discussed. Black boys

Table 4.6

Mean Instances of Approaches to Teachers by Each Race–Gender Group, per Child
per 20 Observation Hours

Class[a]	Mean per white female	Mean per white male	Mean per black female	Mean per black male	All students	
					$\bar{X}$	SD
Maxwell	5.44	6.24	3.29	4.14	5.36	4.41
Avery	8.05	6.62	7.42	1.19[b]	6.74	4.74
Delby	6.74	4.36	5.95	9.92[b]	6.37	4.13
Todd	7.78	2.86[b]	9.52[b]	5.52	7.14	4.73
Horton	10.88	6.36	9.54	11.30	8.89	5.27
Douglas	0.00[c]	28.52[b]	3.34	4.67	5.13	6.14

[a] Teacher names are fictitious.

[b] Mean for this group differs 0.5 or greater standard deviations from the mean for all students in the classroom.

[c] Douglas' classroom contained no white females and only one white male.

were below in four of six rooms. Patterns for white boys and for black girls fluctuated across the rooms. Overall these data offer only weak support for an interpretation that boys, especially black boys, approached teachers less often than most students and that white girls approached more often.

Three types of approaches were particularly revealing of students' orientations toward teachers and were examined in greater detail, although the detailed data are not provided here (see Grant, 1981). These were chats, challenges, and enforcements.

Chats were personal-level interchanges between students and teachers in which each participant moved beyond the formal role relationship of teacher and student to exchange information on out-of-school life. I have argued that chats are beneficial to students because they help to develop and display verbal interaction skills and enhance social comfort in classrooms as a result of the personal bond formed with teachers (Grant, 1983; Grant & Rothenberg, in press). White females chatted with teachers more frequently than other students. Black females attempted to draw teachers into chats, especially early in the term, but were likely to be brushed off. Over time, their bids for chats in most rooms diminished (Grant, 1984). White males rarely instigated chats. Teachers in some rooms attempted to draw black males into chats, but typically were resisted or cut short with monosyllable replies (Grant, 1981).

Challenges were public objections or resistances raised by students to teachers' statements of fact or applications of classroom rules. Male students were the most likely challengers in all rooms (Grant, 1981), although black females sometimes raised challenges on behalf of peers more typically than on behalf of self. Although white males and black males overall were about equally likely to challenge, their challenges tended to be framed around different issues. White males challenged statements of fact, while black males more typically challenged application of rules, or in some instances the teacher's right to impose rules.

Enforcements were spontaneous attempts by students to gain peers' compliance with teacher or classroom rules. Although they might be thought of as peer interactions, they required the actual or symbolic backing of the teacher to make them successful and are discussed as teacher–student interactions. Contextual materials suggested that voluntary enforcements stemmed from diverse motivations, ranging from protecting a peer from a teacher sanction to garnering favorable teacher attention for oneself. Whatever their motivation, however, they indicated knowledge of classroom rules and a willingness to aid the teacher with social control of the classroom. Female students were the primary enforcers in all rooms, with black females especially likely to take on this role (see Grant, 1984).

Patterns apparent in student-initiated teacher contacts are similar to those found for teacher-initiated contacts. Girls' especially white girls, appear closer, more loyal, and more obedient to teachers. Boys, and especially black boys, were more estranged and less obedient. Once more, as individuals the superstar blacks and the bad girl whites were deviant cases. The superstar black boys engaged in substantially more teacher chats than other black boys in their classes, although they rarely enforced rules. Bad girls avoided teacher chats, almost never enforced rules, and challenged teachers at rates far higher than classroom averages. Overall, however, white girls appeared closest to teachers, black girls the next closest, white boys slightly less close than girls of either race, and black boys the most distant.

Peer Interactions

Peer interactions in some respects were related to children's experiences in teacher–student interaction networks. For example, being the "teacher's pet" sometimes brought one sanctions from peers. However, peer interactions also constituted a quasi-autonomous component of classroom life not directly regulated (and sometimes not even fully observable) by teachers. Two excerpts from field notes demonstrate the range of variation which peer interactions could have in orienting students toward or away from the teacher and her agenda for the classroom. The first is an interchange among white girls from Maxwell's class. The children are having recess time indoors on an especially cold day. The four girls, all in the highest reading group, are recreating a reading lesson with Clarissa playing the teacher role:

Clarissa says to the group (Her voice and manners seem to imitate those of Maxwell): "Did everyone bring crayons today?" Emily replies (sing-song type voice): "We always bring our crayons. You don't have to tell us." Clarissa holds up what appears to be a supplementary reading text which this group uses for extra work when they finish assignments. Emily turns to Maribeth (tying her shoe): "Pay attention. She's telling us which story to read." Clarissa taps pencil on table (another gesture imitative of Maxwell), tells group: "Now everyone should read [title of story]. Read carefully; I'll have some dittoes later."

The next excerpt comes from Delby's room and involves an interchange among Andre (black male), Ralph (black male), and Mickey (white male):

Children are assembled on a rug, while Delby reads a story. She tells them: "Pay attention. I'll be asking you some questions about what I'm reading." Andre attempts to attract Ralph's attention and engage him in a pencil-poking fight. Ralph says: SSHH. Janet (white female) tells them: SSHH. Ralph finally fights with pencils with Andre. Mickey giggles. Delby frowns at them, says nothing, keeps reading. Ralph whispers to Andre: "It's snowing out there (looks out window). Let's you and me throw snowballs at recess." Andre grins, nods to indicate yes. Mickey says: "Mr. _____ [the principal] won't let you throw snowballs." Andre tells Mickey: "Well, man, he ain't going to see us."

As the session continued, Andre successfully distracted Ralph's attention from the lesson three more times in the next 10 minutes.

The two excerpts offer strikingly different portraits of the impact of peer involvements on children's orientations to the classroom. The white girls' group advocated loyalty and obedience; their rehearsal of classroom procedures and imitation of the teacher likely strengthened their attentiveness to teachers and their agendas. The reverse pressures were apparent in the boys' interchange. Here students' attention was being diverted from the teacher and the lesson, and peer activities encouraged defiance, rather than conformity, to system rules.

Orientations of peer interchanges were difficult to analyze numerically, and not all peer interactions had direct relevance for students' orientations to classroom activities. However, again with some exceptions, repetitive patterns were discernible across classrooms. Girls' interchanges, especially those of white girls, supported attentiveness to teachers and conformity to rules more so than did those of boys. Boys spent more time, in and out of class, discussing issues unrelated to classroom activities. Themes of defiance and nonconformity appeared more frequently in their interchanges than in those of girls. The latter pattern was especially noticeable in peer interactions involving black boys only.

The data suggest that not only were students in each race–gender group differentially attentive to teachers and peers, as illustrated by ratios reported in Table 4.3, but the orientations of peer networks in which they were involved were qualitatively different. Some children, most notably white girls, were encouraged by peer interchanges to be attentive to teachers; other, most notably black boys, were discouraged by peer interchanges from accepting the teacher's influence. Furthermore, these peer exchanges competed with teacher interactions for time, attention, and loyalty.

Students also held different statuses in peer networks based on their race–gender characteristics, which may have influenced their willingness to invest time in interactions with teachers and peers. I have reported that girls, and especially white girls, are disadvantaged in comparison to boys in peer interchanges (see Grant, 1983). Girls give boys more academic and nonacademic aid and more emotional support than they receive from them. Girls also are overrepresented as victims but not perpetrators of verbal and physical aggression and of racist and sexist remarks. Status and power differentials are less apparent among black as compared to white children by gender. Black children of both genders engage in more reciprocal exchanges of aid. Furthermore, black girls are less apt than white girls to be intimidated by aggression, and retaliate rather than back down when this occurs. The generally more favorable experiences in teacher–student interactions for girls, in comparison to experiences in peer networks, might reinforce their tendency to spend time with teachers. For boys, however, peer networks in comparison to teacher contacts are more consistently rewarding, perhaps reinforcing their tendency to invest time in this domain of classroom life.

IMPLICATIONS FOR STUDENTS' ROLES

The findings of this study suggest that students' schooling experiences are differentiated in systematic ways by their race–gender status. Limitations of data and sample do not permit tracing to what extent variations in children's experiences stem from in-classroom processes and to what extent they stem from forces external to the school. An example of the latter might be parental socialization of different race–gender children or cultural conceptions about appropriate roles of each race–gender group.

The data suggest that students' race–gender status affects their "location" in classrooms and the roles they come to play in this interactive environment. White girls seemed most strongly attached to teachers and most attentive to their influence. They were relatively more involved with teachers than with peers. In cross-gender interactions they were less powerful than boys. Black boys, in contrast, seemed most distant from teachers and most tightly intergrated into close-knit peer cadres which often resisted influence by the teacher. These alliances and orientations influence the manner in which members of these race–gender groups experience daily classroom life.

The effects of classroom location and differing schooling experiences of each race gender group on future adult behavior is less clear, although speculation is possible. Schooling experience, for the most part, seems to contribute to socialization of each race–gender group in a manner consistent with prevailing societal norms about appropriate roles for adults of each ascribed-status group (see Grant, 1984).

Scholars have disagreed about the probable effects of schooling on social stratification. Some (e.g., Dewey, 1966) view public schools as open mobility systems offering advancement based on merit. Others (e.g., Jencks, Smith, Acland, Bane, Cohen, Gintis, Heyns, & Michelson, 1972; Kelly & Nihlen, 1982), argue that schooling has little impact on future social standing, which is related most strongly to family socioeconomic status. Still others (e.g., Bowles & Gintis, 1976; Chesler & Cave, 1981; Rowan, 1982) see schools as significant forces in creating, maintaining, and legitimating current status arrangements in each new generation of students. Schools thus function as transmitters of status arrangements.

While this study does not provide an adequate test of the validity of these theories, its findings are consistent with the transmission of status arrangements argument. However, they also suggest that such conceptualizations perhaps overemphasize the extent to which social differentiation by race–gender status is imposed on students and underemphasize the extent to which students' actions contribute to such differentiation (see Apple, 1979; Giroux, 1981). The process seems to be one of "the sociology of becoming" (Abrams, 1982). Although this concept has not been applied previously to an analysis of educational processes, it is applicable here. Within educational institutions persons are presented with choices that are differentially stratified by the individual's ascribed statuses. For example, white girls might have had an easier time gaining teachers' favorable attentions because teachers expect them to be good students and to be interested in such interchanges.

Despite a stratification of options, however, individuals retain power to make choices. The deviance of the black male superstars and the bad girl white females are examples of students whose experiences differ from those of most members of their race–gender groups. Once a choice is made, however, a person moves along a particular channel, and away from others, where further stratified choices are offered, accepted, or resisted. At each stage it becomes more difficult for individuals to make an atypical choice or to move to another channel.

This study offers numerous examples of such contingent choices and stratification of options. Black boys, who show heavier peer involvements

than other race–gender students, also experience greater hostility in interactions with teachers. The teacher–student contacts may intensify involvement with peers and encourage a nonconforming orientation on the part of
peer networks.

Movement toward social differentiation in classrooms by race–gender
status is thus a multistaged process. It involves actions of the system, reactions of individuals, further responses of the system, and so on. Actors make
choices, and the system exerts pressures, at each stage. Choices and pressures are skewed and are differentially available to persons of the various
race–gender groups. Future choices and pressures are contingent on prior
actions.

IMPLICATIONS FOR CLASSROOM
INTERACTION RESEARCH

This study also points to future directions for classroom interaction research. First, analysis of classroom experiences as they differ for children of
each race–gender group should be more fully developed. The small sample
size and single geographic location of the classrooms analyzed in this study
limit its generalizability. It would be of interest to discover whether or not
patterns discerned in these classrooms also appear in others. The impact of
other variables, such as social class, ability level, and other ethnic statuses,
should be more fully explored.

Second, classroom interaction research might benefit from taking the
classroom, rather than the individual student, as the unit of analysis. This
study suggests classroom-level effects may influence in profound ways experiences of students, and even degrees of differentiation within classrooms
by race–gender group. Yet interaction studies most typically are focused at
the level of the individual student or the small classroom group. More
explicit analysis of classrooms as social systems would illuminate not only
interrelationships among actors and networks in classrooms but also the
extent to which classrooms are influenced by their external social environments.

The trend in interaction research towards analysis of peer interactions
and student's perspectives on classroom life, apparent in several papers in
this volume, holds promise for enriching our knowledge of classroom environments and for designing more effective change strategies to achieve
equity. Knowledge of particular aspects of classroom life that are most
central to various groups of children not only helps in understanding classrooms as ongoing social systems but also can aid effective teaching.

Finally, research addressing the impact of public schooling on intergenerational status arrangements could be enriched by greater attention to processes within schools that affect stratification. Until such mechanisms can be identified, and their sources pinpointed accurately, little can be done to alter outcomes of schooling. The research on stratification and schooling too frequently has taken a macro perspective alone, failing to specify how transmission of status arrangements occurs at the face-to-face level.

NOTES

[1] The Maxwell and Avery classrooms were observed as a part of the larger "Socialization into the Student Role" project, directed by Phyllis Blumenfeld, Steven Bossert, and V. Lee Hamilton. This project was funded by the National Institute of Education. The other four classrooms were observed independently of this project, funded in part by a predoctoral grant to Linda Grant from the National Institute for Mental Health.

[2] I appreciate the aid of Joe Roszak and Mark Wichlin in completing reliability coding.

[3] The derivation of these roles are explored more fully in Grant (1981, 1983). The "superstar" role seems to be related to pressures at the school-level in certain communities to demonstrate that black children could perform well. One result was a single token black boy superstar in each of one school's (Dawson's) three classrooms. The "bad girl" role seems to be related to teacher attributional patterns regarding these children. Teachers expected white girls on the average to be more mature than other students. Positive behaviors were seen as reflections of this greater maturity, but so were negative behaviors. Negative behaviors of white girls were seen as accurate reflections of their "mature" personalities, while comparable behaviors and performances of other children were dismissed as stemming from immaturity or problems in adjusting to school, situational attributions admitting the possibility of reassessment.

REFERENCES

Abrams, P. (1982). *Historical sociology.* Ithaca, NY: Cornell University Press.

Anyon, J. (1983). Intersections of gender and class: Accommodation and resistance by working-class and affluent females to contradictory sex-role ideologies. In S. Walker & L. Barton (eds). *Gender, class, and educations.* Sussex, England: The Falmer Press.

Apple, M. (1979). *Ideology and Curriculum.* London: Routledge & Kegan Paul.

Becker, H. (1953). The teacher and the authority system of the public school. *Journal of Educational Sociology, 27,* 128–141.

Becker, H. (1958). Problems of proof and inference in participant observation. *American Sociological Review, 23,* 652–660.

Berger, J., Rosenholtz, S., & Zelditch, M. (1980). Status organizing processes. *Annual Review of Sociology, 8,* 479–508.

Bidwell, C. (1965). The school as a formal organization. In J. March (Ed.), *Handbook of organizations.* Chicago: Rand-McNally.

Boocock, S. (1980). *Sociology of education: an introduction* (2nd ed.). Boston: Houghton Mifflin.

Bossert, S. (1979). *Tasks and social relationships.* Cambridge, MA: Cambridge University Press.

Bowles, S., & Gintis, H. (1976). *Schooling in capitalist America.* New York: Basic Books.

Brophy, J., & Good, T. (1974). *Teacher–student relationships: Causes and consequences.* New York: Holt, Rinehart & Winston.

Chesler, M., & Cave, W. (1981). *Sociology of education: Access to power and privilege.* New York: Macmillan.

Clement, C., Eisenhart, M., & Harding, J. (1979). The veneer of harmony: Social–race relationships in a desegregated elementary school. In R. Rist (Ed.), *Desegregated schools: appraisals of an American experiment.* New York: Academic Press.

Crain, R., & Mahard, R. (1978a). Desegregation and black achievement: A review of the research. *Law and Contemporary Society, 42,* 17–56.

Crain, R., & Mahard, R. (1978b). School racial composition and black education. *Sociology of Education, 81,* 6–88.

Dewey, J. (1966). *Democracy and education.* New York: Free Press.

Epstein, J., & McPartland, J. (1977). *Sex differences in family and school influence on student outcomes* (Report No. 236). Baltimore: Center for Social Organization of Schools, Johns Hopkins University.

Feldman, S. (1979). Nested identities. In N. Denzin (Ed.), *Studies in symbolic interaction* (Vol. 2). Greenwich, CT: JAI Press.

Giroux, H. (1981). *Ideology, culture, and the process of schooling:* Philadelphia: Temple University Press.

Glaser, B., & Strauss, A. (1967). *The discovery of grounded theory: Strategies for qualitative research.* Chicago: Aldine.

Gordon, C. (1957). *The social system of the high school: A study of adolescence.* Glencoe, IL: Free Press.

Grant, L. (1981). *Race, sex, and schooling: Social location and children's experiences in elementary school classrooms.* Unpublished doctoral dissertation, University of Michigan. Ann Arbor.

Grant, L. (1983). Gender roles and statuses in school children's peer interactions. *Western Sociological Review 14:* 58–76.

Grant, L. (1983, April). *The socialization of white females in classrooms.* Paper presented at the meeting of the American Educational Research Association, Montreal, Canada.

Grant, L. (1984). Black females' 'place' in desegregated classrooms. *Sociology of Education 57:* 98–110.

Grant, L., & Rothenberg, J. (in press). *The enhancement of ability differences: Interactions in first- and second-grade reading groups. Elementary School Journal.*

Guttentag, M. & Bray, H. (1976). *Undoing sex-stereotypes.* New York: McGraw-Hill.

Jencks, C., Smith, M., Acland, H., Bane, M., Cohen, D., Gintis, H., Heyns, B., and Michelson, S. (1972). *Inequality: A reassessment of the effects of family and schooling in America.* New York: Basic Books.

Kelly, G., & Nihlen, A. (1982). Schooling and the reproduction of patriarchy: Unequal workloads, unequal rewards. In M. Apple (Ed.), *Cultural and economic reproduction in education.* London: Routledge & Kegan Paul.

Lancy, D. (1978). The classroom as phenomenon. In D. Bar-Tal & L. Saxe (Eds.), *The social psychology of education.* New York: Wiley.

Lee, P., & Gropper, N. (1974). Sex role culture in the elementary school curriculum. *Harvard Educational Review, 44,* 369–410.

Leggon, C. (1980). Black female professionals: Dilemmas and contradictions of status. In L. Rodgers–Rose (Ed.), *The black woman.* Beverly Hills. CA: Sage.

Lightfoot, S. (1978). *Worlds apart: Relationships between families and schools.* New York: Harper Colophon.

Ogbu, J. (1978). *Minorities and caste.* New York: Academic Press.

Paley, V. (1979). *White teacher.* Cambridge, MA: Harvard University Press.

Patchen, M. (1982). *Black–white contact in schools: Its social and academic effects.* Lafayette, IN: Purdue University Press.

Persell, C. (1977). *Education and inequality.* New York: Free Press.

Rist, R. (1970). Student social class and teacher expectations: The self-fulfilling prophecy in ghetto education. *Harvard Educational Review, 40,* 411–451.

Rodgers–Rose, L. (Ed.). (1980). *The black woman.* Beverly Hills: CA: Sage.

Rowan, B. (1982). The status organizing work of schools. *Social Science Quarterly, 63,* 477–491.

Sadker, M., & Frazier, M. (1973). *Sexism in school and society.* New York: Harper & Row.

Schmuck, R. (1978). Applications of social psychology to classroom life. In D. Bar-Tal & L. Saxe (Eds.), *The social psychology of education.* New York: Wiley.

Schofield, J. (1982). *Black and white in schools: Trust, tolerance, or tokenism?* New York: Praeger.

Scrupski, A. (1975). The social system of the school. In N. Shimahara & A. Scrupski (Eds.), *Social forces and schooling: An anthropological and sociological perspective.* New York: David McKay.

Thomas, G., Alexander, K., & Eckland, B. (1979). Access to higher education: The importance of race, sex, social class, and academic credentials. *School Review, 87,* 133–156.

Classroom Experiences and Student Gender: Are There Differences and Do They Matter?*

JACQUELYNNE S. ECCLES and PHYLLIS BLUMENFELD

INTRODUCTION

The link between achievement beliefs and academic performance has been amply documented (cf. Crandall, 1969; Dweck & Elliott, 1983; Eccles, 1983; Eccles & Wigfield, in press; Stein & Bailey, 1973). Within this literature, males and females are often found to have differing beliefs, which are assumed to account in part for sex differences in achievement behaviors. For example, the higher achievement levels of older boys and men is often

---

* The research reported herein was supported by grants from the National Institute of Education (NIE-G-78-0022) and the National Institute of Mental Health (RO1-MH-31724) to the first author and by a grant from the National Institute of Education (NIE-G-78-0190) to the second author. Grateful acknowledgment goes to all of those who helped design these studies, gather and analyze the data, and provide the classrooms and cooperation necessary to run studies.

79

GENDER INFLUENCES
IN CLASSROOM INTERACTION
ISBN: 0-12-752075-9

attributed to the fact that boys have higher expectations than girls for success on some achievement tasks. Similarly, the lower incidence of behavior problems exhibited by girls has been attributed to the compatability between girls' gender-role orientation and the demands inherent in the student role. The developmental origin of these sex differences in beliefs and attitudes has interested psychologists for many years. Concern over the possible role of schools in socializing these differences has increased during the last 20 years and several investigators have suggested a variety of mechanisms that might yield sex-differentiated socialization in the classroom (e.g., Brophy, see Chapter 6, this volume; Dweck, Davidson, Nelson, & Enna, 1978; Parsons, Ruble, Hodges, & Small, 1976). The research reported in this chapter was designed to evaluate some of these mechanisms; in particular, the mechanisms that might yield sex differences in students' attitudes toward school and toward themselves as learners.

Over the past 6 years, we have observed teacher–student interaction in over 50 elementary and junior high school classrooms in an effort to investigate the impact of sex-differentiated classroom experiences on students' beliefs and motivation. This chapter presents a summary of our findings and some suggestions for classroom practices that might increase sex equity in educational outcomes. We expected to find rather blatant sex differences in children's school experience. We also expected to find evidence linking these differences in experience to children's attitudes toward school and learning. Surprisingly, we found few blatant sex differences. All of the sex differences we found were small; and even these were not consistent across the classrooms we studied. In addition, these differences were not particularly strong predictors of any of the student attitudes and beliefs that have been found to be sex-differentiated.

Based on our experiences, we now believe that teachers play a rather passive role in the maintenance of sex-differentiated achievement patterns. Students start school with sex-differentiated goals and attitudes (Eccles & Hoffman, 1984; Huston, 1983). These attitudes appear to consolidate into sex-differentiated beliefs regarding math and scientific abilities some time around early adolescence (Eccles Parsons, 1984). The role teachers play in this consolidation process is rather subtle. Although teachers do not appear to be the major source of these beliefs, they also do very little to change them or to provide boys and girls with the types of information that might lead them to reevaluate their sex-stereotyped beliefs. In this way teachers passively reinforce the sex-typed academic and career decisions made by their students, thus contributing to sex inequity in children's educational attainment.

These conclusions are based on two extensive observational studies: (1) an elementary school study conducted by Blumenfeld and her colleagues, and (2) a junior high school math classroom study conducted by Eccles and her colleagues. The elementary school study was designed to investigate early socialization of sex-differentiated attitudes and beliefs. The junior high study was designed to investigate the socialization of sex-differentiated attitudes toward math and science during early adolescence. Two types of data were gathered in both studies: (1) detailed observational data on teacher–student interaction patterns and (2) detailed questionnaire information from students regarding their attitudes toward school and learning. Because integrating these two types of data allows us to assess the impact of interaction patterns on students' beliefs and attitudes, these two studies provide a unique look at socialization in the classroom. Furthermore, because the two studies cover such a wide grade range, they provide a test of the possibility that the process of sex-differentiated socialization varies with grade.

The results of these two studies are summarized in the next two sections. In each section we present an overview of the methods, a summary of the observational data, a summary of the student-attitudinal data, and a summary of the relations between the classroom interactional data and the student-attitudinal data. The final section of this chapter outlines suggestions for increasing sex equity in school outcomes. For brevities sake, we have not detailed our hypotheses. These can be found in the various articles we refer to throughout this chapter and most specifically in Parsons, Kaczala, and Meece (1982). And since Brophy (see Chap. 6, this vol.) provides an excellent review of the previous literature on sex-differentiated socialization in the classroom, we have not included a detailed literature review.

SOCIALIZATION IN ELEMENTARY SCHOOL: GRADES 1 AND 5

Study One involved 2 years of data gathering. The first year was designed to examine the relation of teacher communication patterns to children's perceptions of the student role. Consequently, a coding system for teacher communication was needed. Teachers talk to students about many things and try to provide both academic and citizenship training. Academic training involves instruction in both academic content and work procedures. Citizenship training involves instruction in the social and moral procedures necessary to facilitate working with or in the presence of others. Given these considerations, teacher communication was coded in terms of four domains: academic performance, academic procedure, social procedure, and social-moral norms. Furthermore, since there are both theoretical and empirical reasons for expecting sex differences in each of these domains, we coded the communication patterns for the sex of the student recipient of each communication. This procedure made it possible to explore teachers' emphasis on one normative domain versus another as well as differences among domains in socializing strategies used with boys and girls.

Since the major goal of this study was the investigation of socialization into the student role, student perceptions of the student role were also assessed. We wanted to find the extent to which children had incorporated positive academic norms, social norms, and expectations and to explore the reasons children give for conforming with these norms. We expected to find evidence of increased understanding and more questioning of these norms with increasing age. More central to this chapter, we expected girls to evidence greater incorporation of and conformity to these norms than boys. Finally, we expected to find a relation between sex-differentiated teacher communication patterns and sex differences in the students' endorsement of the traditional good student role.

Teacher Communication Patterns

To gather teacher communication data, we recorded 10 hours of verbatim statements made by teachers in each of 9 first- and 9 fifth-grade classrooms representing both middle-class and working-class districts. Teacher statements were coded for domain of reference (academic performance, academic procedure, social procedure, and social-moral norm); for timing (whether the remark was proactive or reactive); for the quality of the behavior from the teacher's viewpoint (positive, negative, or ambiguous); for the target of the remark (male, female, small group, whole class); and for the affective intensity of the remark (whether the teacher raised her/his voice or appeared especially pleased or angry). Finally, the presence of additional information, such as explanations for role expectations, causal attributions, and sanctions, was coded into a set of categories labeled informatives. Results of this study are summarized below; more details can be obtained from Blumenfeld, Hamilton, Bossert, Wessels, and Meece (1983).

OVERALL FLOW OF TEACHER TALK

In order to provide a picture of the general classroom patterns, we summarize the general patterns of teacher communication before discussing gender differences. Since there were few grade-level differences, this general description represents a composite picture across grade levels.

Teachers were quite verbose (emitting an average of 59 clauses per hour). This communication was largely reactive and negative; it focused predominantly on procedures (57%) and academic performance (41%). Since reference to moral concerns occurred rarely, it is not discussed further. In addition, fully 98.5% of all statements were low in affective intensity.

Not surprisingly, characteristics of communication varied across domains. Academic performance communication was more reactive and more positive than communication in the other domains, primarily because performance communication typically occurs after a response and responses are correct slightly more than half the time. In contrast, academic procedure communication tended to be proactive, typically involving directions for upcoming assignments or activities; when academic procedure communication was reactive, it was invariably negative. Communications regarding social procedures were typically reactive (78%) and negative (76%). Procedural conformity was almost never praised.

From the viewpoint of both attribution and social learning theory, causal attributions, explanations for compliance, and threats of potential sanctions are important socialization messages. Students' acceptance of norms of behavior and students' perceptions of their own academic potential should be influenced by these types of informatives. To our surprise, only a small proportion of teacher communications (14% on the average) contained such informatives. In addition, informatives were dramatically more negative and procedural than the other types of teacher communication, even though they were about equally reactive.

The types of informatives varied by domain. Causal attributions occurred primarily in the domain of academic performance; these attributions were predominately positive and effort-related; attributions to ability (either positive or negative) were rare. Whereas explanations about the value or interest of lessons were infrequent, explanations and sanctions were more common in the procedural and moral domains; these statements often referred to circumstances or to potential negative consequences to the self or others as justification for compliance with normative expectations.

Overall, then, the initial picture of teacher communication is mixed. It is reactive and overwhelmingly focused on procedural infractions. Informatives occur rarely and are even more negative and procedural in emphasis than the overall flow of talk. Communications regarding academic performance, although outnumbered by procedural concerns, were the most positive; but even in this domain, it is perhaps most honest to conclude that communications were simply less negative than in the other domains of teacher communication. We have replicated this study on another sample with almost identical results. The patterns of results from both samples are consistent with the reports of others (e.g., Jackson, 1968; Doyle, 1979) in suggesting that the everyday demands of the institution of the classroom,

84   Jacquelynne S. Eccles and Phyllis Blumenfeld

rather than the long-term goal of socializing scholars and citizens, drive classroom interaction. The teacher is primarily a manager of the ongoing activities, and the immediate institutional imperatives of conducting these activities while preventing chaos override what might be judged the ideal socialization practices by those of us outside the classroom. Indeed, the teacher appears to be a manager who mainly reacts to those behaviors that interfere with the flow of classroom events (though generally with low affect). It is against this background of activity that we must evaluate sex differences in the experience of students.

GENDER DIFFERENCES

The major sex differences reflect the fact that boys are the recipients of more teacher talk than are girls: 39% of all communications was directed at boys, only 29% was directed at girls; the remaining communications were directed at mixed groups of students. This imbalance is even more pronounced in looking at informatives: 39% of which were directed at boys compared to 21% directed at girls.

Such differences in communication patterns could reflect several factors (e.g., the teacher might like boys better or boys might create more behavior problems). To get a clearer understanding of the possible cause, we examined the quality and the distribution of concerns addressed to boys and girls. Results indicate that the communications directed to both boys and girls were mostly, and about equally, reactive. There was a slight tendency for boys to receive proportionately more negative feedback than girls, a difference that may be explicable in terms of the concerns addressed to boys and girls. Girls received an appreciably higher proportion of their communications regarding academic performance, whereas communications to boys focused more on procedural issues. Since procedural communication tends to be more negative than academic performance communication, it is not surprising that boys were the recipients of more negative communication than girls.

For the most part, the picture of informatives for boys and girls resembled that for the overall remarks. Like other forms of communication, the informatives directed at boys and girls were equally reactive. However, in contrast to other forms of communication, boys and girls received equivalent proportions of negative informatives (approximately 80% of the informatives addressed to boys and girls were in reaction to violations of norms). Distribution of the informatives across domains was somewhat more skewed, with girls receiving a higher relative proportion of their informatives about academic performance (37%) than boys (22%). Given these differences in concerns addressed to the two sexes, it is not surprising that only 17% of the negative informatives addressed to boys concerned academic performance compared to 33% of the negative informatives to girls. Since attributions were concentrated in this domain, it follows that girls received proportionately more attributions among their informatives (40%) than boys (28%). The majority of these attributions linked academic difficulties to insufficient effort.

In summary, despite some differences between the sexes in the nature and distribution of teacher talk received, the overall message of these data is similar to that reached by Brophy (see Chap. 6, this vol.). The striking difference in teacher handling of girls versus boys concerns the amount of attention paid to boys. Within that background fact, there are relatively more subtle tendencies for girls to receive disproportionately more academic performance communication and perhaps slightly more positive communication. Teachers do not appear to be attending to boys because they are disruptors—although they might be attending to boys in order to prevent them from becoming disruptors. In any case, although a simple explanation does not emerge from these data, the fact remains that boys are the recipient of more teacher communication than girls, especially teacher communications regarding proper procedure.

Student Perceptions of Classroom Norms

To assess student perceptions, 360 first- and fifth-grade students were questioned regarding their views of the importance of various classroom norms, their feelings about meeting these norms, and their reasons for comforming to these norms. Each child was presented with a series of pictures illustrating classroom behaviors in each of the four domains. Since responses to conformity were expected to differ from responses to norm violations, both good and bad behaviors were illustrated. The children were asked to assess how good (or bad) each behavior was, to show how good (bad) they would feel if they did what was pictured, and to explain why the behavior is good or bad. The first two responses were assessed on quantitative scales; the third response was recorded verbatim and coded into intrinsic and extrinsic categories.

OVERALL PATTERN

Children responded to the various domains as expected. Moral norms received significantly higher importance ratings and elicited more extreme affective responses for both adherence and violation. Apparently children believe that the domain receiving the least emphasis in the classroom is the most important, suggesting that moral concerns are learned outside the classroom and are carried into the classroom as they are into any other setting the child encounters.

Although children rated achievement norms as least important, their affective response to these norms was more intense, placing achievement norms in an intermediate position between morals and procedures with respect to affect. In addition, children responded less to norm violation than to norm adherence both in terms of importance and affect. This asymmetry was especially marked for achievement norms. Apparently, children neither consider day-to-day academic failures very important nor feel very intensely about them relative to success, a pattern consistent with communication and sanctions in the elementary classroom.

GRADE LEVEL EFFECTS

Children's perceptions of the student role differed more by grade level than did the teacher talk variables. As anticipated, first graders reacted with greater conformity, more extreme affect, and less differentiation across domains than the fifth graders; first graders also reasoned more externally about the norms than the older children. The decline in ratings was most marked for social conventions and least marked for moral norms. Despite these grade level effects in the extremity of the ratings and in the externality of the reasons offered for compliance with the norms, the rank order of the norms in terms of importance and affective response to both violations and conformity were identical across these two grade levels. These findings, although surprising, are consistent with the fact that teacher communication about these school-related behavior norms differed little across these grade levels. The children's social cognitions apparently mirror these invariant realities of classroom life.

GENDER DIFFERENCES

There was a consistent pattern of sex differences in the student perceptions: Compared to boys, girls consistently reported that they would feel worse about violating procedural and moral norms. There were also some scattered instances in which girls reported that they would feel better about fulfilling a norm, but these effects were not as consistent as the pattern associated with norm violation. There were no sex differences in the reasons offered for complying with the norms.

Interestingly, the pattern of sex differences that emerged was unrelated to the pattern of differential treatment the sexes received from their teachers. Girls reported greater conformity to the norms, despite receiving much less socializing attention than the boys. Girls were also most different from boys in the social-moral domain, the one domain that is least salient in the classroom life. Boys and girls differed least in the domain of academic performance, the domain in which teachers target the highest proportion of effort at girls. For example, there was a significant relationship between the percentage of attributions focused on academic performance and students' ratings of the importance of success on academic tasks. Girls received a higher percentage of their attributions for academic performance. One might expect therefore that girls would rate academic success as more important than the boys. They did not. Thus, despite the fact that they were recipients of the positive teacher communication pattern, they did not evidence the expected advantage in their attitudes. In general, evidence from the student perception measures supports a relatively "sugar and spice" picture of girls—certainly more so than is true of the teacher talk data, and in ways not particularly consistent with teacher talk. These results suggest that girls acquire their values outside the classroom just as students in general appear to acquire their moral values and norms outside school.

But what about boys? Recall that a higher percentages of boys' informatives were focused on social procedural explanations and sanctions. In addition, these informatives tended to be negative. Overall, this pattern of informatives (high percentage on social procedural explanations and sanctions and high percentage negative) was associated with low endorsement of academic and social procedural norms. Consequently, one might expect boys to rate the importance of adhering to these norms lower than did the girls. This was not the case. Once again, the sex difference in classroom communication patterns did not translate into the expected sex difference in student attitudes.

What can we conclude? Despite the fact that there are some consistent sex differences in teacher communication patterns, these differences do not translate into the expected sex differences in student attitudes. These results suggest that the sex differences in student attitudes that do exist are not created by differential teacher communication patterns. Instead, like moral norms in general, we believe these sex differences are acquired in daily life. They reflect widely held cultural beliefs that children are exposed to in a variety of settings. Children bring these beliefs with them to school and continue to believe them unless they are forced to reconsider their validity. If teachers are guilty of sexism, it is their failure to get students to reconsider these beliefs that condemns them.

SOCIALIZATION INTO THE STUDENT ROLE: GRADES 2 AND 6

The second year of the elementary school study was designed to explore in more depth the relation of classroom experiences to student perceptions. The study population included 158 students (101 second graders and 57 sixth graders) and their 11 teachers. Data were obtained from three sources: student interviews, teacher ratings, and classroom observations. Student interviews consisted of both open- and closed-end quantitative questions tapping perceptions of the teacher, of the other students in the class, of schoolwork, of the causes of success and failure in school, and of one's own ability, effort, and conduct. Teachers rated each of the students in terms of their achievement, conduct, work habits, social skills, and personality characteristics. To gain detailed information on classroom interaction patterns, 85 of the children were observed individually for 120 minutes per child. Codes similar to those of Brophy and Good (1974) were used to record (1) the frequency and quality of academic and behavioral feedback from teachers and peers, (2) the frequency and quality of instructional interaction with the teacher, and (3) the frequency of personal conversations with the teacher. Peer interaction codes concerned (1) seeking and giving help, (2) social comparison, (3) negative interchanges like enforcing, fighting, or provoking, (4) positive interactions like stroking, and (5) personal conversations. Every 5 minutes students were rated as to their on-task behavior. These observations were conducted during academic work times, especially during math and reading periods. No child was observed for more than 20 minutes at one time. Whenever an interaction was recorded the activity structure in which it occurred also was noted. These structures were defined as individual seatwork, small group with teacher, whole-group recitation, and transition.

Interactional Patterns

The observational measures yielded data very similar to other reports of teacher and child interactions. The number of interactions for any one child ranged from 7 to 124 over the 2 hours, with a mean of 44. The quality and focus of teacher feedback to individuals was similar to that reported by Blumenfeld, Hamilton, Wessels, and Falkner (1979), Brophy and Evertson (1981), and Parsons et al. (1982). Sixteen percent of a child's interactions with the teacher involved praise. Other frequent teacher behaviors were negative feedback (21%) and commands (20%). The peer interactions also paralleled other descriptions of student classroom behavior (e.g., Hoge &

Luce, 1979). Children were most likely to be talking socially to a peer (19%), seeking help (21%), or seeking to play or work with a peer (11%). Finally, the frequency and quality of children's social comparison behavior (about 9%) was similar to that reported by Ruble and Frey (1982). Although there were some differences in teacher and student behavior associated with student characteristics, the differences were not large. On the whole, different types of children were treated and acted more similarly than differently. A more detailed description of these results can be found in Pintrich (1982).

GENDER DIFFERENCES

There were few sex differences in the students' behavior. Contrary to what one might expect, boys and girls did not differ in the frequency of disruptive behaviors such as defying, fighting, or arguing. They also did not differ in the frequency of off- or on-task behaviors. The only noteworthy sex difference was that boys engaged in more social comparisons of all kinds than girls.

Surprisingly, given the general lack of sex differences in social behavior, boys were the targets of more negative statements from the teacher. Teachers criticized boys more for misbehavior, even though boys did not misbehave more than girls. Boys also got more interactions in general. However, when the larger frequency of teacher behavioral feedback to boys is taken into consideration using proportion variables, there was only one sex difference in the pattern of teacher feedback: Compared to girls, a higher proportion of boys' conduct feedback was negative. Consequently, although boys received more of many kinds of feedback, the sexes did not differ markedly in the general pattern of their feedback.

Sex differences become even more elusive when activity is taken into account. Teachers did not treat boys and girls differently except during periods of transition in which boys received more negative feedback than girls. These results are especially interesting because although boys' and girls' behavior varied by structure, it was quite similar during transitions. This greater teacher reactivity to boys may be a carry-over from recitation periods, during which boys misbehaved more than girls, and may reflect the teachers concern over preventing possible disruptions from the boys during managerially difficult transition periods.

Teachers did not respond differently to boys and girls during other activities, even though student behavior varied by sex. In small-group settings boys talked more than girls; in contrast, girls sought more help than did boys. In seatwork, boys engaged in more social comparisons than girls. Thus, compared to boys, girls seem more conforming, behave more appro-

priately during recitation and small groups periods, and appear less interested in social comparison.

Student Perceptions of Classroom and Self

We examined the relation of students' perceptions of teachers and peers
to their satisfaction. We also explored the impact of classroom experiences
on these and on self-perceptions for the sample as a whole and for each sex
separately. Results are summarized below. More details can be found in
Blumenfeld, Pintrich, and Meece (1983) and Pintrich and Blumenfeld
(1983).

PERCEPTIONS OF TEACHERS, PEERS, AND SCHOOLWORK

In general, children, regardless of age, sex, or socioeconomic status, rated
teachers and peers similarly. In addition, both boys and girls were most
satisfied when they thought their teacher was good-tempered, funny, interesting, enthusiastic, and did special things for the class. Older children
(both boys and girls) were less satisfied if they felt their teacher was over-
reactive and too controlling.

Generally, perceptions of schoolwork differed somewhat by grade but
not by sex. As anticipated, most students thought it extremely important to
do well in school, but the chief reason mentioned, namely, avoiding failure,
suggests a rather negative motivational set. Older children focused more on
future considerations than did younger children. When asked specifically
about topics they like and dislike working on, math was the subject many
children (31%) preferred, especially second graders. However, about the
same number chose math as the subject they liked least. In addition, in
response to the question, "What do you work hardest on?" children over-
whelmingly answered, "math" (61%). Finally, contrary to what we had
expected, responses regarding specific subject matter did not differ by sex
at either grade level. Not surprisingly, older children evidenced greater
concern both with their marks and with their ability to do the work.

Impact of Classroom Experiences on Student Perceptions

We used stepwise regression to examine the relation of classroom experiences to children's perceptions of their teachers and peers and to their

satisfaction with their class. Variables were selected on the basis of high zero-order correlations between the classroom interaction variables and student perceptions. Contrary to expectations, teacher praise did not significantly influence students' perceptions of their teacher. Not surprisingly, children who were the target of more teacher commands and reprimands concerning behavior rated their teacher as more strict and less nice. Since teachers are basically reactive to student behavior, students who elicit more negative feedback are also likely to be the ones who most often misbehave (Brophy & Evertson, 1976). Congruent with this finding, students who were on task more, and talked, defied, or acted out less, reported higher levels of overall satisfaction.

There were some interesting differences in the pattern of predictors of satisfaction depending on grade level and students' sex. We had assumed that younger children and girls would be more affected by teacher behaviors, because both groups are assumed to be more adult-oriented. This was only partially confirmed. Younger children's ratings were more influenced by the amount of negative feedback and commands they received, but positive interaction had similar effects at both grade levels. Most significantly, and contrary to our predictions, there were no sex differences in the impact of teacher interactions on either student perceptions or satisfaction.

In contrast, there were some sex differences in the student behaviors associated with satisfaction. Social comparison with peers and enforcement behaviors designed to keep one's peers in line were both related to satisfaction but in opposite directions for boys and girls. These student behaviors were positively associated with boys' satisfaction and negatively associated for girls'. Since social comparisons generally focused on work completion rate, both of these student behaviors may indicate a concern with conforming with classroom norms. Given that girls feel more strongly about meeting classroom norms, display of these behaviors by girls may reflect anxiety about and dissatisfaction with other students' failure to do assignments and behave properly. The same behavior on the part of boys, who feel less strongly about these matters, may signal higher levels of commitment or concern and thus be associated with more satisfaction.

Self-Perceptions

Since one major goal of this study was to investigate the socialization of students' perceptions of themselves as learners, we examined students' ratings of their own ability, effort, and conduct, the linkages among these, and the criteria used for each rating. In addition we tested the impact of classroom experiences on these ratings. Our findings concerning age and sex

differences parallel those of other studies in that (1) students' self-perceptions corresponded significantly with their teacher's assessments of their
achievement, which, in turn, are closely related to the students' actual
performance; (2) students used grades, speed, work habits, and completion
rate as criteria for assessing their own ability; (3) students' self-ratings
showed a general decline with age; (4) grades increased in importance as
evaluative criteria with age; and (5) girls rated themselves as better behaved. There were no sex differences in the students' ratings of their own
ability and all students primarily used absolute rather than comparative
standards in assessing their ability, effort, and conduct.

The pattern of relations among self-ratings did not differ by age or sex.
Moreover, contrary to our expectations, girls and boys did not differ in the
link of conduct and ability perceptions, the sources of information for judg-
ing each, or their overlap. Congruent with other studies, girls did see themselves as better behaved. But they did not confuse this with being smart or
trying hard. This finding suggests that girls do not form ability perceptions
in a different manner than boys. Although they care about being good and
see themselves that way, this perception has little to do with their self-
ability ratings.

The Impact of Classroom Experience on
Self-Perceptions

Once again, stepwise regression analyses were used to assess the impact
of classroom experience on self-perceptions for the group as a whole and
for each grade level and each sex separately (see Pintrich, 1982, for more
detail). Selection of variables for inclusion in these analyses was again based
on high zero-order correlations of classroom interaction variables with the
three self-perceptions scores studied. Perceptions of ability and effort were
positively influenced by achievement level and by work praise; work criticism negatively influenced perceptions of effort but not of ability. Negative
feedback about behavior also depressed effort perceptions but had its largest impact on conduct ratings. Conduct perceptions were, however, most
closely tied to level of misbehavior exhibited.

The results for the subsamples showed the same basic relationships as for
the total sample. However, there were some interesting sex differences.
Compared to boys, achievement level (as rated by the teacher) accounted
for more variance in the girls' ratings of their ability, their effort, and their
conduct. Classroom experiences also affected boys' and girls' ratings differently, but the nature of the difference depended on the particular rating
being made. Classroom experiences had similar effects on boys' and girls'

ability ratings; namely, positive academic feedback increased these self-perceptions. And as was true for the group at large, conduct feedback had no impact on either boys' or girls' ability ratings. In contrast, the classroom experiences relating to effort and conduct ratings differed for boys and girls. On the one hand, negative feedback about work and positive feedback about conduct depressed boys' effort ratings; on the other hand, girls' effort ratings were depressed most by teacher-monitoring behaviors. A boy's self-conduct rating was not affected by either teacher feedback patterns or by his own achievement level; instead, it covaried with the boy's own level of misbehavior. In contrast, girls' self-conduct ratings were enhanced by their achievement level and by their own good conduct, and were depressed by negative conduct-related feedback from the teacher.

In summary, classroom perception and self-ratings seem to be affected primarily by factors related to teacher control and student performance. As Jackson (1968) suggested, life in classrooms is predominantly one of rules, regulations, and routines that do not vary much by grade level or sex of the child. Teacher communication patterns are remarkably similar across grade level and sex of student. Consequently, although students' experiences do affect their perceptions, these effects do not appear to differ substantially for boys and girls, at least during the elementary school years. Not surprisingly, then, there were also no major differences in boys' and girls' self-perceptions during these years. As noted earlier, sex differences in self-perceptions do not appear consistently until late in elementary school, and even then they depend on the subject area. Consequently, sex differences may be more marked in junior high school and in subject areas that are sex-typed. This hypothesis is explored in the next section.

SOCIALIZATION OF SEX DIFFERENCES IN JUNIOR HIGH SCHOOL MATH CLASSROOMS

The junior high school study was designed to investigate the socialization of sex differences in students' attitudes toward mathematics. Previous studies have shown that sex differences in attitudes toward both oneself as a math learner and mathematics as a subject area emerge in junior high school (see Eccles Parsons, 1984, and Meece, Eccles-Parsons, Futterman, Goff, & Kaczala, 1982, for reviews). Several investigators have suggested that classroom experiences in the upper elementary grades and in junior high school might contribute to this decline in girls' attitudes toward math. In particular, they have suggested that teachers, especially during these years, pay more attention to boys than girls and engage boys in more of the kinds of interactions that foster self-confidence and interest in math and science. Furthermore, they have suggested that these differences in teacher–student interaction may be most marked among the brightest students in the class (for reviews, Brophy, see Chapter 6, this volume; Eccles Parsons, 1984; Meece et al., 1982). The junior high school study was designed to evaluate these hypotheses using low-inference observational procedures derived from the coding systems of Brophy and Good (1974) and Dweck et al. (1978), a teacher questionnaire, and student record data.

Like the elementary school study, the junior high school study was designed to test the relation of classroom experience and teacher expectations for individual students to students' beliefs and attitudes. Too often researchers interested in the socialization of sex differences in achievement behaviors seem content to document the existence of sex differences in the socialization variables they are studying. However, the mere existence of a sex difference on a socialization variable does not prove its importance in explaining sex differences in achievement behavior. The difference might be important, but then again it might not be. Indeed, it may be that boys and girls develop different achievement patterns not only because they are treated differently but also because similar teacher behaviors affect boys and girls differently. If so, then an interactional variable that does not discriminate between boys and girls may play just as important a role in shaping or reinforcing sex differences in achievement behaviors as an interactional variable that does differ by sex of student. The importance of any socialization experience for explaining sex differences in achievement behaviors needs to be established rather than inferred. The junior high school study was designed with this goal in mind.

To accomplish this goal, we had a subset of the students in our sample fill out an extensive questionnaire assessing their achievement-related beliefs and attitudes regarding both math and English. Because the student–teacher interaction data were coded at the level of the individual student, we were able to correlate summary scores derived from the student questionnaire with the student–teacher interactional data in order to estimate the magnitude of the relation between particular classroom experiences and subsequent student beliefs and attitudes. Although not proving the causal impact of classroom experience achievement outcomes, these correlational procedures can confirm or disconfirm the existence of a relation between these sets of variables thus providing a first step in the investigation of the causal impact of classrooms experience on boys' and girls' achievement beliefs and behavior.

The main student sample discussed in this chapter consisted of 428 students from 17 math classrooms in Grades 5, 6, 7, and 9. All of these students are included in the descriptive analyses of classroom interactive patterns.

There were 3 fifth- and sixth-grade classrooms, 8 seventh-grade classroom, and 6 ninth-grade classrooms. Ten hours of observations, coded at the individual student level, were completed in each of the classrooms. Teachers' expectations for each student were measured by having the teacher rate each child in his/her class in terms of the child's math ability, the child's potential performance in future math courses, the level of the child's effort in math that year, and the grade the teacher expected the child to earn that year. Students' beliefs and attitudes regarding math were assessed with a survey questionnaire; 275 students filled this questionnaire out in their classroom about 2 weeks after the completion of the observations. Results of this study are summarized here. More details on the classroom findings can be found in Heller & Parsons, (1981) and Parsons et al. (1982). Results from a second sample of approximately 200 junior high school students given the same questionnaire and observed using the same coding system are discussed where appropriate. These students were members of 12 different seventh- to ninth-grade math classes.

Classroom Interaction Patterns

The coding system, derived from the Brophy–Good Dyadic Interaction Coding System (Brophy & Good, 1974), focused on academically relevant student–teacher interactions that involved a student and the teacher in direct dialogue with one another. Table 5.1 outlines major coding categories. Each interaction was coded in terms of the initiator (student or teacher); whether the interaction was private or public; the type of question being asked (academic, discipline, self-referrant); how the student got into the interaction (raised a hand, called out an answer, was called on without volunteering); the nature of the student's response (correct, incorrect, nonresponsive); the nature of the teacher's feedback (no explicit response, simple affirm or negate, prolonged interchange with additional opportunites for the student to respond, ask another student the answer, provide explanatory feedback, provide correct answer); and the affective intensity and direction of the feedback (positive and negative; high, medium, low). Based on the work of Dweck et al. (1978), we also coded whether academic feedback focused on the academic content of the answer or on the form in which the answer was given. In addition, all incidences of conduct feedback (both positive and negative) were recorded as well as all explicit incidences of causal attributions for any student's performance and all explicit statements regarding the teacher's expectations for a student's, or a group of students', performance on an upcoming task. Finally, we began by noting all incidences of a teacher explaining why a child might want to be able to do

Table 5.1

Overview of Observational System

I. Response opportunities: Situation in which teacher publicly questions students in the class
  A. Type of question
    1. Discipline: Teacher calls on student to redirect student's attention
    2. Direct: Teacher calls on student who has not volunteered
    3. Open: Teacher calls on student who has raised his/her hand
    4. Call-out: Student calls out the answer without permission
  B. Level of question
    1. Response: Questions that have a right or wrong answer
    2. Self-reference: Questions that ask for opinion or prediction
  C. Type of student response
    1. Answer
    2. Don't know
    3. No response at all
  D. Teacher's feedback
    1. Praise or criticism directed to quality of the work
    2. Praise or criticism directed to the form of the work
    3. Praise or criticism directed to conduct
    4. Affirm
    5. Negate
    6. No feedback
    7. Give answer
    8. Ask other: Calls on another student to answer the question
    9. Sustaining feedback: Gives the student another opportunity to answer the question
    10. Attributions to ability, effort, and task difficulty
II. Student-initiated questions
  A. Type of question
    1. Content
    2. Procedural
  B. Teacher's feedback (same as #I.D. 1–10)
III. Dyadic interactions: Situations in which teacher interacts privately with student
  A. Initiator of interaction
    1. Teacher
    2. Student
  B. Feedback
    1. Brief
    2. Long
    3. Same as #I.D. 1–10
IV. Explicit expectation statements

---

the assigned math work, or doing something explicit to make the assignment enjoyable, or tying the assignment to some enjoyable quality of mathematics. These incidences were so rare we stopped recording them.

This observational system yielded approximately 70 distinct raw frequency codes that were converted into 50 more meaningful units by summing across categories and by creating proportional variables describing the relative frequency of various interaction types. To facilitate interpretation of the student–teacher interaction data, we divided the interactional variables into three categories: (1) Teacher style variables (interactions primarily under the teacher's control, e.g., praise following a correct answer, use of public criticism); (2) Student style variables (interactions controlled primarily by the student, e.g., student-initiated private interactions); and (3) Joint style variables (interactions requiring initiative of both the student and the teacher, e.g., number of interactions initiated by the teacher with a student who has raised his/her hand). These three categories acknowledge the fact that student–teacher interaction depends on characteristics of both students and teachers. Many of the differences we found in interaction patterns were as much a consequence of student characteristics as of any sexist orientation of the teacher. By explicitly pointing out the major controlling party or parties for each of our interaction variables, we hope to sensitize the reader to the need for caution in interpreting the meaning and origin of any differences that might emerge.

Based on previous research, on our theoretical predictions, and on the frequency of occurrence, we focused our analyses on 36 variables: 28 frequency count variables and 8 proportional variables (see Parsons et al., 1982, for more details on the selection of these variables). The 28 frequency count variables are listed in Table 5.2 by category. The eight proportional variables focused on the relative frequency of praise and criticism and on the relative focus of one's praise and criticism on academic content, academic form, and conduct (e.g., percentage of one's praise or criticism focused on academic content, proportion of one's interaction yielding praise or criticism). These variables were used to compare our results with those of Dweck et al. (1978) and to provide an estimate of the general affective experience of each student. The proportional variables were either teacher style or joint style variables.

Because several investigators have suggested that teacher–student interactions depend on the teacher's perceptions of the student's ability level as well as on the student's gender, we included both student's gender and the teacher's expectation for the student in our analyses. To obtain the teacher's expectation for each student, we summed the teacher's ratings for each student and divided the class into two groups, high teacher-expectation students and low teacher-expectation students, based on each classes' median teacher-expectation score.

The total frequency count data (summed across all 10 observational periods) for these four groups of students and for the sample as a whole are summarized in Table 5.2. Since a very high proportion of students do not participate in most types of teacher–student dyadic interactions, Table 5.2 also lists the number of students actually represented in each frequency count. In general, these classrooms appear slightly more work-oriented than the elementary school classrooms discussed earlier, but this may be an artifact of the coding system. Certainly, the general impression of the observers was one of only slightly controlled chaos; and in support of this impression, 34% of all public response opportunities contained some degree of criticism, almost always focused on misbehavior, and almost always mild in its intensity. As was true of the elementary school classrooms, the level of affect associated with academic work was very low; academic work was rarely criticized and only occasionally praised (8% of the time). Causal attributions were also rare and almost always (94% of the time) focused on lack of sufficient effort or attention.

GENDER DIFFERENCES

To assess differential treatment of boys and girls, we compared the actual distribution of each interaction variable across our four expectancy by sex-of-student groups to the expected distribution using a 95% simultaneous confidence interval (Goodman, 1965). Low teacher-expectancy girls received more praise and asked more procedure questions than expected; high teacher-expectancy girls received fewer teacher-initiated private dyadic interactions but asked more questions, engaged in more total interactions, and had more of their public responses negated (announced publicly as incorrect) than other groups. Girls in both groups received less criticism and asked more questions than boys.

Low teacher-expectancy boys received more criticism, more teacher-initiated interactions, engaged in fewer response opportunites, and received fewer affirms than the other three student groups. In contrast, high teacher-expectancy boys received fewer teacher-initiated interactions but received more affirms than other students.

As was true with the elementary school classrooms, one is struck in these data by the relative lack of sex differences in teacher treatment of the students. With the exception of criticism, of which the low teacher-expectancy boys clearly got more than their share, boys and girls were treated differently in only four ways: Teachers initiated an unusually high number of private dyadic interactions with low teacher-expectancy boys, they ad-

Table 5.2

Frequencies of Observation Variables for Boys and Girls for Whom Teachers Have High and Low Expectancies[a]

Variables	Total frequency	Female		Male	
		Low expectancies frequency	High expectancies frequency	Low expectancies frequency	High expectancies frequency
Teacher style behaviors					
Teacher-initiated dyadics[b]	291 (155)	60 (36)	51[c] (33)	126[d] (47)	54[c] (39)
Direct questions[e]	671 (224)	172[d] (47)	179 (61)	153 (58)	167 (58)
Teacher-initiated interactions	1078 (306)	253 (67)	265 (79)	309[d] (80)	251[c] (80)
Response opportunities yielding criticism[b]	672 (207)	107[c] (36)	131[c] (44)	272[d] (62)	162 (65)
Response opportunities yielding work criticism	18 (16)	1 (1)	3 (3)	6 (5)	8 (7)
Conduct criticism[b]	619 (189)	98[c] (32)	123[c] (38)	253[d] (56)	145[c] (63)
Total work criticism[b]	41 (34)	4 (4)	6 (6)	19[d] (14)	12 (10)
Total criticism[b]	727 (219)	117[c] (41)	137[c] (47)	297[d] (64)	176 (67)
Response opportunities yielding praise	174 (92)	49 (23)	35 (18)	40 (23)	50 (28)
Response opportunities yielding work praise	154 (86)	45 (23)	30 (17)	32 (19)	47 (27)
Total work praise	295 (137)	83[d] (32)	63 (32)	72 (34)	77 (39)
Total praise	319 (141)	90[d] (32)	69 (33)	80 (36)	80 (40)
Attribution statements	88 (64)	13[c] (10)	22 (19)	26 (18)	27 (17)
Negates with feedback[b]	97 (59)	13 (7)	22 (13)	34 (18)	28 (21)
Ask other	129 (86)	28 (22)	41 (21)	30 (23)	30 (20)
Sustaining feedback	263 (154)	58 (34)	65 (42)	59 (32)	81 (46)
Negates with sustaining feedback	36 (29)	10 (6)	12 (10)	5 (5)	9 (8)

(*continued*)

Table 5.2 (*continued*)

Variables	Total frequency	Female		Male	
		Low expectancies frequency	High expectancies frequency	Low expectancies frequency	High expectancies frequency
Student style behaviors					
Student-initiated procedure questions[e]	221 (106)	66[d] (25)	73 (33)	38[c] (23)	44[c] (25)
Student-initiated dyadics	1491 (321)	311 (67)	416 (86)	364 (78)	400 (90)
Student-initiated questions[e]	969 (199)	219 (38)	409[d] (59)	157[c] (48)	184[c] (54)
Joint style behaviors					
Total response opportunities	2003 (309)	413 (63)	563 (83)	433[c] (75)	594 (88)
Open questions	950 (180)	188 (41)	279 (47)	199[c] (43)	284 (49)
Total dyadics	1780 (349)	371 (73)	467 (90)	488[d] (87)	454 (99)
Total interactions[e]	5034 (413)	1052 (85)	1520[d] (112)	1150[c] (101)	1312[c] (115)
Affirms	1340 (275)	268 (58)	377 (72)	277[c] (64)	418[d] (81)
Negates	277 (132)	46 (25)	96[d] (32)	72 (37)	63 (38)
Student-initiated questions yielding praise	14 (12)	0 (0)	6 (4)	2 (2)	6 (6)
Student-initiated questions yielding criticism	7 (6)	2 (2)	1 (1)	2 (2)	2 (1)
Total N	428	89	114	105	120

[a] Number of students having nonzero frequencies is shown in parentheses.
[b] The proportion of interactions involving males significantly greater than that involving females, $p < .05$.
[c] Lower frequency than one would expect based on proportion of sample included in this group, $p < .05$.
[d] Higher frequency than one would expect based on proportion of sample included in this group, $p < .05$.
[e] The proportion of interactions involving females higher than that involving males, $p < .05$.

dressed an unusually high number of direct questions and work praise at low teacher-expectancy girls, and they were more likely to provide boys with some form of short feedback following an incorrect answer than girls. Since the other differences reflect student or joint style variables, they cannot be attributed to the teacher. Furthermore, high teacher-expectancy boys and girls were involved in fairly comparable patterns of interactions with their math teachers.

Although we cannot determine from our data the reasons teachers might have for the patterns of differential treatment that did emerge, three of the four differences make sense in light of Cooper's (1979) analysis of teacher strategies. Cooper argued that teachers use strategies that direct potentially disruptive students into private interactions rather than encouraging them to participate in public interactions. The low teacher-expectancy boys appeared to be *the* group that was giving these teachers the most trouble. It makes sense then for these teachers to try to discourage these boys from public interactions through the use of public criticism and to encourage them to engage in more private dyadic interactions by initiating such interactions with them. In contrast, the low teacher-expectancy girls did not appear to be a source of disruption; instead the teachers may have perceived them as too docile and uninvolved. If so, then the teachers' treatment of this group also seems an appropriate remedial strategy.

The data just described are aggregated at the group level. Since we are primarily interested in psychological processes that occur at the level of the individual student, we needed interactional data aggregated at the level of the student. Since not all students were present for all 10 days of observation, we could not use each student's frequency counts; instead, the frequency counts for each of the 28 frequency variables were converted to mean frequencies per session observed. The eight proportional variables were already in a form that could be used for analysis at the level of the individual student. These are the scores discussed in the remainder of this chapter. Every student has a score for each of these 36 variables; even though for many of the variables this score is zero.

To test for sex and teacher expectancy group differences at the individual level, analyses of variance were run on each of the 36 interactional variables discussed thus far and on a measure of each student's past performance in math. By and large these effects mirror the findings obtained using the raw frequency count data: The girls received less criticism and asked more questions than the boys; the low teacher-expectancy boys, in particular, received more criticism, especially conduct criticism, and more teacher-initiated dyadics than any of the other three student groups.

One additional result emerged: High teacher-expectancy girls received praise in a smaller percentage of their interactions than any of the other three student groups. This result probably reflects a student style variable rather than differential teacher treatment. High teacher-expectancy girls asked more questions and, as a consequence, had more total interactions with the teacher than the other three student groups; praise, however, was rare in student-initiated questions. Thus, despite the fact that on the average these girls engaged in more teacher–student interactions, they did not receive more total or more work praise than the other student groups. Consequently, a smaller proportion of their total interactions involved praise than was true for the other three student groups, not because the teacher praised their academic performance less but because they asked more questions.

As was true with the frequency code data, by and large teachers treated these boys and girls, especially the high teacher-expectancy boys and girls, in a fairly similar manner. In addition, the boys and girls had done equally well in math in previous years; and not surprisingly, the teachers expected the boys and girls to do equally well in that year's math course.

Contrary to what we had predicted, we did not find any evidence that teachers were praising and criticizing boys and girls for different behaviors. Dweck et al. (1978) suggested that girls receive a disproportionate amount of their praise for good conduct and good form rather than good work, while boys receive most of their praise for good work; in contrast, they suggested that boys receive most of their criticism for bad conduct, whereas girls are more likely to be criticized for bad work as well as for bad conduct; we did not find either of these patterns. Both boys and girls got most of their praise (93%) for good work and most of their criticism (92%) for bad conduct. Boys did, however, get more of the latter, and we could not determine whether they deserved more or not.

The general pattern of few sex differences other than amount of criticism was replicated in our second sample of junior high school classrooms. In this sample, the low teacher-expectancy boys again stood out in terms of the level and amount of criticism directed at them by their teacher. In addition, in this second sample, the girls had a higher percentage of their praise directed at the quality of their academic work than did the boys. No other interactional variables yielded sex differences consistent enough across classrooms to be significant.

Student Beliefs and Attitudes

The majority of students in the main sample ($N = 275$) filled out an extensive questionnaire assessing their achievement-related attitudes and beliefs regarding both math and English (see Eccles, 1983; and Parsons et al., 1980, for more details on the questionnaire and on the scale construction procedures). In particular, scales on this questionnaire assessed self-concept of math ability, self-concept of English ability, perceptions of how difficult both math and English are to master, perceptions of the value and importance of studying both math and English, estimates of the likelihood of success in future math and English courses and on jobs requiring either math or English skills, and perceptions of how well the student's math teacher expected him/her to do on math in the future. Since English is not the focus of this chapter and since there were no sex differences of note on the English scales, only the math scales are discussed here.

To be consistent with the analyses reported thus far, analyses of variance were conducted on each of the math scales using student sex and teacher expectancy group as the independent variables. The results form a consistent pattern favoring the boys. Boys thought math was easier to master than did the girls; boys also had higher expectations for success in future math courses and in jobs requiring math skills. To make matters even worse, the high teacher-expectancy girls had less confidence in their math ability than did the high teacher-expectancy boys, despite the fact that they had done as well as the boys in previous math courses and that their math teachers had equally high expectations for them. Finally, these sex differences were more marked among the ninth graders than among the seventh graders. In fact, by ninth grade, the girls also felt it was less important and useful to study math than did the boys.

Relations between Interactional Variables and Student Attitudes

Correlations across the sexes and within each sex provided the first test of the relations between classroom interaction variables and attitudes. Very few significant relations emerged and the general pattern was similar for boys and girls. Positive attitudes were associated most strongly with the teacher expectation measures taken from the teacher rating form. These positive correlations held up even when the relations of past performance to both the teacher expectation measure and the students' attitudes were statistically controlled. Apparently, teacher expectations are being conveyed to the students and are influencing the students' attitudes. Exactly how is not clear from our data, since only two of the observational variables correlated significantly and substantially ($r > .20$) with the teacher expectation measure; and even these two correlated only for boys.

Among the observed interactional variables, work criticism had the strongest, most consistent effect on student attitudes. Boys and girls who received more work criticism had more positive attitudes toward math; they thought math was easier, had more confidence in their own math ability, and had higher future expectations. Although this result may seem counterintuitive and is certainly at odds with the findings in the elementary study, it can be explained. Work criticism occurred very rarely in this group of classrooms. Perhaps these teachers used work criticism only when they expected a student to do better. If so, then work criticism could convey a positive message despite its surface negativity. Some support for this interpretation is offered by the elementary school results. While work criticism did not relate positively to ability concepts in this group, it also did not relate negatively. Clearly, even the elementary schoolchildren were not incorporating the negative surface message into their self-concepts.

The relation between praise and students' attitudes was less clear and varied by sex. In particular, high levels of praise and high proportions of praise focused on work were associated with confidence in one's math ability for boys *only*. Praise did not appear to have similarly positive effects on girls' self-concepts. Recall that praise was used most liberally with low teacher-expectancy girls. These girls were also the recipients of unusually high levels of teacher-initiated response opportunities. If this pattern of teacher behavior reflected a strategy to draw these girls into classroom discussion, as suggested earlier, then it is unlikely that these girls would interpret this praise as a sign of high teacher expectations. Rather, they probably interpreted it for what it was, a positive gesture designed to make them feel comfortable and more willing to volunteer to participate in the future.

The use and interpretation of student-initiated questions also distinguished boys and girls. Among boys the number of questions asked related positively to how hard they thought math was, whereas the number of questions girls asked was unrelated to their estimates of difficulty. Finally, a high number of affirms related to high ability concepts *only* for boys.

To shed additional light on these relationships, we asked the students to give us their estimate of their teachers' expectations for them. If teachers' influence on students' attitudes was mediated by inferential processes, then there ought to be a relation between the interactional variables and the students' perceptions of their teachers' expectations for them. To test this hypothesis, we correlated the interactional variables with the students' perceptions of their teachers' expectations for them. For both boys and girls, the frequencies of both direct questions and teacher-initiated interactions were positively related to the students' perceptions of their teachers' expectancies. In contrast, the percentage of student questions yielding praise was positively related to the students' perceptions of their teacher's expectations among the girls but negatively related among the boys. In addition, total work praise was positively related to the students' perceptions of their teacher's expectations among the boys *only*.

What does all this mean? If you are a girl, you think the teacher has high expectations for you to the extent that the teacher asks you many academic questions and considers your questions worthy of the rare praise that is given out in response to a student's question. In contrast, if you are a boy, you think the teacher has high expectations for you to the extent that the teacher asks you many academic questions and praises your answers but does not praise your questions.

Interestingly, only the relation between work praise and boys' perceptions of their teachers' expectations for them coincides with the relations existing between the interactive variables themselves and the students' own attitudes: Praise was related to self-concept of math ability for boys *only*. Even more interestingly, amount of teacher praise did not in fact relate significantly to the teacher's expectations for either boys or girls. The girls appear to be aware of this fact and to discount the meaning of teacher praise accordingly. The boys, in contrast, are not aware of this fact and appear to be incorporating the praise into both their perception of their teachers' expectations for them and their own self-concept.

REGRESSION ANALYSES

Since we were most interested in the biasing effect of teacher–student interactions, we needed to find a way to separate the effects of teacher–student interactions from the effects of previous performance level. Teachers treat high- and low-expectation students differently. To a large extent, teachers base these expectations on the students' performance in previous math courses. Consequently, it is quite possible that any relations that might emerge between the interactional variables and students' beliefs, attitudes, and subsequent performance are an artifact of the relation of both the interactional variables and student beliefs and attitudes to previous performance. To test for this possibility and to provide an unconfounded estimate of the relation of interactional variables to subsequent attitudes, the variables identified in the correlational analyses were entered along with past performance into stepwise regression analyses of self-concept of ability and future expectancies.

The results were essentially the same for both attitudinal variables. For both boys and girls, past performance accounted for the largest share of the variance. But, contrary to the results in the elementary school study, past performance accounted for more variance in the boys' self-perceptions (between 16 and 27%) than in the girls' (between 7 and 9%). Among girls the number of student-initiated questions yielding criticism was the only interactional variable that accounted for an additional significant amount of variance in their self-perceptions; it depressed their self-perceptions to a very limited degree (accounting for an additional 3 to 5% of variance). In contrast, among boys three interactional variables added significantly to the regression equation (adding between 6 and 10% to the variance accounted for); the number of negates with feedback related negatively, while both the amount of praise and number of response opportunities yielding work criticism related positively to their self-perceptions. In interpreting this latter relationship, recall that work criticism was a rare event. In this context it may convey high teacher expectations, leading to its positive relation with self-concept. Finally, both past performance and interactional variables accounted for more variance in the attitudes of boys (between 22 and 37%) than of girls (between 10 and 14%).

Summary

Student sex was related to student–teacher interaction patterns but not in the manner predicted by Dweck et al. (1978). Instead, the effects largely replicated the findings reported by Brophy and Good (1974): Girls as a group received less criticism than boys and high teacher-expectancy girls received less praise than other student groups. Low teacher-expectancy boys received a disproportionate amount of criticism and teacher-initiated dyadics, whereas low teacher-expectancy girls received more praise especially in response to teacher-controlled questioning. Thus, although these teachers treated high-expectancy boys and girls similarly, they appeared to be using different control strategies for low-expectancy boys and girls. They acted as though they were trying to draw the low teacher-expectancy girls into public participation and the low teacher-expectancy boys into private interaction. This pattern mirrors the pattern of preventive control for boys and proactive control for girls reported in the elementary study. Other than these few differences, boys and girls were treated similarly, and even these differences were small.

Although classroom experiences appeared to have some effect on student attitudes, these effects were not very large and were clearly less powerful than students' own performance and teachers' expectations, neither of which differed by sex of student. And for both boys and girls, the impact of any particular experience seemed to depend on the subjective meaning the child attached to the experience. These meanings may well differ across boys and girls, especially since teachers' behaviors relate to their own attitudes differently depending on whether the target child is male or female.

Students' are undoubtedly aware of these subtle variations in the meaning of teacher behavior and should respond accordingly.

To the extent that boys and girls were influenced by different experiences, the girls seemed more reactive to criticism and less receptive to the effects of praise than the boys; but these differences again were slight and not consistent across measures. As was the case in elementary school study, these sex differences seemed as much a consequence of student characteristics as a consequence of differential treatment by teachers.

One major discrepancy emerged between the junior high school and elementary school studies: In the elementary school study, girls' self-perceptions were more strongly related to their achievement level than were boys'; in contrast, among the junior high school students, girls' self-perceptions related less strongly to their previous grades than did the boys'. The reason for this discrepancy is not clear. Possibly girls form more stable self-concepts than do boys at a young age but become less certain of their self-evaluations as they enter early adolescence. Alternatively, this discrepancy could reflect the difference in the level of specificity of the perceptions being assessed. The elementary school students were asked to rate their general level of academic ability; in contrast, the junior high school students were asked to rate their math ability. At any rate, the self-perceptions of the boys in both age groups seem to be more affected by the immediate situation, especially positive teacher feedback, than the girls' self-perceptions. This difference might make boys' self-concepts more resilient to negative classroom experiences during these school years.

Comparison of Classroom Types

The analyses reported thus far were performed on the entire sample. It is probable that the effects of teachers' behaviors are different across classrooms. For example, some teachers may treat boys and girls differently, whereas others may not. By combining across all of our teachers, these effects would be masked. To explore this possibility, we selected from the sample of 17 classrooms the 5 classrooms with the largest sex difference in the students' expectations for themselves and the 5 classrooms with no significant sex difference on the measure of student expectations and compared them on two levels. First, we compared the two types of classrooms in terms of general teaching practices, teacher style, and student behavior in order to get a picture of variations in general classroom climate. Then we compared the classrooms in terms of the specific behaviors of the students within the classrooms.

However, before proceeding to discuss these comparisons, it is important to note whether it was the boys' or the girls' expectations that were related to classroom-type. To test this we used analysis of variance with classroom-type and student sex as the two independent variables and student expectations as the dependent variable. Boys' expectancies did not differ across the two types of classroom while girls' did; in fact, girls' expectancies in the high-difference classrooms were lower than the expectancies of the other three student groups.

CLASSROOM LEVEL COMPARISONS

Although few significant differences emerged, these classrooms clearly differed from one another. Stepwise regressions were performed to determine which interactional variables best discriminated between these two classroom-types. To add generalizability, three stepwise regressions were performed, each using a random 60% of the sample. Six variables emerged as significant predictors in all three samples: total dyadics, total open questions (questions answered by a student who raised his/her hand prior to being called upon), total criticism, total conduct criticisms, total criticisms in teacher-initiated response opportunities, and total work praises (listed in order of importance). In general, teachers in the high sex-differentiated classrooms were quite critical, in many cases using very pointed sarcasm to put a student in his or her place; they also tended to use a public teaching style rather than a more private teaching style and to rely heavily on student volunteers for answers. In contrast, teachers in the low sex-differentiated classes were less openly critical toward their students, tended to rely on a more private teaching style characterized by a high proportion of student– teacher conferencelike interactions, and took a more active role in calling on specific students for answers rather than relying on volunteers.

These results suggest that girls' attitudes toward math are more positive in a class characterized by a high proportion of private teacher–student dyadic interaction relative to the time spent in public recitation, and by relatively high levels of teacher control over the public recitation when it occurs. This same pattern emerged in our second sample of junior high school classrooms. Using a similar procedure, we divided these 12 classrooms into two groups: the 6 with the least sex difference in the students' self-perceptions and the 6 with the most extreme sex difference in the students' self-perceptions. These two types of classrooms also differed primarily in terms of the proportion of time spent in private student–teacher interactions versus the time spent in public recitation and in terms of the degree to which the teacher controlled who participated in public recitation rather than relying on volunteers. And, once again, the girls' self-perceptions were highest in the more private and teacher-controlled recitation classrooms.

There is some evidence that girls are less likely than boys to thrive, academically speaking, in an environment that is competitive and male-dominated (see Fennema & Peterson, Chapter 2, this volume; Petersen, & Fennema, 1983; Webb & Kenderski, Chapter 10 this volume; Wilkinson, Lindow, & Chiang, Chapter 9, this volume). It is quite possible that classrooms characterized by relatively high reliance on public recitation and on student volunteers seem relatively more competitive and threatening to students than classrooms characterized by relatively high reliance on private student–teacher interactions and on teacher-controlled recitation, provided that the teacher uses this control to encourage participation from everyone rather than a chosen few (Brush, 1980). If this is true, then we should expect that girls would find these more private classrooms more congenial and, consequently, would develop more positive attitudes toward math in such environments.

It is important to note that the logic underlying this proposal does not depend on sex-differentiated treatment by the teacher as a causal explanation of sex-differentiated beliefs and attitudes among the students. Instead, it suggests that sex differences in student learning and in students' attitudes could come about because similar environments affect boys and girls differently, primarily because boys and girls enter those environments with different views of the world and different learning histories. The extent to which this process is operative raises intriguing questions for those of us interested in fostering sex equity in education.

STUDENT LEVEL COMPARISONS

In the next set of comparisons we used the student level data to assess whether boys and girls were treated differently in either of these two types of classrooms and whether these sex differences varied across the two types of classrooms. Several interesting sex differences emerged in these analyses. In the low-difference classrooms, girls interacted more than boys (gave more responses, asked more questions, initiated more interactions); they also received more praise for work and criticism for form than boys. In high-difference classrooms, boys interacted more and received more praise for their work and criticism for their form.

We next divided the sample into the high and low teacher-expectancy groups discussed earlier. In general, high teacher-expectancy boys and girls were treated quite differently in these two types of classroom. High teacher-expectancy girls interacted the most, answered the most questions, received the most work and form praise, and the least criticism in the low sex-differentiated classrooms. In contrast, high teacher-expectancy boys were accorded the most praise and interacted the most in the high sex-differentiated classrooms. High teacher-expectancy girls were accorded the least amount of praise of any of the eight sex by teacher expectancy by classroom-type groups in the high sex-differentiated classrooms.

The Sex × Teacher Expectancy interactions were particularly interesting in the high-difference classrooms. In these classrooms, the classic teacher expectancy effects emerged only among the boys; that is, high teacher-expectancy boys in these classrooms received more attention, more rewards, and less criticism than low teacher-expectancy boys. In contrast, the high teacher-expectancy girls in these classrooms were not treated in the manner predicted by the teacher-expectancy literature. In fact, if anything the low teacher-expectancy girls in these classrooms were accorded the classic high teacher-expectancy pattern, especially in terms of response opportunities and praise, while the high teacher-expectancy girls were basically ignored and given virtually no praise or encouragement.

What about the low-difference classrooms? The high teacher-expectancy girls fared very well in these classrooms; they dominated the interactions and received the most praise. But while the high teacher-expectancy boys got less praise in these classrooms than did the high teacher-expectancy girls, the pattern of its distribution across high and low teacher-expectancy children was equivalent for the two sexes. In this social climate, there was no overall sex difference in expectancies despite the fact that the girls both got more praise and interacted more than the boys.

These data suggest that being in a classroom in which praise is used differently for boys and girls has a detrimental effect on all girls but not on boys. Only the girls' expectations differed across these two types of classrooms. Furthermore, the relatively high levels of praise given to the low teacher-expectancy girls in the high sex-differentiated classrooms did not appear to have the facilitative effect on their attitudes one would expect; they had lower expectations for their own future success in mathematics than any of the other seven sex by teacher expectancy by classroom-type groups.

One cannot infer from these data that praise itself is responsible for the expectancy differences in these two classrooms. In fact, the correlation between amount of praise and attitudes was nonsignificant for girls in either type of classrooms. Rather, it appears that the pattern of praise across the various subgroups is critical. Boys and girls had equivalent expectancies when the relative distribution of praise and criticism was similar for both sexes.

Summary

The data from the junior high school study clearly indicate that the impact of classroom experiences on students' self-perceptions depends on their subjective meaning to the students. To advocate that teachers should avoid criticism or give praise more freely overlooks the power of the context in determining the meaning of the message. Praise was positively related to self-perceptions only in the group, in this case boys, in which it in fact conveyed information about the teachers' expectations. Among girls, a group for which the teachers' use of praise did not covary with their expectations, praise was not related to either the girls' self-perceptions or to their perceptions of their teachers' expectations.

What role do the teachers play in perpetuating sex differences in math attitudes? Our data suggest that differential treatment may be one factor, although not a very powerful or ubiquitous factor. Girls have lower expectancies for themselves in those classrooms in which they are treated in a qualitatively different manner than the boys. And while this differential treatment was not characteristic of most of our classrooms, these results suggest that the brightest girls are not being nurtured to the same extent as are boys in some classrooms. The causal implications of this difference need to be established.

Our data also suggest that general classroom climate may play an important role in reinforcing sex differences in achievement attitudes, beliefs, and performance. Certain kinds of educational environments may facilitate boys' achievement while either dampening or having little positive effect on girls' achievement. Relying on public recitation and student volunteers emerged as two such environmental characteristics in the junior high school study. Competitive goal structures and coeducation are two other characteristics that have been suggested as having similar effects (see Eccles, Midgley, & Adler, 1984, for discussion of impact of general classroom level variations on student motivation and self-perceptions). The remedy for such differential effects is not clear. Should we educate boys and girls differently so that each experiences the educational environment best suited for his or her needs? Probably not, especially since variations within sex make identification of such ideal environments for each sex impossible. Instead, educators at all levels need to be aware of the fact that children may respond to similar educational experiences in different ways. Then we can work toward a balance between providing both boys and girls with all types of educational experiences and helping both boys and girls acquire the skills necessary to benefit maximally from various types of learning environments.

GENERAL CONCLUSIONS

In summary, we, like many others, have found small but fairly consistent evidence that boys and girls have different experiences in their classrooms. However, these differences seem as much a consequence of preexisting differences in the students' behaviors as of teacher bias. Nonetheless, when differences occur, they appear to be reinforcing sex-stereotyped expectations and behaviors. In addition, we found some evidence that boys and girls respond differently to similar experiences. These results indicate that similar treatment may not yield equitable outcomes for both boys and girls.

Studies relying more on case-study approaches have provided stronger evidence of the impact of teachers on students' career plans and decisions. For example, women working in male-dominated fields often report that a particular teacher played a very important role in shaping their career choice (Casserly, 1975; Boswell, 1979). Unfortunately, few students encounter a teacher who encourages them to consider a wide range of careers. Instead, most teachers reinforce traditional behavior and occupational plans for both boys and girls independent of where the student's interests or talents might lie (Eccles & Hoffman, 1984). For example, mathematically gifted girls are less likely to be identified as such by their teachers than are mathematically-gifted boys. Similarly, girls who drop out of the math curriculum or out of other nontraditional majors in college often attribute their decisions to a teacher who actively discouraged their interests (Fox, Brody, & Tobin, 1980).

Casserly's (1975) work indicates that teachers can favorably affect girls' preparation for math and science-related occupations if they provide active encouragement, exposure to role models, sincere praise for high ability and good performance, explicit advice regarding the value of math and science, and explicit encouragement to both boys and girls and their parents regarding the importance of developing their talents to the fullest and aspiring after the best jobs they can obtain (Casserly, 1975; Eccles & Hoffman, 1984). Most teachers rarely do any of these things. Certainly none of the teachers we observed did. In addition, we recorded less than a dozen instances of a teacher explaining the value of math and very few instances of a teacher explaining proactively the intrinsic value of engaging in any academic activity. We also rarely observed a teacher providing any form of career counseling. Thus, although teachers can help overcome sex stereotypes and promote more sex-equitable educational outcomes, they rarely do. As a consequence, most students leave each classroom pretty much as they entered it, neither more or less sex stereotyped in their beliefs and future goals.

REFERENCES

Blumenfeld, P., Hamilton, V. L., Bossert, S., Wessels, K., & Meece, J. (1983). Teacher talk and student thought: Socialization into the student role. In J. Levine & M. Wang (Eds.), *Teacher and student perceptions: Implications for learning.* Hillsdale, NJ: Erlbaum.

Blumenfeld, P., Hamilton, V. L., Wessels, K., & Falkner, D. (1979). Teaching responsibility to first graders. *Theory into Practice, 28,* 174–180.

Blumenfeld, P., & Pintrich, P. R. (1983). *The relation of student characteristics and children's perceptions of teachers and peers in varying classroom environments.* Paper presented at the annual meeting of the American Educational Research Association, Montreal, Canada.

Boswell, S. (1979). *Nice girls don't study mathematics.* Symposium paper presented at the annual meeting of the American Educational Research Association meeting, San Francisco.

Brophy, J., & Evertson, C. (1976). *Learning from teaching: A developmental perspective.* Boston: Allyn & Bacon.

Brophy, J., & Evertson, C. (1981). *Student characteristics and teaching.* New York: Longman.

Brophy, J., & Good, T. (1974). *Teacher–student relationships: Causes and consequences.* New York: Holt, Rinehart & Winston.

Brush, L. R. (1980). *Encouraging girls in mathematics: The problem and the solution.* Boston: Abt Associates.

Casserly, P. (1975). *An assessment of factors affecting female participation in advanced placement programs in mathematics, chemistry, and physics* (Report). Washington, DC: National Institute of Education.

Cooper, H. (1979). Pygmalion grows up: A model for teacher expectation communication and performance influences. *Review of Educational Research, 49,* 389–410.

Crandall, V. C. (1969). Sex differences in expectancy of intellectual and academic reinforcement. In C. P. Smith (Ed.), *Achievement-related behaviors in children.* New York: Russell Sage.

Doyle, W. (1979). Making managerial decisions in classrooms. In D. Duke (Ed.), *Classroom management: Yearbook of the National Society for the Study of Education.* Chicago: University of Chicago Press.

Dweck, C. S., Davidson, W., Nelson, S., & Enna, B. (1978). Sex differences in learned helplessness: II. The contingencies of evaluative feedback in the classroom; III. An experimental analysis. *Developmental Psychology, 14,* 268–276.

Dweck, C. S., & Elliott, E. S. (1983). Achievement motivation. In P. Mussen & E. M. Hetherington (Eds.), *Handbook of child psychology* (Vol. 4). New York: Wiley.

Eccles Parsons, J. (1984). Sex differences in mathematics participation. In M. Steinkamp & M. Maehr (Eds.), *Women in science.* Greenwich, CT: JAI Press.

Eccles, J. S. (1983). Expectancies, values, and academic choice: Origins and change. In J. Spence (Ed.), *Achievement and achievement motivation.* San Francisco: W. H. Freeman.

Eccles, J. S., & Hoffman, L. W. (1984). Socialization and the maintainance of a sex-segregated

114   Jacquelynne S. Eccles and Phyllis Blumenfeld

labor market. In H. W. Stevenson & A. E. Siegel (Eds.), *Research in child development and social policy* (Vol. 1). Chicago: University of Chicago Press.

Eccles, J., Midgley, C., & Adler, T. F. (1984). Grade-related changes in the school environment: Effects on achievement motivation. In J. H. Nicholls (Ed.), *The development of achievement motivation.* Greenwich, CT: JAI Press.

Eccles, J. S., & Wigfield, A. (in press). Student expectancies and motivation. In J. B. Dusek (Ed.), *Teacher expectancies.* Hillsdale, NJ: Erlbaum.

Fox, L. H., Brody, L., & Tobin, D. (1980). *Women and the mathematical mystique.* Baltimore: Johns Hopkins University Press.

Goodman, L. A. (1965). On simultaneous confidence intervals for multinomial proportions. *Technometrics, 7,* 247–254.

Heller, K. A., & Parsons, J. E. (1981). Teacher influences on students' expectancies for success. *Child Development, 52,* 1015–1019.

Hoge, R. P., & Luce, S. (1979). Predicting academic achievement from classroom behavior. *Review of Educational Research, 49,* 479–496.

Huston, A. C. (1983). Sex-typing. In P. Mussen and E. M. Hetherington (Eds.), *Handbook of child psychology, Vol. IV.* New York: Wiley Press.

Jackson, P. (1968). *Life in classrooms.* New York: Holt, Rinehart & Winston.

Meece, J. L., Eccles–Parsons, J., Futterman, R., Goff, S. E., & Kaczala, C. M. (1982). Sex differences in math achievement: Toward a model of academic choice. *Psychological Bulletin, 91,* 324–348.

Parsons, J. E., Adler, T., Futterman, R., Goff, S., Kaczala, C., Meece, J., & Midgley, C. (1980). *Self-perceptions, task perceptions, and academic choice: Origins and change* (Final Report. Grant NIE-G-78-0022). Ann Arbor: University of Michigan. (ERIC Document Reproduction Service No. ED 186 477)

Parsons, J. E., Kaczala, C. M., & Meece, J. L. (1982). Socialization of achievement attitudes and beliefs: Classroom influences. *Child Development, 53,* 322–339.

Parsons, J. E., Ruble, D. N., Hodges, K. L., & Small, A. W. (1976). Cognitive–developmental factors in emerging sex differences in achievement-related expectancies. *Journal of Social Issues, 32,* 47–61.

Peterson, P. L., & Fennema, E. H. (1983). Effective teaching, student engagement in classroom activities, and gender-related differences in learning mathematics. Paper presented at the conference on gender-related differences in the classroom. Madison, WI, October, 1983.

Pintrich, P. (1982). *Classroom experience and children's self-perceptions of ability, effort, and conduct.* Unpublished dissertation, University of Michigan, Ann Arbor.

Pintrich, P. R., & Blumenfeld, P. (1983). *Classroom experience and children's perceptions of teachers and peers.* Paper presented at the annual meeting of the American Educational Research Association, Montreal, Canada.

Ruble, D. N., & Frey, K. (1982). *Self evaluation and social comparison in the classroom: A naturalistic study of peer interaction.* Paper presented at the annual meeting of the American Educational Research Association, New York.

Stein, A. H., & Bailey, M. M. (1973). The socialization of achievement orientation in females. *Psychological Bulletin, 80,* 345–366.

Interactions of Male and Female Students with Male and Female Teachers*

JERE BROPHY

INTRODUCTION

American educators have debated gender-related issues throughout the twentieth century. Claims that one sex or the other is not being taught effectively in our schools have been frequent and often impassioned, especially when based on philosophical grounds rather than examination of empirical data. From early in the century (Ayres, 1909) through about 1970 (Sexton, 1969; Austin, Clark, & Fitchett, 1971), criticism was usually focused on the treatment of boys, especially at the elementary level. Critics noted that boys received lower grades in all subjects and lower achieve-

---

* This work is sponsored in part by the Institute for Research on Teaching, College of Education, Michigan State University. The Institute for Research on Teaching is funded primarily by the Program for Teaching and Instruction of the National Institute of Education, under Contract 400-81-0014. The opinions expressed in this chapter do not necessarily reflect the position, policy, or endorsement of the National Institute of Education.

115

ment test scores in reading and language arts. They suggested that these sex differences occurred because the schools were "too feminine" or the "over-whelmingly female" teachers were unable to meet boys' learning needs effectively. More recently, other critics (eg, Becker, 1981; Stallings, 1979) have noted that the advantage enjoyed by girls at the elementary level is not sustained, and that by the secondary level, especially in mathematics and science, boys begin to pull ahead. These critics claim that girls are not reaching their achievement potentials in these areas because of inappro-priate teacher expectations or other aspects of institutionalized sexism in our school system as a whole.

Speculation about possible causes of these gender-related differences in school achievement introduces a broad range of issues (school organiza-tion, curriculum and instruction, academic counseling practices, etc.). This chapter focuses on events occurring at the classroom level and in particular on the quantity and quality of interactions that teachers have with their male and female students. The chapter considers whether teachers treat male and female students differently, and if so, whether this differential treatment is a function of the sex of the teacher. It begins with a summary of the data reported through 1973, and then considers in more detail data reported in the last 10 years.

For simplicity, the data are described in terms referring to biological gender status (male and female teachers interacting with male and female students). However, these behavioral differences are not construed as mani-festations of genetically programmed sex differences; instead they are inter-preted as reflecting gender role behaviors acquired through social learning mechanisms. It is assumed that children of both sexes in any given society are exposed to gender-differentiated behavioral modeling by older children and adults who have already been socialized into the differentiated gender roles favored in that society, and that significant others (of both sexes) tend to socialize individual children into differentiated gender roles by commu-nicating expectations about how children of their sex are expected to behave.

Classrooms are expected to reflect these modeling and socialization ten-dencies seen in society at large. Male and female teachers can be expected to model the characteristics and behavior expected of males and females (respectively) in the society, such as a tendency for males to take an instru-mental role and for females to take an expressive role in social interactions. Most teachers are from (lower) middle-class families and thus were ex-posed to less rigid gender role socialization than individuals from lower class families; nevertheless, they can be expected to show some degree of gender role differentiation. Thus, male teachers as a group can be expected to model somewhat different behaviors than female teachers (although in general, male and female teachers are much more alike than different).

In addition, teachers socialize students by communicating behavioral norms and expectations, including norms and expectations related to gender roles. Sometimes this is done directly, by stating that certain behaviors are appropriate for boys and other behaviors are appropriate for girls. More typically, however, this is accomplished through subtle yet systematic (but often unconscious) differential treatment of boys and girls—treatment communicating the expectation that certain characteristics and behavior are associated with boys, and that other characteristics and behavior are associated with girls. In their general approach to teaching, male teachers usually model masculine role behaviors and female teachers usually model feminine role behaviors. Yet, in their interactions with students (especially their dyadic interactions with individuals), teachers of both sexes tend to socialize students of both sexes to conform to the students' own gender roles. Thus, both male and female teachers tend to project expectations that male students conform to the male role and female students conform to the female role.

PRE-1974 FINDINGS

Brophy and Good (1974) reviewed in detail the research literature dealing with gender-related issues and schooling published through 1973. Their focus was on elementary schooling and the problems of boys because few data on secondary schooling and the problems of girls were available at that time. The conclusions they reached from their literature review follow (see Brophy & Good, 1974, for details and references).

First, there was (and is) a "problem" in that, even though there are no sex differences in general intelligence or ability, elementary school boys do not achieve as highly as girls in reading and language arts, and boys are referred more frequently for remedial reading help or assistance with diagnosed learning disabilities. Furthermore, these sex differences, which are found repeatedly in the United States, are not observed in many other countries. Thus, they are caused by factors in our culture generally or in our system of schooling in particular and not by genetic differences in patterns or rates of maturation of intellectual abilities.

Teacher expectations are one probable factor. Palardy (1969) found that first-grade boys showed reading achievement equivalent to that of first-grade girls in classrooms taught by teachers who expected no sex difference, but that first-grade boys did not achieve as highly as their female classmates in classes taught by teachers who expected the girls to achieve more than the boys. The reading achievement of the girls in the latter classes was equivalent to that of both the boys and the girls in the former classes, but the reading achievement of the boys in the latter classes was depressed, possibly through self-fulfilling prophecy effects of the teachers' lower expectations for boys. The majority of American teachers are apt to see boys as less interested in (and perhaps also as possessing less aptitude for) reading and language arts than girls, so it can be argued that self-fulfilling prophecy effects explain the known sex differences in achievement. If so, there should be evidence that boys and girls are taught differently, particularly during reading instruction.

Another possibility is that elementary school boys see schooling in general as feminine, not only because most of their teachers are female, but because of a poor fit between the culturally prescribed male gender role and the student role that has become institutionalized in American elementary schools. Brophy and Good (1974) reviewed numerous studies suggesting that this student role calls for a primarily passive, recipient learning style rather than a more active or exploratory one, and that teachers tend to prefer students they describe as quiet, mature, orderly, and conforming over students they describe as active, independent, or assertive. These desired attributes of students (hereafter designated collectively as "the student role") clearly overlap much more with the female than the male gender role as traditionally defined by our society; therefore girls should find it easier to adjust to this student role than boys and should be more motivated to do so. This congruence between gender roles and the student role factor probably explains some of the sex differences in achievement mentioned above, although two points should be noted. (1) Although it may explain why elementary school girls tend to get generally higher report card grades than their male classmates, it cannot explain the documented sex differences in objectively measured achievement, because these vary according to subject matter. Thus, girls outperform boys only on tests of achievement in reading and language arts, even at the earliest grades, despite what appears to be a better fit between the female sex role and the student role. (2) Although American elementary student role expectations and associated teacher attitudes can be cited as evidence that elementary schools are primarily feminine-oriented institutions, it should be noted that this student role was institutionalized in the past, when most teachers were male "schoolmasters" and education was seen as important mostly for males.

Another potentially important factor is the sex of the teacher. Perhaps, critics suggest, male students cannot easily identify with female teachers, or female teachers cannot teach male students effectively. On the first issue,

Brophy and Good (1974) reported mixed findings, although with some tendency for students to prefer teachers of the same sex. On the second issue, they reported negative findings. A few studies indicated a tendency for boys to achieve better when taught by male teachers (or more generally for children to achieve better when taught by teachers of the same sex). Overall, however, most studies showed no difference, and the studies showing a slight advantage to same-sex teachers were balanced by other studies showing a slight advantage to opposite-sex teachers. In general, the data did not support the notion that sex of teacher was an important factor determining student achievement.

In addition to these data on historical trends, teachers' attitudes, and students' achievement patterns, Brophy and Good (1974) reviewed the data on student sex differences in classroom experiences and patterns of teacher–student interaction. These data appear complex and conflicting at first, but they concur rather well when level of schooling (preschool vs. elementary school), sex of teacher, and research methodology (especially the issue of whether teacher initiations were separated from teacher reactions to student initiations in recording the data) are taken into account.

Sex Differences in Students' Classroom Interaction Patterns

Studies conducted in nursery schools and preschools often show a tendency for boys to come into conflict frequently with their (female) teachers, who tend to praise and reward children of both sexes for engaging in behavior associated with the female sex role but to criticize or punish children of both sexes for engaging in behavior associated with the male sex role. It is difficult to judge the meaning of such data because the categorizations of children's behaviors as male or female tend to be too broad and to fail to take into account the appropriateness or desirability of the behaviors (both fighting and independent block-building, for example, might be classified as male-oriented behaviors). Thus, it is not clear whether nursery school teachers tend to be inappropriately rigid and feminizing in their interactions with children (because of personal qualities that cause them to become nursery school teachers in the first place or because of factors unique to the training of nursery school teachers), or whether they merely respond appropriately to the behavior of the children (preschool boys may become overtly aggressive or otherwise behave undesirably much more often or intensely than elementary school boys do).

In any case, no parallel feminizing tendency is seen in the data from elementary school classes. In part, this is because interactions between elementary school teachers and their students are focused on teaching and learning the curriculum, which tends to be sexually neutral, whereas many of the play activities in nursery schools tend to be associated with one or the other gender role. Thus, although the elementary school student role has been portrayed as female-oriented, this is a matter of degree. Compared to other roles common in the lives of children, the student role is more neutral or androgynous than sex-typed.

Brophy and Good's (1974) review of elementary school studies indicated that certain consistent sex differences appear, but that these are more accurately construed as student effects on teachers than as teacher effects on students. It is true that teachers criticize and punish boys more often than girls for misbehavior, and that they initiate interactions with them more frequently in order to give them procedural instructions, to check their progress on assignments, or in general to monitor and control their activities. However, this is only part of a larger pattern indicating that boys are more active and salient in classrooms and that they have more of almost any kind of interaction with the teacher that may be measured. Thus, although boys are criticized more often than girls, they are praised as often and sometimes more often. Also, although boys have more behavioral and procedural interactions with their teachers, they also have more academic interactions. Teachers not only check on boys' work more often but also tend to call on them more often during lessons, and boys are also more likely than girls to call out answers without first being recognized by their teacher and thus to coopt response opportunities for themselves. In general, the data suggest that differences between boys and girls in patterns of interaction with their teachers are due to differences in the behavior of the boys and girls themselves (and the effects of this behavior on the teachers) rather than to any consistent tendency of teachers to treat the two sexes differently.

On the average, boys misbehave much more often and intensively than girls, and thus teachers need to criticize or punish boys' misbehavior more frequently (in general, the sex differences in teacher response to student misbehavior are not as large as the sex differences in the misbehavior itself). Measures of the frequency of particular types of interaction typically favor boys whenever a sex difference appears, although certain ipsative or percentage measures favor girls. For example, a greater percentage of girls' total interactions with the teacher are apt to be academic interactions rather than procedural or managerial ones, and a greater percentage of those academic interactions are apt to be initiated by the girls themselves rather than by the teachers.

Ironically, fewer sex differences are noted during reading group interaction than in general class activities. In part, this is because the "reading turns" feature of reading groups tends to equalize the frequency and homogenize the nature of teacher–student interaction during group activities. In any case, the sex differences noted in reading group interactions were similar in direction to but less extreme than the sex differences noted in whole-class activities, and there was no clear tendency for teachers to treat girls more appropriately than boys during reading instruction. One study revealed a teacher tendency to work harder to elicit improved responses from girls during reading group interaction. Here the teachers tended to respond to girls' reading failures by giving clues or providing second-response opportunities, whereas they were more likely to simply give the word or call on someone else in parallel situations with boys. This finding is compatible with the hypothesis that teachers might produce higher reading achievement in girls through self-fulfilling prophecy effects of higher achievement expectations, but the finding is an exception to the more general rule of no significant differences (and in particular, no differences favoring girls) during reading instruction.

Brophy and Good (1974) reported that patterns of teacher–student interaction may be influenced by sex of student not so much as a main effect but as parts of interaction effects also involving student achievement and behavior variables. Although boys regularly receive more criticism and sometimes receive more praise than girls, this criticism and praise is not distributed equally among the boys in the room. A large proportion, sometimes even a majority, of the criticism is directed to a small group of boys who frequently misbehave and usually are low achievers. Meanwhile, a large proportion of the praise (especially praise for good academic accomplishments rather than merely for good behavior) is directed to another small group of boys who are high achievers and usually well adjusted to the student role. Typically, there is no overlap between these two subgroups of boys. These data provide one example of the larger point mentioned above that teachers typically respond to students' behavior, and not their gender, in interacting with them in the classroom.

Interactions of Male and Female Students with Male and Female Teachers

Brophy and Good (1974) located only a few studies comparing male with female teachers in their treatment of male versus female students. These studies all agreed, however, in finding that classes taught by male teachers show the same kinds of student sex differences as classes taught by female teachers. That is, attitude assessments showed that male teachers preferred conforming and obedient students over independent and assertive students;

report card data indicated that male teachers assigned higher marks to girls than to boys; and classroom interaction data indicated that male teachers interacted more frequently with boys, criticized them more often for misbehavior, et cetera.

The largest of these studies (Good, Sikes, & Brophy, 1973) involved 16 junior high school teachers: 4 male and 4 female math teachers, and 4 male and 4 female social studies teachers. Data on 62 measures of teacher–student interaction yielded numerous effects of subject matter and student sex, and interactions between sex of teacher and subject matter. However, there was only one significant interaction between sex of teacher and sex of student, which was less than the number to be expected by chance. Thus, the data did not support the notion that teachers (of either sex) treat same-sex students differently, let alone more appropriately, than they treat students of the opposite sex.

Sex Differences in Teacher Behavior

Data comparing male and female teachers indicated a few differences, although these were in general approaches to teaching rather than in treatment of male versus female students. Data from several studies suggested that male teachers tend to be more direct and subject-centered and female teachers to be more indirect and student-centered. Male teachers appear to do more lecturing and female teachers to do more questioning. In the classrooms studied by Good et al. (1973), for example, students had more public response opportunities, initiated more comments and questions, and initiated more private contacts with the teachers in classes taught by females. They were also more likely to guess when unsure of their answer in female teachers' classes but more likely to remain silent in male teachers' classes (suggesting that the students felt safer in guessing in the female teachers' classes).

Female teachers gave more praise following correct answers but also failed to give feedback more often following incorrect answers (they tended to move on to someone else when the first student failed to respond correctly). Following wrong answers or failures to respond, male teachers were more likely to give explanations designed to clear up the student's misunderstanding and more likely to provide a second response opportunity by asking another question. In general, the female teachers were warmer and more responsive following student success, but the male teachers were more informative and comfortable in sustaining the interaction with the student following failure.

These teacher sex differences are compatible with the traditional notions of the male gender role as instrumental and the female gender role as expressive; however, they do not interact with sex of student nor suggest that teachers of either sex are categorically more effective with students of either sex. Furthermore, these are relatively minor differences within a larger context of similarily. Male and female teachers are much more similar to each other than different, and the variance within sex far exceeds the variance between the two sexes.

PROGRESS IN THE LAST DECADE

The 10 years that have elapsed since Brophy and Good's (1974) review have witnessed not only new empirical contributions but also new approaches to the study of gender-related issues in schooling. One major change has been the switch from males to females as the primary at-risk group of interest. Accompanying this switch has been a switch of focus from elementary to secondary schooling and from instruction in reading and language arts to instruction in mathematics and science. Studies with larger samples and better coding systems have been conducted, often with better control of subject matter and of teacher versus student initiation of interaction. "Thick description" methods have been introduced to focus on subtle qualitative nuances that are not addressed through coding and tabulating discrete behaviors. Finally, a broader range of factors has been taken into account in conceptualizing the quality of students' classroom experiences. In particular, measurement of the frequency and affective quality of teacher–student interaction in public settings has been supplemented by attention to the more purely instructional aspects of teacher behavior, to the kinds of assignments made and the expectations communicated in the process of making them, and to the expectations and attributions communicated in private contacts with students.

Preschool Studies

Several studies were done at the preschool level by Fagot (1977, 1978, 1981). The first (Fagot, 1977) focused on teachers' and peers' reactions to children's play behaviors. The (female) teachers responded positively to boys when they were engaged in task behaviors, but tended to criticize the boys for engaging in behaviors sex-typed as feminine. Teachers were also likely to criticize the girls for joining masculine-role activities with groups of boys. Thus, in contrast to Fagot's earlier study suggesting that teachers tend to feminize children of both sexes, this study suggested that teachers socialize both sexes along traditional lines by criticizing them for engaging in cross-sex play.

Fagot's other studies dealt with the variable of teacher experience in working with young children, because this seemed to explain some of the conflicting findings of earlier studies. Fagot (1978) reported that experienced teachers tended to initiate more activities with children, whereas inexperienced teachers tended to join children's ongoing activities. Furthermore, the experienced teachers tended to interact more with both boys and girls when they were engaged in feminine-preferred activities, whereas inexperienced teachers tended to interact more with boys when they were engaged in masculine-preferred activities and with girls when they were engaged in feminine-preferred activities. It should be noted that many of the feminine-preferred activities included art, small motor coordination skills, and other school readiness activities, so that in effect the data indicate that experienced teachers tend to direct their children into school readiness activities, whereas inexperienced teachers tend to go along with whatever the children's existing play preferences may be.

Fagot (1981) conducted a larger study in which teacher sex and teacher experience were investigated both separately and in interaction with each other. Once again the data indicated that experienced teachers initiated more interactions with the children and interacted more with both boys and girls when they engaged in feminine-preferred activities. This was true of both male and female experienced teachers. Also, inexperienced teachers were once again observed to interact more with boys when they were engaged in masculine-preferred activities but with girls when they were engaged in feminine-preferred activities. Thus, the tendencies of experienced teachers to direct the children into school readiness activities and of inexperienced teachers to join existing play activities were replicated. Male teachers were found to join the play of children more often than female teachers, and to express more physical affection to them. The latter finding was unexpected and probably indicates that males who choose to go into nursery school and preschool education are much more nurturant than typical males. There were no interactions between sex of teacher and sex of child in this study. However, teachers in general were observed to ask more questions and give more information to girls but to join the existing play activity of boys more often. In other words, teachers' interactions with girls were more verbal and school-readiness oriented.

The previous sentence essentially summarizes the differences found in various studies by Fagot. Despite the use of terms "masculine preferred" and "feminine preferred," the operative variable determining teachers' reactions to student activities seemed to be the value of those activities for furthering readiness for school and not the degree to which the activities were associated with one or the other gender role or the degree to which children of different genders preferred the activities. Inexperienced teachers of both sexes tended to join children's ongoing play and thus reinforce whatever they were doing, whereas experienced teachers of both sexes tended to initiate verbal, artistic, fine motor, and other school readiness activities with the children (slightly more with girls than with boys, but essentially with all the children).

Cherry (1975) studied four female preschool teachers' interactions with boys and girls. These teachers initiated and spoke more often to boys than to girls but essentially because they more often spoke with "attentional-marked utterances" that occurred during attempts to focus or control behavior. Thus, this is the typical finding that teachers interact more with boys than with girls because of a need to supervise and intervene to control the boys more often. Cherry also reported that girls received more verbal feedback than boys following their answers to teachers' questions.

Perdue and Connor (1978) observed physical touching patterns in preschool classrooms that contained both a male and a female teacher (all inexperienced undergraduates). They reported that teachers touched children of their own sex more often than they touched children of the opposite sex. Furthermore, many of the male teachers' touches of boys were "friendly" touches involving expression of nurturance or approval or occurring as part of a game, whereas most of their touches of girls were "helpful" touches that occurred when the teacher was helping the child or the child was helping the teacher. Perdue and Connor also found that boys touched male teachers more often than girls did, and that boys touched male teachers more often than they touched female teachers. These differences were sizable. Teachers were twice as likely to touch children of the same sex as children of the opposite sex, and boys were three times as likely to touch male teachers as female teachers. It is not yet clear, however, whether experienced teachers would show the same pattern of differences.

DISCUSSION

Fagot's work indicates that many of the earlier findings from the preschool level need to be cast in a new light, in which preschool teachers are seen more as trying to prepare their children for school than as feminizing them. The teacher experience factor must also be considered: Comparisons of male teachers with female teachers tended to be *de facto* comparisons of inexperienced teachers with experienced teachers in most studies (Fagot's 1981 study is an exception), so it is possible that some findings attributed to teacher sex were actually due to teacher experience. Consideration of these factors suggests that the preschool data may not be as different from the elementary school data as earlier findings suggested. Still, it is at the preschool level that the strongest arguments can be made (on the basis of data) for suggesting that boys may not be treated optimally and that an infusion of more male teachers would be helpful.

The work of Huston and Carpenter (see Chapter 7, this volume) also provides a new perspective on earlier findings from the preschool level. In particular, the differential touching patterns noted by Perdue and Connor (1978), as well as earlier findings suggesting a tendency for preschool teachers to reinforce students more for engaging in feminine-preferred activities, may have been influenced at least in part by the greater preference of girls for activities structured by an adult over unstructured independent or peer-oriented activities.

Elementary School Studies

As part of the evaluation of an in-service program dealing with desegregation, Hillman and Davenport (1978) observed teacher–student interaction in 306 classrooms in kindergarten through twelfth grade. Data were analyzed according to sex as well as race of teachers and students. These data indicated that boys received more public response opportunities (both as volunteers and as nonvolunteers) and more teacher criticism (both for poor answers and for misconduct), and that they asked more questions of the teachers. There were no main effects for sex of teacher, and no interactions between teacher sex and student sex. Thus, once again we see that boys are more active and more apt to be criticized, regardless of the sex of the teacher.

Brophy and Evertson, with Anderson, Baum, and Crawford (1981) studied teacher attitudes, teacher–student interaction, and student effects on teachers in 27 elementary school classrooms taught by female teachers. Teacher attitude data revealed small but statistically significant differences favoring girls over boys in teachers' perceptions of such variables as maturity, persistence, achievement level, cooperation, and attentiveness. About two-thirds of teachers' free response descriptions of girls were positive, but only about half of their comments regarding boys were positive. Still, the significant sex differences were concentrated on traits related to the student role (classroom demeanor, work habits, etc.) rather than on traits relating to likability or moral character.

Interaction data revealed that boys had more total contacts with their teachers, partly because the teachers initiated more contacts with the boys but mostly because the boys had more conduct-related contacts. Boys called out more answers to teacher questions, and teachers initiated more private contacts with boys, especially academic and personal contacts (concerning personal tasks or responsibilities such as clean-up or care of possessions). In general, teachers felt it necessary to monitor the boys more closely and remind them to do things that girls tended to do without having to be told.

Girls initiated more private contacts with the teachers, especially approval-seeking and housekeeping contacts. Thus, the girls were more likely to show completed work or accomplishments to the teachers (anticipating praise or approval) and to approach the teachers to request permission to run errands or perform housekeeping chores. In general, the data suggest that the girls were more teacher-oriented than the boys.

Boys misbehaved not only more often but more disruptively than girls, but they were no more likely to express hostility toward or respond sullenly to the teachers, even during behavior contacts. In general, no sex differences in student affect were expressed toward the teachers. There were no sex differences in teacher praise of students, but teachers directed more academic criticism toward boys during private work contacts. That is, the criticism was not for wrong answers or failure per se but for failure to work carefully or efficiently on assignments (i.e., criticism for poor effort). Of 19 variables concerning teacher affective reactions to or special treatment of students, the only one to show a significant difference indicated that the teachers were more likely to reward boys than girls with special privileges. This finding did not so much suggest favoritism of the boys as more frequent teacher attempts to use behavior modification techniques with them. Measures of teachers' responses to students' requests indicated that teachers were more likely to refuse boys than girls when they requested permission to perform errands or housekeeping chores, sought permission to meet personal needs or desires, or tried to tattle on their classmates. These differences were small, however, and appeared to be produced by differences in the timing or appropriateness of student requests rather than sex differences per se.

Overall, the data from the Brophy et al. (1981) study suggested that sex differences in students' behavior in the classroom and response to the teacher are greater than the sex differences in teachers' response to the students, and that teacher behavior is responsive to student behavior rather than to student sex. Few if any of the sex differences seem inappropriate or reflective of bias or discrimination by the teachers. Most differences were in frequencies and types of contact rather than in teacher or student affect.

Good, Cooper, and Blakey (1980) observed in 16 classrooms in Grades 3–5 at various points throughout the school year. Significant sex differences were seen on only two variables: Girls initiated private contacts with the teacher more often than boys did, and teachers had more conduct-related interactions with boys than with girls.

Stake and Katz (1982) observed classrooms taught by 11 female and 10 male teachers in Grades 4, 5, and 6. The teachers described girls as more obedient and boys as noisier and more disruptive, and classroom observations revealed that boys received more behavioral reprimands. However, there were no sex differences on other measures of teacher–student interaction and no interactions between sex of teacher and sex of student. Thus, these student sex differences in classroom experience were unrelated to the sex of the teacher.

Simpson and Erickson (1983) studied 16 first-grade classrooms taught by female teachers (eight black and eight white) focusing on praise and criticism. The teachers interacted more often with boys and gave them more verbal and nonverbal criticism. The subgroup of white teachers also praised boys more often than girls, although this difference in praise did not hold for the black subgroup or for the total sample. In general, the white teachers differentiated more between boys and girls than the black teachers did.

Lockheed (1982) reported data from 29 fourth- and fifth-grade classes. Each class was observed for eight entire school days, with focus on three male and three female target students selected randomly. Frequency counts of particular behaviors (called "microevents"), showed significant sex differences on only 41 of 312 measures. Boys had higher frequencies than girls on 39 of the 41 measures, most of which dealt with inattention or off-task behavior rather than academic performance. Teachers' responses to boys' and girls' behaviors were generally similar, although the teachers tended to be more managerial and critical when responding to the inappropriate behavior of boys.

Blumenfeld and her colleagues (Eccles and Blumenfeld, see Chapter 5, this volume) report two elementary grade studies in which teachers were found to be more attentive toward and more critical of boys than girls, although the greater criticism of boys was directed toward misbehavior rather than academic failings.

The data reviewed so far in this section mostly replicate findings reported prior to 1973. In addition, however, two other elementary grade studies were conducted that looked at more subtle and qualitative aspects of teacher treatment of boys versus girls. Their findings are provocative, although based on small samples. Dweck, Davidson, Nelson, and Enna (1978) studied the evaluative feedback given by (female) teachers in two fourth-grade and one fifth-grade classroom. The data showed no differences in general frequencies of praise and criticism related to academic work. However, important qualitative differences appeared when evaluative feedback was subdivided according to whether it referred to the intellectual quality of work (competence or correctness) or to nonintellectual aspects (neatness, following instructions, speaking clearly). For positive evaluations of work, about 94% of the statments directed to boys concerned the work's intellectual quality, but the corresponding figure for girls was only about 81%. Thus, boys were almost always praised for having responded correctly or done work competently. Girls were praised for the same reasons most of the time, but on a relative basis they were much more apt to be praised for neatness, following directions, or speaking clearly. Thus, good performance on their part was less often attributed to their own personal competence. Teachers' negative evaluations of students' work showed a different pattern. Here, only about 54% of the criticism directed to boys referred to poor intellectual quality of their work, but the corresponding figure for girls was 89%. Thus, criticism of girls' work almost always indicated that they lacked competence or did not understand the work, whereas criticism of boys' work often referred to nonintellectual aspects that did not imply lack of competence. Taken together, these patterns of evaluative feedback probably have more favorable effects on boys than girls in developing self-confidence, sense of efficacy, and a tendency to attribute academic successes to internal factors (ability and effort) but to attribute failures to external factors (inappropriate or overly rigid teacher responses to the form rather than the substance of the work).

Grant (1983) also made some provocative suggestions based on her observations in five desegregated first-grade classrooms. Her interest was on interactions between sex and race rather than main effects of sex alone, and the Grant (1983) paper concerns the classroom experiences of white girls. The data indicate that teachers have higher academic expectations for these white girls, and place them in higher reading groups on the average. They also expect, however, that these girls will be more obedient and conforming, better dressed and groomed, and more socially mature than other students. These expectations can lead to rigid or stern judgments, however, so that white girls who fail to conform to these expectations may become thought of as "bad girls" and dealt with quite differently from the others.

The teachers did not praise white girls more often nor criticize them less often than other groups. However, there were a few students in each classroom who were praised very often, criticized seldom, and frequently given "trusted lieutenant" duties and other special treatment. Of the 12 students who had this status, 9 were white girls. There was no tendency for teachers to praise white girls more often for good behavior (not just good work), although except for the bad girls, white girls rarely were reprimanded for misbehavior. The teachers chatted socially more often with white girls than with other groups and revealed more knowledge about these girls' personal lives in interviews. The white girls tended to be teacher-oriented, to approach the teachers more often than other groups, and to have these approaches accepted by the teachers (again, bad girls were exceptions). White girls were especially likely to approach the teacher to show off achievements or brag about good behavior. White girls did not tattle more often than other groups, but their tattling was more likely to be successful in the sense that the teacher would punish the target of the tattle. In general, the white girls were relatively closer to the teachers and less close to peers than the other groups.

Although in need of more systematic documentation and replication on larger samples and at higher grade levels, Grant's observations help explain why the advantages enjoyed by girls in the early grades do not seem to do them much good in the long run. These advantages are largely in personal and social relationships rather than in quantity or quality of academic instruction, and they may have the effect of inhibiting rather than stimulating the development of such attributes as intellectual curiosity, achievement striving, or intellectual risk taking. Also, Grant's observations concerning bad girls remind us that, as is the case with boys (cf. Brophy & Good, 1974), student sex may be more informative as a part of an interaction effect than as a main effect in helping us to understand students' classroom experiences.

Grant (see Chapter 4, this volume) discusses her observations of teachers' interactions with white girls and also notes contrasting patterns for black girls, white boys, and black boys. For example, the teachers viewed black girls as having average or below average academic skills, but highly developed social skills, and they encouraged these girls to pursue social contacts rather than to work for high academic achievement. Teacher feedback to these girls stressed classroom behavior more than academic work, and the teachers were unlikely to chat with these girls often (in contrast to their pattern with white girls).

SUBJECT MATTER SPECIFIC STUDIES

In addition to the above studies, which examined teacher–student interaction in various subject matter areas, researchers began to look at teacher–student interaction within subject areas that show sex differences in achievement progress. Leinhardt, Seewald, and Engel (1979) observed in second-grade classrooms during reading and mathematics instruction (these were unusual classrooms using individualized programs, so that the teachers traveled around the room and contacted students one at a time rather than teaching in groups). As usual, they found that teachers had more managerial contacts with boys than with girls (in both subject areas). However, the frequencies of academic contacts varied by subject area. Teachers had more academic contacts and spent more cognitive time with girls than with boys in reading but showed the opposite pattern in math. These differences were small (10% or less) but statistically significant and indicated a tendency to concentrate more on girls in reading instruction but on boys in math instruction.

Pflaum, Pascarella, Boswick, and Auer (1980) studied small-group instruction in reading in elementary classrooms. Observers coded different types of student reading error and the following teacher behaviors: total words teachers assigned children to read, number of teacher corrections, number of teacher pronunciations without correction, frequency of teacher-provided graphemic and phonemic cues, frequency of provision of syntactic and semantic cues at the time of the error, general directions about using particular cues given before the child read, general directions about the volume or speed of reading, positive feedback, and negative feedback. Only one significant effect related to sex of student appeared: Teachers gave suggestions about cues that children should use during their reading more often to the girls than the boys. Thus, the girls received somewhat more specific and detailed instruction than the boys did, although teachers' instructional behaviors were generally related much more closely to students' reading performance than their sex.

Fennema, Reyes, Perl, Konsin, and Drakenberg (1980) studied teacher–student interaction in fourth- and fifth-grade mathematics classes. They found that boys initiated more interactions with their teachers than girls did in these classes, and that the teachers initiated more interactions with the boys than with the girls.

Morse and Handley (see Chapter 3, this volume), in a study of seventh- and eighth-grade science classes, found that boys receive more response opportunities than girls and, in general, that boys are more active in participating in activities and interacting with the teachers.

REVIEWS

Two integrative review articles also appeared in the last decade. Vroegh (1976) reviewed the elementary school literature with an eye toward whether or not sex of teacher made a difference in student achievement or quantity or quality of teacher–student interaction. She concluded that it did not, for the same reasons that Brophy and Good (1974) reached the same conclusion (sex difference patterns are the same in the classrooms of male teachers as in the classrooms of female teachers).

Bank, Biddle, and Good (1980) reviewed the literature with an eye toward explanations of the documented sex difference in American students' reading achievement. They concluded that the data did not support explanations based on maturation or other genetic factors, nor did they support explanations based on the notion that female teachers are biased against male students. The data provided at least some support for the remaining four hypotheses:

1. Discrimination: Teachers treat boys and girls differently because of the differential fit between their respective gender roles and the school's expected student role.
2. Feminization of reading: American teachers and students look upon reading as a feminine activity, and this affects motivation and expectations.
3. Differential response: Teachers do not respond to students' sex per se but do respond to their behavior, and boys and girls behave differently.
4. Sex-relevant teaching styles: Different teachers have different views of what and how teachers should teach, and the teaching styles common in the United States may serve girls more effectively than boys.

DISCUSSION

For the most part, the studies conducted at the elementary school level in the last decade continue to suggest that male versus female student differences in classroom experience are due almost entirely to gender role-related differences in the behavior of the students themselves and not to any general tendency of teachers of either sex to treat boys and girls differently. But there are indications of two possible exceptions to this statement. First, studies that have taken subject matter into account suggest that girls may be getting more or better instruction in reading, and boys may be getting more or better instruction in mathematics. Second, studies that have examined subtle qualitative aspects of teacher behavior suggest that teachers may be socializing boys relatively more toward self-reliance and independent achievement striving while socializing girls relatively more toward conformity and responsibility. These differences are minor and may be due in part to differences in the behavior of the students themselves, but they do suggest that teachers play at least some part in reinforcing (but probably not causing or increasing) traditional gender role stereotypes.

Secondary School Studies

Three studies on the secondary school level have been reported; all deal with sex differences in students' experiences in mathematics classes. Becker

(1981) reported interaction patterns in 10 high school geometry classes (7 of the 10 teachers were female). This work grew out of a pilot study of 22 high school mathematics classes in which Becker observed that the teachers were more likely to call on or otherwise initiate interactions with boys than with girls. The boys also received not only more disciplinary statements but more jokes, praise, and personalized statements, and they were seen to interact socially with the teachers more often.

Similar differences, and others as well, appeared in the study of the 10 geometry classes. There were no differences in student-initiated contacts with the teachers or in the frequencies of lower order questions or questions directed to nonvolunteers. However, the boys had more response opportunities than the girls because teachers more often called on boys as volunteers or allowed them to coopt response opportunities by calling out answers. Furthermore, a greater percentage of the boys' response opportunities involved process (explanation) rather than fact questions. Following incomplete or incorrect responses, the teachers were more likely to stay with boys than with girls in an attempt to elicit an improved response by rephrasing the question or giving clues. Interestingly, some teachers justified this by stating that the boys could not handle the teacher moving on to another student emotionally, or that the boys were less conscientious and required more persistent questioning by the teacher. Nevertheless, the net result was that the teachers worked harder for correct responses from the boys than from the girls.

The teachers spent more time with the boys, approached them more often, and shared not only more discipline contacts but more social and joking contacts with them. They also directed more encouragement and praise to the boys (the latter finding may have occurred because the boys were more likely to answer teachers' questions correctly than the girls were). All in all, Becker describes the environment for boys in these geometry classes as supportive both academically and emotionally, but the environment for girls is described as one of benign neglect. Even though the majority of the teachers were female, much of their behavior suggested that the boys were expected to learn geometry but the girls were not.

Stallings (1979) observed in high school algebra and geometry classes and found similar but weaker patterns to those reported by Becker. Her conclusions are as follows:

> Though few of the differences are significant, the trend is rather clear. Men are spoken to more often than are women. Men ask more questions and teachers ask men more questions. Women volunteer answers as often as do men but the men are called upon to respond more frequently than are women. Men receive a little more individual instruction and social interactions. Acknowledgement, praise, encouragement, and corrective feedback are given slightly more frequently to men than to women.

> The only variable that occurs more frequently with women is positive interactions. Teachers smile or laugh more often with women students than they do with men. (Stallings, 1979, p. 5)

The weaker pattern of differences may be due to the fact that Stallings observed in these classes less frequently than Becker did. Also, questionnaire responses from the teachers indicated that they felt that male and female students were equally good at mathematics and did not differ in spatial ability. These response patterns are unusual and suggest that these teachers may have been less traditional in their sex-role orientations than most teachers.

Parsons et al. (1980) observed 10 sessions in each of 18 mathematics classes (2 fifth-grade, 1 sixth-grade, 8 seventh-grade, and 7 ninth-grade). Surprisingly, these observations revealed even fewer sex differences than usual. Of 51 interaction variables, only 3 yielded a significant effect for sex of student. These indicated that girls received less criticism than boys and, specifically, less work-related criticism and less criticism of the quality plus the form of their work. There were no sex differences in criticism of misconduct, in praise of either work or conduct, or in the frequencies of various types of interactions with the teachers. Furthermore, the sex differences in types of evaluation noted by Dweck et al. (1978) were not replicated here. Almost all work-related praise and criticism were directed at the intellectual quality of the work rather than its form or other aspects unrelated to correctness. Thus, there was no teacher tendency to praise boys more than girls for good intellectual quality of work, nor to criticize girls more than boys for work of poor intellectual quality. Nor did teachers interact more often with boys, ask them different types of questions, or provide different types of feedback to their responses.

These analyses based on the entire sample of 18 classes were supplemented by other analyses comparing the five classrooms showing the largest student sex differences in self-reported expectancies for achievement with the five classrooms that had no significant sex differences in such expectancies. The findings indicated that the teachers in the high sex-differentiated classrooms were more likely to use a public teaching style rather than to rely on private dyadic interactions with individual students, more likely to rely on student volunteers than to call on nonvolunteers, and more likely to criticize the students. In these high sex-differentiated classrooms, the boys had more frequent interactions with the teachers and received more praise. In the low sex-differentiated classrooms, the girls interacted more frequently with the teachers and received more praise. These differences were particularly noticeable among the brighter students. Bright girls interacted more, answered more questions, received more praise and less criticism in the low sex-differentiated classrooms, but received the least praise of any group in the high sex-differentiated classrooms (See Eccles and Blumenfeld, Chapter 5, this volume, for additional discussion of the data from this study.)

DISCUSSION

It is difficult to know how to interpret these confusing secondary school results, particularly the contrasts between the Becker (1981) findings and those of Parsons et al. (1980). Both studies involved 10 observations in each of the classrooms, so the sex differences are probably quite reliable. Differences in the types of teachers included in the studies or in the geographical areas in which the data were collected may explain some of the contrasting findings. The most likely explanation, however, is grade level. Most of the classes studied by Parsons et al. were junior high or ninth-grade math courses taken by all of the students, whereas all 10 classes studied by Becker were geometry courses taken only by the brighter and more mathematics-oriented students. Dramatic sex differences of the kind reported by Becker, if frequent at all, may be frequent only in secondary level courses of this type. In this connection, it should be noted that Stallings' (1979) results, which generally fell between those of Becker and those of Parsons et al., were collected in lower level algebra and geometry classes that fell between the other two samples in terms of the kinds of students represented and their level of progress in mathematics.

Given that 7 of Becker's 10 teachers were female, it seems clear that depressed mathematics achievement of female students cannot be attributed to anything as simple as bias and discrimination by male teachers and is unlikely to be changed through anything as simple as an infusion of more female teachers into mathematics classes.

Interactions between Sex of Teacher and Sex of Student

Etaugh and Hughes (1975) and Stake and Katz (1982) reported no significant interactions between sex of teacher and sex of student in their studies of teachers' attitudes and preferences concerning student traits. Similarly, Fagot (1981), Hillman and Davenport (1978), and Stake and Katz (1982) all reported no significant interactions between sex of teacher and sex of student in their studies of teacher–student interaction in the classroom. Thus, the elementary and secondary level studies of the last decade continue to support Brophy and Good's (1974) conclusions that sex differences in students' classroom experiences are not due to the sex of their teachers and are unlikely to be changed significantly by infusing more male teachers into elementary reading and language arts courses or more female teachers into secondary mathematics and science courses. Gold and Reis (1982) reached similar conclusions in their review.

Some of the findings from nursery school and preschool settings, however, although based on small samples, suggest the possibility of significant sex of teacher by sex of student interactions at this level. Also, studies of teacher–student interaction in college classrooms (Karp & Yoels, 1976; Sternglanz and Lyberger-Ficek, 1977) suggest that female college students may participate more often (and more equally with male peers) in classes taught by female instructors.

Sex Differences in General Teaching Styles

Fagot (1981) reported that male preschool teachers were more likely than female preschool teachers to interact with the children, join their play, and dispense praise and physical affection. These findings are atypical, however, and probably indicate that the males who choose to enter preschool education are more child-oriented and nurturant than most males (and perhaps, most females).

Data in the last decade from elementary and secondary school settings replicate and elaborate the teacher sex differences reported by Brophy and Good (1974). Amidon and Picogna (1975) reported that female teachers used less criticism and produced more student-initiated talk than male teachers. Stake and Katz (1982) found that female teachers were more positive than male teachers in their attitudes and behaviors toward students. The female teachers dispensed more praise and encouragement, gave fewer reprimands, and less often failed to respond to a student when a teacher response was appropriate.

College level studies show similar findings. Kajander (1976) found few differences in the behaviors of male versus female teaching assistants but noted that students in classes taught by female teaching assistants initiated more contacts, answered more questions, and received more feedback. Richardson, Cook, and Macke (1981) found that female university professors were more accepting, less harsh, and more likely than their male colleagues to engage in the give and take of classroom discussion. The male professors were more apt to correct students directly or publicly repimand them. In general, these data continue the pattern noted earlier indicating that male teachers tend to be relatively more teacher-centered and direct, and female teachers tend to be relatively more student-centered, indirect, and supportive of students.

DISCUSSION

The last decade has witnessed important additions to the literature on gender-related issues in education as well as the development of some newer perspective on older research. Yet, the data continue to indicate that male and female teachers are much more similar than different, both in their general approaches to instruction and in their interactions with male and female students. Teachers do not systematically discriminate against students of the opposite sex.

Male and female students do have somewhat different experiences in most classrooms, although these sex differences are relatively minor and tend to interact with other status variables and especially with students' individual academic achievement and classroom conduct. Although teachers do not seem to be major factors in causing or broadening student sex differences, they probably sustain or reinforce the differences that do exist, at least to some degree. This is because most teacher behavior, especially in interactions with individual students, is situationally determined and reactive rather than proactively planned and systematic (Brophy & Good, 1974).

Although methodological progress has been made, several additional improvements are needed. One is a broadening from an almost exclusive focus on teacher–student verbal interaction toward consideration of other factors, such as the activities and assignments that teachers use to instruct their students, the classroom organization and peer interaction patterns they establish or allow, and the special projects they make available to the students. Several chapters in this volume report progess in these areas.

Thicker description with more attention to qualitative aspects of classroom events is also needed. Research using the Brophy–Good dyadic interaction coding system and similar systems for low-inference recording of discrete behaviors that occur frequently in classrooms have produced useful information (e.g., most of the information reviewed in this chapter), but they do not allow for capturing the subtleties and qualitative aspects of classroom events that are important for studying gender-related issues. Thick description approaches, such as those used by Grant (see Chapter 4, this volume), seem to have more potential for identifying and documenting subtle gender differentiation in classroom experience, especially if care is taken to distinguish teacher effects on students from student effects on teachers and to express as many of the qualitative findings as possible in quantitative form.

Findings also might become clearer if teachers' expectations were measured rather than merely inferred. The chapters by Grant (see Chapter 4, this volume) and by Fennema and Peterson (see Chapter 2, this volume) describe teachers' beliefs and expectations about students that (if measured) might predict differential behavior toward boys and girls in their classrooms.

Most of the research reviewed in this chapter looked only at sex of teacher and sex of student, without measuring gender role adoption or other individual characteristics. Yet, other research has shown that individuals of both sexes vary considerably in the degree to which they adopt the attitudes and behaviors associated with the modal gender roles in their societies. Studies that classify teachers according to sex role adoption might yield more clear-cut results than studies that merely classify teachers as male or female. Furthermore, such classifications might interact with grade level and subject matter. There are hints, for example, that males who go into nursery school teaching are unusually nurturant. Perhaps teachers of either sex who teach subject matter traditionally associated with their own sex tend to be traditional in their gender role adoptions and teachers who choose to teach subject matter traditionally associated with the opposite sex tend to be more androgynous in their gender role adoptions.

A combination of better characterization of the teachers with thicker description of their activities might shed light on a seeming paradox in the data presently available. As noted in this chapter, studies of teachers' general approaches to instruction do show some consistent teacher sex differences, but studies focused on interactions between sex of teacher and sex of student typically do not find such interactions and conclude that student sex differences in classroom experience are due to the students themselves and not to the sex of the teacher. Yet, it may be that teacher sex (or more specifically, teacher gender role adoption) asserts itself not only on general dimensions, such as tendency to lecture versus question or tendency to be subject-oriented versus student-oriented, but also on more subject matter-specific dimensions. Thick description of how different types of teachers (e.g., teachers who have adopted the masculine gender role, androgynous teachers, and teachers who have adopted the feminine gender role) teach particular subject matter (such as tenth-grade geometry) might yield consistent patterns indicating differences not only in interactions with male versus female students but also in the attitudes and beliefs expressed toward the subject matter, the way the subject matter is approached, and so on.

Another weakness in the existing literature is that it is almost exclusively descriptive and correlational. Enough information may be available now to attempt treatment studies designed to improve the achievement of boys in elementary reading and language arts and of girls in secondary mathematics and science. One caveat about such studies comes to mind: The criteria for success should be expressed in terms of absolute levels of achievement rather than only in terms of the achievement of one sex relative to that of the other sex. In other words, the goal should be to raise the scores of the presently lower achieving sex to at least the levels presently enjoyed by the higher achieving sex and not merely to eliminate the sex difference (the latter approach might result in lower scores for the presently higher achieving sex rather than higher scores for the presently lower achieving sex).

To be effective, the treatment in such a study needs to be powerful enough to overcome the existing tendencies of boys and girls to act differently in classrooms and thus create sex differences in outcomes. If teachers are to counteract existing sex differences, it is not enough for them merely to treat boys and girls the same ways in the same situations, because sex differences in student behavior create differences in the types of situations with which the teachers are presented (Huston & Carpenter, see Chapter 7, this volume). Thus, the teachers would have to treat boys and girls differently (consciously calling on boys more often in reading and language arts and on girls more often in mathematics and science, for example). In effect, teachers would have to exert steady pressure on both boys and girls to depart from their customary behavior patterns.

This can be difficult, because gender role expectations and behavior, like any other entrenched expectations and behavior that develop slowly over time and become "second nature," are not easily changed. Furthermore, this is even more true of teachers than students (the teachers have been socialized more traditionally than the students, and for a longer time), so that even those teachers who want to change long-standing patterns may find it difficult to do so. They may find the experience threatening, experience role confusion, or encounter other problems that may occur when established coping styles break down. For many teachers, provision of emotional support and opportunities to talk out the situation at length may be necessary before any fundamental changes in gender role-related behaviors can occur.

In this regard it should be noted that both male and female teachers (and male and female students, for that matter) have been exposed to the same gender role socialization pressures and thus have come to share essentially the same views of what males and females should be like. This is why students' gender-related classroom experiences tend to be the same whether the teacher is male or female. Teachers of both sexes project the same differential expectations toward boys and girls and show the same tendencies to respond differently to gender-related student behavior. Thus, though gradual change can be expected, drastic changes are unlikely. Not only is the disintegration of established roles threatening, but schools as institutions are inherently conservative, and most teachers come from conservative home backgrounds. Yet, things are changing. Teachers of both sexes are less traditional than in the past and more sensitized to sexism issues. Students seem to be much less sex-typed than in the past, at least in the middle and upper socioeconomic status segments of the population.

In general, I believe there is reason for optimism. Although I cannot prove it, my sense is that much progress has been made in recent years concerning the adjustment of young boys to school in general and reading in particular. Changes in staff ideology and in the play opportunities available and types of activities conducted in preschools have brought balance (perhaps a better word is androgyny) into what was formerly a feminized milieu. *Sesame Street* and similar programs, the advent of home computers and games, and the emphasis on basic skills in the elementary school, among other factors, have probably reduced any tendency to see reading as a primarily feminine activity. Schools are much more attractive and less regimented places than they used to be. Gesellian and related theories of child development that placed great emphasis on physical maturation and sex differences have receded in favor of Piagetian and other cognitive approaches that do not assign any great importance to sex differences.

Related changes in the ideology of the public at large and of teachers in particular probably have already had some positive effects on the problem of depressed achievement of girls in secondary mathematics and science. The problem may even disappear in 10 years. However, there are some reasons to believe that the problem is more serious and more difficult to deal with than the problem of boys' achievement in elementary reading. For one thing, there seems to be a difference in how the problem is perceived by the students themselves. Boys' problems with elementary reading seem to be primarily motivational—many boys acquire the idea that reading is primarily for girls and that they will not enjoy it. Relatively few boys, however, construe the problem as one of ability (acquiring the belief that boys lack aptitude for reading). If boys are aware of any problem with reading, they are likely to say that they do not like it, not that they cannot do it. In secondary mathematics and science, however, girls' depressed achievement is often attributed to lower aptitude, not just lower motivation. If students (and teachers) have this perception, it is necessary to motivate not only in the sense of developing interest in and willingness to take these subjects but also in the sense of developing the expectation that success can be achieved with relative ease if reasonable effort is applied.

The problem may also prove to be more entrenched from the viewpoint of teacher behavior. Most of the concerns expressed about elementary school teachers' treatment of boys have involved issues of regimentation of behavior, not the quality of instruction. Even in reading, there is very little evidence that elementary teachers provide more or better instruction to girls than to boys. However, the jury is still out concerning the quantity and quality of instruction girls receive in secondary mathematics and science. If the findings of Becker (1981) prove to be typical, achieving change in these secondary school classrooms may require changing teachers' approaches to instruction and not merely their attitudes toward gender-related behavior.

REFERENCES

Amidon, E., & Picogna, J. (1975). *Personality, sex, and classroom behavior.* Unpublished manuscript, Department of Education, State of New Jersey.

Austin, D., Clark, B., & Fitchett, G. (1971). *Reading rights for boys.* New York: Appleton-Century-Crofts.

Ayres, L. (1909). *Laggards in our schools.* New York: Russell Sage Foundation.

Bank, B., Biddle, B., & Good, T. (1980). Sex roles, classroom instruction, and reading achievement. *Journal of Educational Psychology, 72,* 119–132.

Becker, J. (1981). Differential teacher treatment of males and females in mathematics classes. *Journal of Research in Mathematics Education, 12,* 40–53.

Brophy, J., & Evertson, C., with Anderson, L., Baum, M., & Crawford, J. (1981). *Student characteristics and teaching.* New York: Longman.

Brophy, J., & Good, T. (1974). *Teacher–student relationships: Causes and consequences.* New York: Holt, Rinehart & Winston.

Cherry, L. (1975). The preschool teacher–child dyad: Sex differences in verbal interaction. *Child Development, 46,* 532–535.

Dweck, C., Davidson, W., Nelson, S., & Enna, B. (1978). Sex differences in learned helplessness: II. The contingencies of evaluative feedback in the classroom; III. An experimental analysis. *Developmental Psychology, 14,* 268–276.

Etaugh, C., & Hughes, V. (1975). Teachers' evaluations of sex-typed behaviors in children: The role of teacher sex and school setting. *Developmental Psychology, 11,* 394–395.

Fagot, B. (1977). Consequences of moderate cross-gender behavior in preschool children. *Child Development, 48,* 902–907.

Fagot, B. (1978). Reinforcing contingencies for sex-role behaviors: Effect of experience with children. *Child Development, 49,* 30–36.

Fagot, B. (1981). Male and female teachers: Do they treat boys and girls differently? *Sex Roles, 7,* 263–271.

Fennema, E., Reyes, L., Perl, T., Konsin, M., & Drakenberg, M. (1980, April). *Cognitive and affective influences on the development of sex-related differences in mathematics.* Symposium presented at the annual meeting of the American Educational Research Association, Boston.

Gold, D., & Reis, M. (1982). Male teacher effects on young children: A theoretical and empirical consideration. *Sex Roles, 8,* 493–513.

Good, T., Cooper, H., & Blakey, S. (1980). Classroom interaction as a function of teacher expectations, student sex, and time of year. *Journal of Educational Psychology, 72,* 378–385.

Good, T., Sikes, J., & Brophy, J. (1973). Effects of teacher sex and student sex on classroom interaction. *Journal of Educational Psychology, 65,* 74–87.

Grant, L. (1983, April). *The socialization of white females in classrooms.* Paper presented at the annual meeting of the American Educational Research Association, Montreal, Canada.

Hillman, S., & Davenport, G. (1978). Teacher–student interactions in desegregated schools. *Journal of Educational Psychology, 70,* 545–553.

Kajander, C. (1976). The effects of instructor and student sex on verbal behaviors in college classrooms. *Dissertation Abstracts International, 37*(5-A), 2743–2744.

Karp, D., & Yoels, W. (1976). The college classroom: Some observations on the meanings of student participation. *Sociology and Social Research, 60,* 421–439.

Leinhardt, G., Seewald, A., & Engel, M. (1979). Learning what's taught: Sex differences in instruction. *Journal of Educational Psychology, 71,* 432–439.

Lockheed, M. (1982, March). *Sex equity in classroom interaction research: An analysis of behavior chains.* Paper presented at the annual meeting of the American Educational Research Association, New York City.

Palardy, J. (1969). What teachers believe—what children achieve. *Elementary School Journal, 69,* 370–374.

Parsons, J., with Adler, T., Futterman, R., Goff, S., Kaczala, C., Meece, J., & Midgley, C. (1980). *Self-perceptions, task perceptions and academic choice: Origins and change* (Final Report, Grant NIE-G-78-0022). Ann Arbor: MI: Department of Psychology, University of Michigan. (ERIC Document Reproduction Service No. ED 186 477)

Perdue, V., & Connor, J. (1978). Patterns of touching between preschool children and male and female teachers. *Child Development, 49,* 1258–1262.

Pflaum, S., Pascarella, E., Boswick, M., & Auer, C. (1980). The influence of pupil behaviors and pupil status factors on teacher behaviors during oral reading lessons. *Journal of Educational Research, 74,* 99–105.

Richardson, L., Cook, J., & Macke, A. (1981). Classroom management strategies of male and female university professors. In L. Richardson & V. Taylor (Eds.), *Issues in sex, gender, and society.* Lexington, MA: Heath.

Sexton, P. (1969). *The feminized male: Classrooms, white collars and the decline of manliness.* New York: Random House.

Simpson, A., & Erickson, M. (1983). Teachers' verbal and nonverbal communication patterns as a function of teacher race, student gender, and student race. *American Educational Research Journal, 20,* 183–198.

Stake, J., & Katz, J. (1982). Teacher–pupil relationships in the elementary school classroom: Teacher-gender and pupil-gender differences. *American Educational Research Journal, 19,* 465–471.

Stallings, J. (1979). *Factors influencing women's decisions to enroll in advanced mathematics courses: Executive summary* (Final Report, Grant NIE-G-78-0024). Menlo Park, CA: SRI International.

Sternglanz, S., & Lyberger-Ficek, S. (1977). Sex differences in student-teacher interactions in the college classroom. *Sex Roles, 3,* 345–352.

Vroegh, K. (1976). Sex of teacher and academic achievement: A review of research. *Elementary School Journal, 76,* 389–405.

Gender Differences in Preschool Classrooms: The Effects of Sex-Typed Activity Choices*

ALETHA C. HUSTON and C. JAN CARPENTER

INTRODUCTION

For increasing numbers of American children, the first school experience occurs in preschools and day care centers long before the age of 5 or 6. These school environments are distinctly different from most elementary schools in that much of the children's time is spent in "play" activities (which are the curriculum of the preschool), and children often exercise a considerable amount of choice in selecting their own activities. Other chapters in this volume suggest that many sex differences in classroom behavior are already formed by the time children enter elementary school. Therefore, preschool classroom experiences and play activities may have important implications for sex-typed socialization.

---

* This research was supported by a grant from the National Institute of Mental Health and by a grant from the Graduate Research Fund of the University of Kansas.

RATIONALE

The research reported in this chapter is directed primarily toward two goals: (1) to identify some of the ways in which the socialization experiences of girls and boys differ in the preschool and in other settings where play activities are available, and (2) to determine how those socialization experiences influence social and task-oriented behavior.

Sex Differences in Play Experience

Observational studies in preschool classrooms and home environments have demonstrated two fairly consistent sex differences in socialization experience. From age 2 onward, boys and girls (on the average) play with toys and games that are culturally defined as appropriate for their gender more than with toys and activities defined as appropriate for the other gender (Huston, 1983). Second, on the average, girls spend more time than boys in close proximity to adults (Fagot, 1978; Serbin, 1980). By the elementary school years, girls are supervised more closely than boys, as a result they have more contact and guidance from adults (Huston, 1983). These two areas of sex-differentiated experience—participation in sex-stereotyped play activities and different amounts of close contact with adults—are potential arenas for learning different types of social and cognitive behaviors.

Theoretical Framework

Feminine-stereotyped play activities and activities that are closely supervised by adults are both relatively structured in comparison to masculine play activities and activities with minimal adult involvement. Structure, as used in this theoretical framework, refers to rules, guidelines, or suggestions regarding how to go about performing the activity. Structure may be provided directly by an adult who gives instructions, suggestions, praise, criticism, or other verbal feedback about the activity or the child's performance. Because girls spend more time in proximity to adults, they probably experience more adult-imposed structure than boys do. Structure may also be provided by models who demonstrate how to carry out the activity. Many stereotypically feminine play activities entail role play of maternal and household activities that children can observe frequently; by contrast, children may have fewer opportunities to observe the adult analogs of masculine sex-typed activities, such as driving a truck or construction. Therefore, feminine activities may have more structure resulting from observation of models than masculine activities.

In this formulation, activity structure is defined by the social environment (adult input and modeling) rather than by the nature of the materials themselves. Ecological psychologists sometimes define structure by the nature of the physical materials (Gump, 1980). Both social cues and physical properties in play activities are probably important. For instance, a baby doll with openings at both ends and a small bottle could be considered highly structured because it strongly suggests pouring water in the mouth and collecting it in a diaper. But a child must have some familiarity with bottles, babies, or similar dolls in order to be guided in such a specific way by the toy itself. The research reported here is focused on the social components of structure, without in any way suggesting that other properties of play activities are unimportant.

This theoretical framework is influenced by social learning theory and by ecological psychology. These two theoretical orientations share the assumption that the external environment is an important influence on human behavior. Social learning theorists (e.g., Mischel, 1968, 1973) have asserted that social behaviors, such as aggression and altruism, are dependent on the environmental cues in a particular situation. Therefore, social behavior varies from one situation to another depending on the individual's particular learning history in each setting. Children and adults learn stimulus–response associations so that different environmental settings instigate different behaviors.

In ecological psychology, the physical and social properties of the environment are also considered primary contributors to behavior. Barker's (1968) construct, the behavior setting, is defined by three components: a physical setting, human components, and "standing patterns of behavior." In a formal sense, there are appropriate actions or behaviors and particular roles for participants. In a school classroom, there are opening rituals, for instance, when announcements are made, the flag is saluted, and the roll is taken. There are roles for teachers, students, student helpers who take the roll sheets to the office, and the like. The behaviors in each of these actions and roles are coerced by the setting; that is, they are fairly similar regardless of the characteristics of the people in the setting. The important theoretical point for our purposes is that a physical–social setting provides a context in which certain behaviors are relatively likely and others are fairly unlikely, regardless of the individual differences among participants in the setting.

Environments differ not only qualitatively in the types of behavior they encourage but also quantitatively in the degree to which they contain cues, direction, or rules about behavior of participants. Some settings have highly specific behaviors and roles; others have less clearly specified guidelines for behavior. This quantitative dimension, that is, the degree to which there are rules, expectations, or guidelines for behavior or the specificity of those rules, is the amount of structure.

Although social learning and ecological theories share an emphasis on environmental influences, they differ in two important respects. Social learning theory is focused on individual differences in learned responses to particular stimuli, while ecological psychology is concerned with the features of an environmental setting that have a common impact on participants. Of course, social learning theory might also predict a common response if participants had similar histories of reinforcement. Second, in ecological psychology the constant and enduring properties of a setting are stressed, while in social learning theory a stimulus environment may change frequently. The analysis presented here is closer to the ecological view: It is concerned with structure as a relatively enduring property of activities that operates similarly for all participants.

A preschool classroom is a behavior setting, and the play activities within a classroom are subsettings. Each activity has materials, rules for appropriate behavior, and an expected behavior pattern, but activities differ in the specificity of these guidelines (i.e., in the amount of structure). Some of these activity characteristics depend on the physical materials involved, but many of them are based on the guidance and modeling provided by adults in the preschool. The amount of structure in an activity is a relatively stable property of that activity; even the amount of adult feedback and guidance is reasonably constant within any particular classroom.

Effects of Structure on Behavior

A few studies of preschools have demonstrated that particular activities are associated with certain behaviors. For instance, aggression is more likely when children are using blocks than when they are painting or making something at a table (Gump, 1975). These findings are usually interpreted as showing that the play materials or the activity context encouraged or discouraged particular forms of social behavior. However, the dimensions or properties of the activities that might be responsible for their apparent effects on the behavior of participants are not well understood. In addition, such studies are open to the alternative explanation that different types of children congregate in different activities. There is a good deal of evidence, for instance, that boys play more often with blocks than girls do (Serbin, 1980). The higher level of aggression in blocks might simply be a function of the fact that boys are generally more aggressive than girls, and they often play with blocks (Maccoby & Jacklin, 1974, 1980).

Structure is proposed here as one dimension of activities that affects behavior. Highly structured environments or activities may encourage children to fit into structures provided by others, play according to established rules, follow instructions, and allow control by others. High structure is expected to cultivate compliance to adults, seeking recognition and approval, requests for help, and proximity seeking. Low structure, by contrast, should encourage children to create their own structure. If there are few guidelines about how an activity is to be performed, then the child must decide what to do and how to do it. In such settings, therefore, they are expected to be active and assertive, to devise their own rules or procedures, to take initiative, and to attempt to exert control. The behavioral manifestations of creating structure are leadership attempts, aggression, independence, initiation of social encounters, initiation of new components in the play activity, and novel uses of materials. Children in low-structure activities are expected to be more peer-directed and less adult-directed than children in high-structure activities (Carpenter, 1983a; Carpenter & Huston-Stein, 1980).

Some support for this model appears in the literature. In one study, 13 Head Start classrooms were rank ordered according to the amount of time spent in teacher-directed activity (i.e., adult structure). Children in high-structure classrooms took more responsibility for following class rules and were more attentive during group instruction, while in low-structure classrooms, children manifested more prosocial behavior, aggression, and imaginative play (Huston-Stein, Friedrich-Cofer, & Susman, 1977). In another series of studies by Smith & Connolly (1980), classrooms were assigned to high or low structure for an entire semester. The behavior patterns in the two classes differed in ways that are consistent with the model presented here.

Play activities not only have immediate effects on the behavior of participants; they may also provide practice or learning opportunities for particular behavior patterns which have long-term consequences. Children who spend much of their time in high-structure settings gain experience in compliance to adults, recognition seeking, and following rules, but little experience in leadership, independence, and the like with their peers. They may become relatively skilled and comfortable in behaviors we define as "fitting into others' structures" and may have less skill in creating their own structures. This imbalance may be perpetuated if children then avoid settings that require behaviors with which they have little experience or skill. The converse could, of course, be true for children who spend most of their time in low-structure settings. This hypothesis is similar to earlier proposals that children may develop cognitive skills, such as visualizing spatial relationships, from spending time in play activities that promote those skills (Serbin & Connor, 1979; Sherman, 1967).

Activity Structure and Sex Differences in Behavior

In summary, the model predicts that because girls spend more time than boys in proximity to adults and play in feminine-stereotyped activities, girls are exposed to highly structured activities more often than boys. As a result they practice different types of behavior. Girls' more frequent experience in high-structure settings cultivates compliance to adults, recognition seeking, and imitation of adult models. Boys' more frequent experience in low-structure settings enables them to practice and become skilled in peer-direct leadership, initiating new interactions or activities, novel uses of materials, aggression, and other behaviors that are encouraged in low-structure settings.

The model deals only with possible outcomes of participation in settings of different structure levels; it does not provide an explanation for how girls and boys come to engage in sex-differentiated activities in the first place. There is an accumulating body of evidence that parents, mass media, and other socializing influences train children to select sex-stereotyped toys and to exhibit different amounts of proximity to adults from infancy on (Huston, 1983). This chapter explores the kinds of behavior children learn as a consequence of their experiences in different play activities.

EMPIRICAL STUDIES

A series of four studies was conducted to test the model for preschool and elementary school-age children. These studies follow a multimethod approach in order to provide a more solid basis for conclusions than is possible from any single method. Both observation in natural settings and experimental manipulations were used; analysis of group trends as well as single-subject analyses were employed. The methods, age groups, and variables measured in each of these studies are summarized in Table 7.1.

The first study consisted of observations of naturally occurring patterns in five preschool classrooms during three semesters. Children's choices of activities were coded, and the behaviors associated with high- and low-structure activities were analyzed. The second study was a laboratory experiment to provide a more controlled test of the effects of structure. The third study consisted of experimental manipulations of structure in a pre-

Table 7.1

Summary of Methods and Results

Age group and setting	Method	Results
	Study 1	
Preschool classrooms; ages 2½–5 years	Observation; structure varied naturally; children chose activities	1. Boys selected low-structure; girls selected high-structure activities 2. Children in high-structure complied, sought recognition; in low-structure, attempted leadership
	Study 2	
Laboratory; ages 3–5 years	Structure manipulated experimentally; children assigned to treatments	1. In high-structure, more compliance, seeking recognition, leadership to adults 2. In low-structure, more compliance, seeking recognition, leadership to peers
	Study 3	
Preschool classroom; ages 3–5 years	Structure manipulated experimentally; children assigned to treatments	1. In high-structure, increased recognition seeking to adults 2. In low-structure, increased leadership attempts to peers
	Study 4	
Summer day camp; ages 7–11 years	Structure manipulated experimentally; children chose activities	1. Girls selected high-structure; boys selected low-structure 2. In high-structure, more compliance, recognition seeking, leadership to adults 3. In low-structure, more compliance, recognition seeking, leadership to peers

school classroom to determine whether the laboratory findings generalize to a real classroom setting. The fourth study was an experimental manipulation of structure in a day camp for elementary school-age children to determine whether the findings among preschool children also occur among older children.

Study 1. Observation in Preschool Classrooms

The major purposes of this observational study were (1) to determine whether preschool activities could be reliably classified along the structure dimension, or whether the adult-imposed structure in particular activities varied widely across classrooms; (2) to determine whether girls and boys spent different amounts of time in high- and low-structure activities when they had a choice of activities; and (3) to determine whether patterns of social and task-oriented behavior in high- and low-structure activities differed.

METHODS

The methods used are described in detail elsewhere (Carpenter, 1983b; Carpenter & Huston-Stein, 1980). Observations were collected for three different semesters in each of five preschool classrooms. Three classes were in a university laboratory facility, and two were in a university-affiliated day care center. The number of children observed in each semester was 46, 83, and 85. They ranged in age from $2\frac{1}{2}$ to 5 years. Because many of the personnel were students, there was considerable turnover of teachers from one semester to the next.

Children were observed individually using a time-sampling technique. For each interval, adult feedback (instructions, praise, or comments related to the play activity) and the activity in which the child was participating was recorded. Predefined categories of social and task-oriented behavior were coded if they occurred. In all three semesters, compliance to adult demands and novel uses of materials were coded. In the third semester, recognition seeking, leadership attempts, and some other behaviors (not presented in this chapter) were also recorded.

Because compliance, recognition seeking, and leadership attempts are the principal categories of behavior that were investigated in subsequent studies, they have been chosen for detailed explication here. Compliance was scored whenever an adult or child asked the target child to do something and the target child did it. Recognition seeking was defined as any statement or action that was likely to bring recognition or praise about the child or the child's accomplishments. It included verbalizations of pride in behavior, objects, and the like, but recognition seeking did not include simple attention seeking. Leadership attempts were defined as behaviors that cued or prompted behavior by another person.

Activity structure was defined by two separate indices: the amount of adult feedback and the amount of adult modeling. In each classroom, play activities were classified according to the average rate of *adult feedback* provided to all children in the activity. That rating constituted the adult feedback index of structure. This index reflected the typical structure level for that activity; it was not a measure of fluctuations in structure over time or for different children participating. It was designed to describe the stable, enduring properties of the activity in any particular classroom and was therefore closer to the ecological psychology emphasis than to the approach of most social learning theorists.

The second index of activity structure was *model availability.* Play activities that resemble adult jobs or activities that children observe frequently in everyday life are highly structured by modeling even without direct instruciton or feedback. Activities were classified as high or low on model availability on the basis of ratings by parents of how often children see adults performing similar activities in their everyday lives.

RESULTS

The first question was whether activities could be classified reliably along the structure dimension. Approximately 20 types of activities appeared in most classrooms, and the rates of adult feedback for different activities were fairly consistent within classrooms. That is, in any one classroom, different children in the activities tended to receive similar amounts of feedback, and the amounts of feedback were reasonably consistent from one semester to another. However, the rates of feedback for particular activities varied considerably across classrooms. In each classroom, the 20 activities were rank ordered by the amount of adult feedback received. Correlations between pairs of classrooms were generally low, suggesting that the same activities received different amounts of structure in different classrooms. For instance, art in one class might have high rates of teacher feedback, while in another class it might have intermediate or low rates of feedback (Carpenter & Huston-Stein, 1980). This finding supported the assumption that structure as defined by the rate of feedback was reasonably independent of the particular properties of the materials or the nature of the activity.

The second question was whether there were sex differences in participation in high- and low-structure activities. In all three semesters, girls spent more time in high-structure activities and boys spent more time in low-structure activities. When activities were classified by the rate of adult feedback, there were significant Sex $\times$ Feedback interactions in all three studies. The mean levels of participation appear in Table 7.2. In Figure 7.1 the level of participation in individual activities, arranged by the amount of adult feedback, is shown. When model availability was used as an index of structure, there were also Sex $\times$ Structure interactions that reached significance in two of the three semesters (see Table 7.2).

The third prediction was that children's behavior would vary as a function of activity structure. Sex differences within structure levels were not expected. These predictions were supported. Children were more often compliant and showed more bids for recognition in high-structure activities. They exhibited more attempts at leadership in low-structure activities

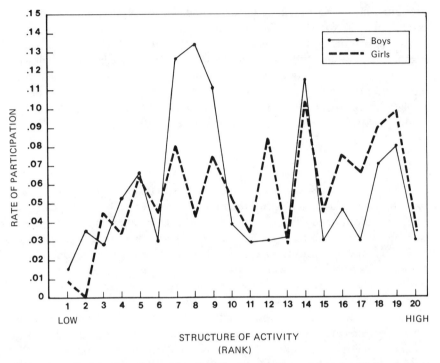

Figure 7.1. Girls' and boys' rate of participation in activities as a function of the structure provided by adult feedback in preschool classrooms (Study 1).

(Carpenter, 1983b; Carpenter & Huston-Stein, 1980). The means are shown in Figure 7.2.

SUMMARY OF STUDY 1

These observations provide reasonably strong support for the theoretical model. Girls chose more high-structure activities and boys chose more low-structure activities in free play. The fact that this finding held true even when the particular content of the high- and low-structure play activities varied from one classroom to the next provides strong support for the hypothesis that activity structure has effects that are independent of other features of specific activities.

The results also provide evidence that both girls and boys exhibit compliance and bids for recognition more often in high-structure activities, and that they display leadership attempts more often in low-structure activities. Because these findings are correlational, however, one cannot conclude with certainty that activity structure led to the observed behavior differ-

Table 7.2

Frequency of Participation in Activities Varying in Structure for Boys and Girls: Study 1

Semester	Gender	Low	Medium	High	F (Sex × Structure)
			Structure level[a]		
			Adult feedback		
I ($n = 46$)	Boys	.30	.36	.22	15.24**
	Girls	.12	.34	.45	
			Model availability		
	Boys	.35	.27	.25	5.15**
	Girls	.24	.43	.24	
			Adult feedback		
II ($n = 85$)	Boys	.35	.31	.23	6.16**
	Girls	.23	.38	.29	
			Model availability		
	Boys	.32	.41	.18	ns
	Girls	.18	.47	.18	

		Low	Medium low	Medium high	High	
			Adult feedback			
III ($n = 83$)	Boys	.21	.27	.22	.15	8.96**
	Girls	.15	.20	.29	.23	
			Model availability			
	Boys	.28	.18	.24	.13	11.37**
	Girls	.16	.19	.39	.13	

[a] Numbers represent proportion of intervals observed. Proportions do not add to 1.0 because intervals outside any activity were not included.

** $p < .01$.

ences. It is possible that children of both genders who enjoyed leadership and taking initiative sought out low-structure settings, while children who were compliant or dependent sought high-structure settings. Therefore, the next step was a laboratory experiment in which structure was manipulated.

Study 2. Experimental Manipulation of Structure in the Laboratory

The purposes of this experiment were to test the immediate effects of activity structure on children's behavior and to test the prediction that

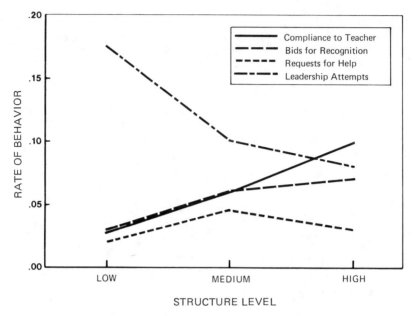

Figure 7.2. Rates of compliance, bids for recognition, requests for help, and leadership attempts as a function of activity structure in preschool classrooms (Study 1).

experience in high or low structure would produce some behavior patterns that carry over into other situations.

METHODS

Subjects were 60 preschool children ranging in age from 3 to 5 years. Pairs of children of the same gender and approximately the same age were randomly assigned to three treatments: high structure, low structure, or control. Children in the high- and low-structure treatments participated in four play sessions lasting 10–15 minutes on four different days. Four types of play materials were used, one for each session. In the high-structure treatment, an adult participated actively in the play session, providing high rates of feedback to both children and demonstrating ways of using the play materials. In the low-structure treatment, the same materials were available to the two children, but the adult sat at one side of the room apparently engaged in some work of her own. The control group did not have any treatment sessions.

All three groups participated in a posttest play session in which the materials from the treatment sessions were available. For part of the posttest session the adult was relatively inactive, and for part of it she participated actively. The purpose of the posttest was to determine whether any effects of the treatments endured beyond the immediate treatment setting.

All of the sessions were videotaped, and the tapes were coded for categories of behavior similar to those used in the preschool observational studies. A major change, however, was that behavior directed toward the other child was coded separately from behavior directed toward the adult.

RESULTS

During the four treatment sessions, the structure manipulation had clear effects on children's social behavior. Children directed more of almost every type of social behavior toward the adult in the high-structure treatment than they did in the low-structure treatment. The means for compliance, seeking recognition, and leadership attempts are shown in Figure 7.3. That result is not surprising, given the greater availability of the adult in the high-structure treatment and the fact that the adult initiated many comments and remarks about the activity.

By contrast, children directed more compliance, bids for recognition, and leadership attempts toward their peer in the low-structure treatment than they did in the high-structure treatment. The means are shown in Figure 7.3. In fact, the rate of peer interaction was extremely low during the high-structure sessions. This result is not so obvious. The peer was equally available for interaction in both sessions. However, the active direction and feedback provided by the adult seems to override the children's tendencies to direct social interactions toward one another. In a high-structure situation, they interact primarily with the adult and very little with one another.

The quality of the adult interactions are probably different than the quality of peer interactions. The adult's greater skill and experience almost inevitably means that she leads and the child follows. By contrast, peers are more equal in skill and experience, so it is more likely that each can exhibit some independent leadership toward the other.

In the posttest sessions, there were no effects of prior treatment on adult-directed behavior. However, children who had experienced low structure showed higher rates of peer compliance and tended to exhibit more leadership to peers than those who had experienced high structure or the control group. The difference appeared primarily when the adult was not participating actively (see Figure 7.3). That is, low-structure children had learned the skills for a low-structure situation and demonstrated them more than children who had not had that treatment. Once the adult became an active participant, however, most of the treatment differences disappeared. The immediate effects of an active, highly involved adult obliterated the tendencies learned by the children in the treatment sessions.

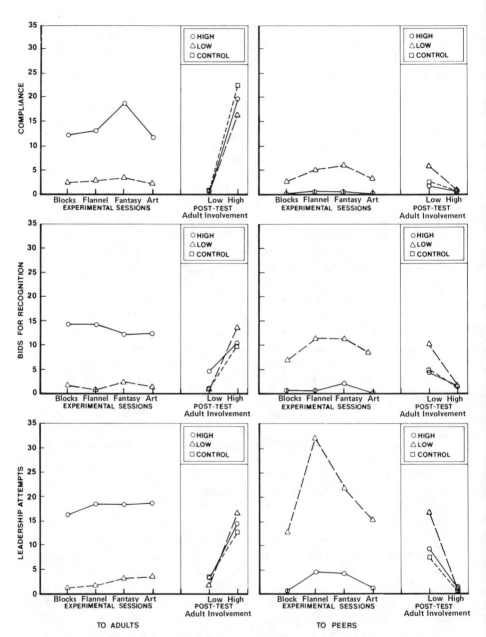

Figure 7.3. Rates of compliance, bids for recognition, and leadership attempts to peers and adults in high- and low-structure activities (Study 2).

SUMMARY OF STUDY 2

The results of this laboratory experiment establish that structure has a causal relation to children's social behavior. The effects occurred in a situation in which children were randomly assigned to treatments and in which the properties of the activities were identical in the high- and low-structure treatments. In high-structure settings, children directed their bids for recognition and other interactions to the adult and rarely interacted with each other. In the low-structure settings, children were much more likely to engage in leadership attempts, compliance, and bids for recognition toward one another. There were few sex differences or interactions of sex with treatment. Behavior was largely a function of the activity structure rather than of the child's gender. In this short-term experiment, some slight evidence for lasting effects of experience in low-structure settings appeared, but a more extended period of treatment might be necessary to observe clearly enduring effects.

Study 3. A Field Experiment

Although the effects of structure were quite marked in the laboratory study, there is always a question about how well laboratory findings generalize to real-world settings. The next step in this research program, therefore, was a field experiment in which the structure of activities was experimentally manipulated in a real classroom (Carpenter, Huston, & Holt, 1981). Single-subject methods of study were used to complement the group analyses used in earlier studies.

METHODS

Activity structure was manipulated during a 1-hour free play period each day for most of a semester in a preschool classroom containing 15 children. On any given day, four different activities were available in different parts of the room. Two of the activities were highly structured, that is, the teachers provided high rates of feedback and some modeling. The other two activities were low in structure, an adult supervised from the sidelines, but tried to remain relatively uninvolved. The particular activities assigned to high and low structure varied from day to day, and each activity was presented at both structure levels several times during the semester. These manipulations were slight exaggerations of the usual variations in structure that occur in preschools, but they fell well within the normal range observed in naturally occurring settings.

During the first 15 minutes of the 1-hour free play period, children were assigned to one of four activities. This was accomplished by giving children colored necklaces made of snap beads that signified the activity they were to participate in. Because the assignment was standard procedure from the beginning of the semester, and because children had an additional 45 minutes of free choice, the procedure did not appear to produce dissatisfaction. At the end of 15 minutes, children were allowed to move to other activities. The structure levels remained in effect for the entire hour.

Two behaviors were selected as the primary focus of observation: recognition seeking and leadership attempts. Some additional behaviors were observed, but they are not reported here. Two observers conducted time-sampled observations during the entire free play period each day.

For the first 11 days, baseline observations were collected for all 15 children. On the basis of these observations, eight children were selected for individual analysis. Four children had high rates of leadership attempts to peers and low rates of seeking recognition from adults. Two had high rates of seeking recognition from adults and low rates of leadership attempts to peers. The remaining two were low on all types of social interaction. Children with these extreme patterns were selected because it was expected that low rates of interaction with either adults or peers might be modified by exposure to high or low structure, respectively.

The experimental method was a within-subject reversal design (ABCBC). After the baseline period, half of the children were placed in high-structure treatments each day and the other half in low. After 2 or 3 weeks, the treatments were reversed. At the end of another 2 or 3 weeks, they were again reversed. For some children, there was time for a fourth reversal. Each child remained in a given treatment until behavior appeared to have stabilized, then a reversal was instituted.

RESULTS

The results for each of the eight children are shown in Figure 7.4. On the whole, high-structure experiences led to increased recognition seeking toward adults, often accompanied by decreased rates of peer interaction. In low-structure activities, most of the children demonstrated increases in leadership attempts toward their peers. There were two children who did not show the expected patterns. Subject 1 showed generally decreased peer interaction in both experimental treatments, and her recognition seeking to adults remained relatively low as well. In fact, this child played alone a good deal of the time, often initiating her own activities. Subject 6 was one of two

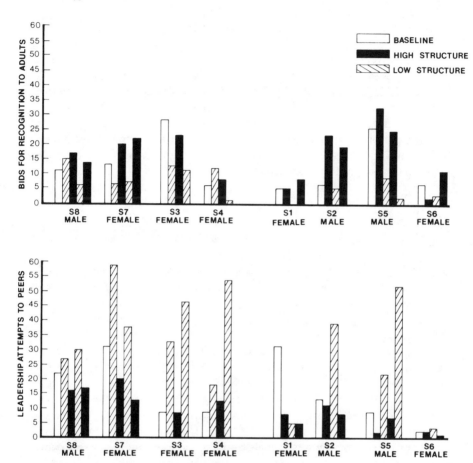

Figure 7.4. Rates of bids for recognition to adults and leadership attempts to peers in high-
and low-structure activities in a preschool classroom (Study 3).

socially withdrawn children at the outset. Although the other withdrawn
child, Subject 4, did show increased peer interaction during low structure,
Subject 6 remained socially inactive throughout most of the observations. It
appears that low structure can provide the occasion for increased leadership to peers but may sometimes be ineffective for children who lack the
skills or the motivation to engage in that behavior.

The means for each child when in high- and low-structure treatments
were compared using a Wilcoxon signed ranks test. The difference between
treatments was significant, $p < .01$, one-tailed test, for both behaviors measured.

Study 4. Activity Structure in Middle Childhood

The most recent investigation in this series was a study of the effects of activity structure during middle childhood (Huston, Carpenter, Atwater, & Johnson, 1985). The major purpose of this study was to determine whether elementary school-age children demonstrate patterns that were similar to preschool children. Specifically, would boys and girls show the same pattern of participation in high- and low-structure activities in a free choice situation, and would children's leadership and recognition-seeking show the same relation to activity structure?

METHODS

As part of a follow-up investigation of children who had been observed during preschool, 110 children ranging from 7 to 11 years old attended a 1-week summer day camp. Each group had from 8 to 12 children in attendance. The day camp was designed to provide an environment that was parallel to preschool, that is, a setting in which the activities included arts and crafts, construction, and dramatic play and in which children had some choice of activities as well as freedom to interact socially.

In the day camps, structure was manipulated experimentally. However, children were free to choose between high- and low-structure activities. The first hour of each half-day session was devoted to a craft or construction activity, and the second activity hour was spent preparing the script and props for a marionette play which was performed at the end of the week. The materials for the current activity were arranged on two large tables near each other. Two adults, a male and a female, served as the day camp teachers. They stayed at or near one of the tables, providing frequent feedback, modeling, and social interaction to the children there. The other table was low in adult structure. The adults did not stay at the table, and they responded briefly to initiations from children who were there. In one corner of the room there were bookshelves containing board games which children were free to use. Children in this area also received low rates of adult feedback.

RESULTS

Children were free to choose activity areas at all times. Girls spent more time in the high-structure activities (i.e., the table where adults provided high rates of feedback), and boys spent more time in the low-structure activities (i.e., the activity table with low rates of adult feedback and the

Table 7.3

Mean Rates of Participation and Behavior in High- and Low-Structure Activity Settings for Elementary School-Age Children: Study 4

| Behavior category | Gender | Structure level | | F^a |
		Low	High	
Participation (percentage of time)	Boys	0.55	0.36	A × B = 34.88**
	Girls	0.33	0.60	
Compliance to adults		1.3	8.8	A = 624.85**
Recognition seeking to adults		2.5	19.2	A = 709.26**
Leadership attempts to adults		1.5	12.7	A = 788.06**
Compliance to male peers	Boys	4.2	1.5	A = 98.23**
	Girls	1.9	1.2	A × B = 14.99**
Recognition seeking to male peers	Boys	9.5	2.5	A = 110.18**
	Girls	2.6	1.5	A × B = 19.61**
Leadership attempts to male peers	Boys	18.3	5.0	A = 105.24**
	Girls	4.6	2.2	A × B = 7.42*
Compliance to female peers	Boys	1.5	1.2	A = 62.30**
	Girls	3.7	1.5	A × B = 18.72**
Recognition seeking to female peers	Boys	2.4	2.0	A = 34.42**
	Girls	8.1	3.4	A × B = 14.85**
Leadership attempts to female peers	Boys	3.4	2.8	A = 36.74**
	Girls	12.3	4.6	A × B = 16.19**

^{a} A = Structure effect; B = Sex effect; A × B = Sex × Structure.
* $p < .05$.
** $p < .01$.

board game area). The means are shown in Table 7.3. Because the activity materials at both tables were similar during any one time period, these differences cannot be attributed to activities. They are also not a function of the sex of the adults. There were virtually no differences in children's social behavior toward the male and female adult, nor did participation vary depending on adult gender.

The second hypothesis was that children in high-structure activities would demonstrate more compliance and recognition seeking toward adults, and children in low structure would demonstrate more leadership to peers. As shown in Table 7.3, these predictions were supported. As in the laboratory experiment with preschoolers, children in high structure displayed more of all types of social interaction toward adults than did those in low-structure activities. By contrast, in low-structure activities, children displayed more of all types of social interaction toward peers than they did in high-structure activities. In addition, most of their peer interactions were directed to same-sex peers.

As in earlier studies, boys and girls behaved similarly when they were observed in similar levels of activity structure. There were few sex differences. Most of the peer interactions occurred among children of the same gender.

SUMMARY OF STUDY 4

This study demonstrates that the patterns observed in the preschool years continue and may become more pronounced during middle childhood. Boys continue to select low-structure activity settings, while girls more often select high-structure settings. In high-structure settings, both sexes not only display high rates of interaction with adults but tend to have low rates of peer interaction. In low-structure settings, both genders demonstrate leadership attempts, recognition seeking, and compliance to their peers, primarily those of their own gender.

DISCUSSION

The theoretical perspective used in this research appears to provide a useful means of conceptualizing the impact of classroom activities on young children. The level of structure, defined by the amount of adult feedback, is one major dimension with important consequences for the behavior of children in those settings.

The nature of the behavior fostered by variations in activity structure can now be described in some detail. In the original model it was proposed that high- and low-structure activities would encourage qualitatively different types of behavior. High-structure settings would lead to compliance and recognition seeking—behaviors that entailed fitting into structures created by others—while low-structure settings would encourage independence, leadership attempts, and initiative—behaviors that involved creating one's own structure. The findings of these investigations indicate, however, that compliance, recognition seeking, and leadership efforts occur in both high- and low-structure settings, but that the targets of those behaviors are different. In high-structure settings, children interact with adults. Even when peers are participating in the activity, they do not direct social behavior to one another. The adult forms the pivot for interactions with each child. In low-structure settings, children interact primarily with their peers. They not only exhibit leadership and initiations toward each other, but they comply with peer requests and seek recognition from each other.

Despite the similar labels for the types of behavior directed to adults and peers, it is likely that the quality of any one of these behaviors is different in a child–adult interaction than it is in a child–child interaction. Complying to a peer is more likely to be a reciprocal process than complying to an adult. Leadership efforts directed to an adult are efforts to get the adult to do something or suggestions about the adult's participation in the task. Nevertheless, adults are generally assumed to have superior knowledge and skills, so children do not believe that they can lead the interaction in the same fashion that they lead a peer. Our observation categories are apparently insensitive to this qualitative difference between adult and peer interactions, but there is good reason to believe that it exists. Therefore, the nature of a child's experience in these two types of interactions is probably qualitatively different.

In both the preschool years and middle childhood, girls select highly structured activities more often than boys do. Boys more often select low-structure activities when they have a choice. The antecedents for this sex difference are probably a combination of very early socialization experiences, but they are not addressed directly in this research. Nevertheless, because the difference exists, boys and girls receive different amounts of experience engaging in the behaviors cultivated by low and high structure. Over the long run, it is likely that these differences cumulate. Girls feel increasingly confident and comfortable interacting with adults, attending to adult directions, and complying with adult requests. Boys feel increasingly confident and comfortable in peer interactions, particularly with other boys, as they learn to exchange leadership attempts, comply with one anothers' requests, and engage in other forms of reciprocal interaction.

At the same time, activity structure is sufficiently powerful that sex differences in behavior within a high- or low-structure activity are minimized. Both boys and girls can and do engage in high rates of adult interaction when exposed to high structure; conversely, both exhibit leadership and peer interaction when placed in a low-structure setting. One implication of this finding is that activity structure could be planfully varied to produce changes in children's classroom behavior. Children who are overly compliant and dependent on adult direction might profit from some exposure to low structure; those who are overly assertive and involved primarily with peers might profit from more high-structure experiences.

Two sources of activity structure form the core of this model: adult feedback and modeling. The separate effects of these two cannot be identified easily. Adult feedback has a strong, immediate impact. When an adult is present and giving active feedback, children's behavior is affected dramatically. The effects of modeling are more difficult to tease out. The natural observational study demonstrated that girls participated more than boys in activities that are seen frequently in everyday life. More information about the behavioral consequences of cumulative observational experiences is needed, however.

Finally, a few comments on the implicit or explicit values guiding this research are in order. Much research on sex differences is guided at least partly by social and political concerns about sex discrimination. It is often focused on the detrimental effects of a particular set of variables or conditions on females. At the outset, that orientation flavored our approach as well. It seemed that males were learning skills in taking initiative, planning, and creating structure that were particularly important for achievement in adulthood. Females, by contrast, were being taught to conform and depend on other people to define the parameters of their world. Further examination of these findings and their implications for children's socialization in school settings raises serious questions about the assumption that creating structure is better or more useful than fitting into others' structures. Assuming that males' skills are superior may be yet another instance of the tendency by social scientists to value masculine attributes more highly than feminine attributes.

It seems more reasonable to argue that being able to create structure and to fit into structures created by others are both adaptive. In school situations, learning can be fostered by skills in attending and complying with adult directions, seeking praise and recognition from adults, and directing leadership efforts toward adults. Similarly, social and intellectual competence can be gained by exercising skills in complying with peer requests, leading peers, and seeking the praise and recognition of one's peers. The implication of this view is that, to the extent that these different skills are practiced in high- and low-structure settings, children of both genders can profit from a balance of experience in settings with different amounts of adult structure.

REFERENCES

Barker, R. G. (1968). *Ecological psychology.* Stanford, CA: Stanford University Press.
Carpenter, C. J. (1983a). Activity structure and play: Implications for socialization. In M. B. Liss (Ed.), *Social and cognitive skills: Sex roles and children's play.* New York: Academic Press.
Carpenter, C. J. (1983b). *Patterns of behavior and sex differences associated with preschool activity structure.* Unpublished doctoral dissertation, University of Kansas.
Carpenter, C. J., Huston, A. C., & Holt, W. (1981). *The use of selected activity participation to modify sex-typed behavior.* Paper presented at the annual meeting of the Association for Behavior Analysis, Milwaukee, WI.
Carpenter, C. J., & Huston-Stein, A. (1980). Activity structure and sex-typed behavior in preschool children. *Child Development, 51,* 862–872.

Fagot, B. I. (1978). The influence of sex of child on parental reactions to toddler children. *Child Development, 49,* 30–36.

Gump, P. V. (1975). Ecological psychology and children. In E. M. Hetherington (Ed.), *Review of child development research* (Vol. 5). Chicago: University of Chicago Press.

Gump, P. V. (1980). The school as a social situation, *Annual Review of Psychology, 31,* 553–582.

Huston, A. C. (1983). Sex typing, In P. H. Mussen & E. M. Hetherington (Eds.), *Handbook of child psychology: Vol. 4. Socialization, personality, and social behavior* (4th ed.). New York: Wiley.

Huston-Stein, A., Friedrich-Cofer, L., & Susman, E. J. (1977). The relation of classroom structure to social behavior, imaginative play and self-regulation of economically disadvantaged children. *Child Development, 48,* 908–916.

Maccoby, E. E., & Jacklin, C. N. (1974). *The psychology of sex differences.* Stanford, CA: Stanford University Press.

Maccoby, E. E., & Jacklin, C. N. (1980). Sex differences in aggression: A rejoinder and reprise. *Child Development, 51,* 964–980.

Mischel, W. (1968). *Personality and assessment.* New York: Wiley.

Mischel, W. (1973). Toward a cognitive social learning reconceptualization of personality. *Psychological Review, 80,* 252–283.

Serbin, L. A. (1980). Sex role socialization: A field in transition. In B. Lahey & A. Kazdin (Eds.), *Advances in clinical child psychology* (Vol. 3). New York: Plenum Press.

Serbin, L. A., & Connor, J. M. (1979). Sex typing of children's play preferences and patterns of cognitive performance. *Journal of Genetic Psychology, 134,* 315–316.

Sherman, J. A. (1967). Problems of sex differences in space perception and aspects of intellectual functioning. *Psychological Review, 74,* 290–299.

Smith, P. K., & Connolly, K. J. (1980). *The ecology of preschool behavior.* Cambridge: Cambridge University Press.

Some Determinants and Consequences of Sex Segregation in the Classroom*

MARLAINE E. LOCKHEED

INTRODUCTION

In the decade since the implementation of Title IX of the Elementary and Secondary Education Act, administrators and teachers have expended considerable energy in an effort to eliminate overt sexism in the policies, programs, practices, and materials of the public schools. While great strides have been made in opening programs to both girls and boys, in promoting gender-fair textbooks and other educational materials, and in raising the

---

* Support for the research reported in this chapter was provided by the National Institute of Education (NIE), under Contract 400-80-0032 to Educational Testing Service (ETS) and by ETS. The views and conclusions expressed in this chapter are the author's and do not necessarily reflect those of either NIE or ETS. The collaboration of Abigail M. Harris in conducting the study and the research assistance of Kenneth Rosenblad, Karen Jensen, Leta Davis, and William Nemceff are gratefully acknowledged.

167

consciousness of teachers and administrators regarding subtle inequities, a more fundamental form of sexism—one that threatens to undermine these positive gains—has remained untouched and unchanged: the universal tendency of children to segregate themselves on the basis of sex for virtually all social and academic activities.

This self-selected sex segregation is well documented as a widespread phenomenon among elementary and junior high school-aged children. It has been demonstrated in studies of student friendship choices and work partner preferences that utilize sociometric techniques, in surveys of student attitudes, and by direct observation of student seating, play, and interactive behaviors. The results of these studies show that students identify same-sex but not cross-sex classmates as friends (Hallinan, 1977; Hallinan & Tuma, 1978), choose to work with same-sex but not cross-sex classmates (Lockheed, Finkelstein, & Harris, 1979), sit or work in same-sex but not cross-sex groups (Schofield & Sagar, 1977; Lockheed & Harris, 1984), and engage in many more same-sex than cross-sex verbal interchanges (Day & Hunt, 1974; Berk & Lewis, 1977; Grant, 1982; Wilkinson & Subkoviak, 1981). Similar findings have been reported in numerous other studies, which are summarized in Table 8.1.

Despite the extensive documentation of the existence of sex segregation, only a few studies examined either its determinants or its consequences and none distinguished between *observed* sex segregation and the sex segregation that is *inferred* from analyses of sociometric instruments. In this chapter, which examines both observed and inferred sex segregation, observed behavior is referred to as "cross-sex interaction" and the inferred social structure of the class (as calculated from student sociometric choices) is described in terms of a sex segregation–sex integration continuum.

Determinants of Cross-Sex Interaction

Cross-sex interaction in the classroom is largely determined by three factors: (1) the opportunity to interact, (2) the students' willingness to interact with cross-sex peers in general, and (3) the students' willingness to interact with the specific individuals in their class. In addition, cross-sex interaction is increased by teacher reinforcement.

OPPORTUNITIES TO INTERACT

A number of experimental studies have sought to reduce sex segregation in the classroom by increasing cross-sex interaction. In these studies, cross-

Table 8.1

Recent Studies of Sex Segregation in Elementary Classrooms by Dependent Variable[a]

Author	Sample	Measure	Results
1. Observed work group or seating composition			
Campbell (1979)	~250 elementary students in 11 classrooms	Voluntary group composition	78% of students joined same-sex groups
Lockheed & Harris (1983)	29 4th- and 5th-grade classrooms	Observation of target students in groups	14% of observations indicated cross-sex groups
Marquis & Cooper (1982)	2 preschool classes	Selection of work partner for self-disciplined work session	Virtual sex segregation in choices of partners observed on six occasions
Schofield & Sagar (1977)	7th- and 8th-grade students at lunch	Seating patterns at 32 tables in cafeteria	Cross-sex adjacencies were extremely rare
Wilkinson & Subkoviak (1981)	23 boys and girls in 4 first-grade reading groups	Seating charts	Same-sex preference in seating
2. Observed interactions			
Berk & Lewis (1977)	22 boys, 22 girls, age 4–8 years, in 4 school types	Observed social contacts, interchanges	Girls engaged in more same-sex interchanges than boys. The proportion of same- to cross-sex interchanges = 4:1 to 3:1 in 3 schools. Progressive schools = 1:3
Campbell (1979)	11 six-person, cross-race, cross-sex groups	Observed amount of interaction	63% of all interactions were same-sex interactions; 20% of all interactions were cross-sex, cross-race interactions
		Observed type of interactions	43% of cross-sex, cross-race interactions were negative; 78% of same-sex, same-race interactions were positive

(*continued*)

Table 8.1 (*continued*)

Author	Sample	Measure	Results
Damico (1975)	30 students, 8–10 years in university lab school	Ethnography	No recorded incidence of spontaneous cross-sex academic helping behavior. Two separate sex-segregated social systems identified
Fagot (1977)	106 boys, 101 girls in preschool	Fagot–Patterson observation	Boys who showed cross-gender preference were given more peer criticism and fewer positive reactions. No peer criticism of cross-gender girls
Grant (1982)	6 first-grade classrooms	Ethnographic observations	Fewer actual cross-sex interactions than expected (~10% fewer in 4 classes, 3% fewer in 1 class, and 22% fewer in 1 class) Cross-sex helping was rare, and cross-sex academic helping was more frequently F → M (>7.0% in 3 classes, >50% in 2; in 1 class M → F greater)
Lockheed & Harris (1982)	29 4th- and 5th-grade classrooms	Observation of target student verbal interaction	Same-sex responses to target student behavior twice as frequent as cross-sex response
Serbin, Tolnick, & Sternglanz (1977)	2 nursery school classes	Cross-sex cooperative play	Baseline showed low rate of cooperative cross-sex play
Singleton & Asher (1979)	39 white, 39 black, 3rd-grade students	Observation of teacher–student cross-sex and single-sex interaction	77.8% of peer interaction was same-sex peer interaction

(*continued*)

170

Table 8.1 (*continued*)

Author	Sample	Measure	Results
3. Self-reported preferences			
Lockheed, Finkelstein, & Harris (1979)	211 4th-grade boys 266 4th-grade girls	Choice of three work partners	Same-sex choice made by 72% of boys and 67% of girls
	234 5th-grade boys 223 5th-grade girls	Choice of three work partners	Same-sex choice made by 65% of boys and 57% of girls
4. Sociometric ratings			
Hallinan (1977)	51 classes in Grades 5–8	Sociometric	A total separation by sex existed in the cliques in every class
Hallinan & Tuma (1978)	4th-, 5th-, and 6th-grade students in 18 classrooms	Sociometric of best friend, friend, not a friend	77% of Best Friends were of same sex peer
Lockheed & Harris (1982)	29 4th- and 5th-grade classrooms	Sociometric rating	Mean cross-sex ratings lower than mean same-sex rating
Phillis (1971)	30 boys, 30 girls, age 5–8 years, in laboratory summer school	Sociometric	Sex differences in choice of play partners and leader of physical education team
Singleton & Asher (1977)	197 white, 48 black 3rd-grade students	Sociometric	Same-sex peer play and work partner ratings were more positive than cross-sex ratings

[a] Complete citations for papers listed in this table are available from the author upon request.

sex interaction was increased by reorganizing the classroom into small cooperative groups for learning, generally using peer tutoring to promote interaction (DeVries & Edwards, 1974; Hansell, 1983; Oishi, Slavin, & Madden, 1983; Sharan, 1980; Raviv, 1982). Unfortunately, most of these studies used student sociometric choices to assess segregation. Although the experimental treatment was designed to promote cross-sex interaction, actual interaction was rarely observed. Only the study conducted in Israel by Sharan's student Raviv used cross-sex behavior as a dependent variable. In that study, students spent several weeks working together in small interdependent learning groups, completing group projects using Sharan's "investigative method." After the intervention, student behavior was assessed in experimentally composed cross-sex and cross-ethnic groups. The intervention was successful in increasing cross-sex cooperative behavior and reducing cross-sex competetive behavior.

The remainder of the studies cited previously inferred that the intervention produced greater cross-sex interaction, and assessed the effect of the intervention by examining changes in the ratings given classmates on sociometric scales. In general, both same-sex and cross-sex ratings became more positive in the experimental classrooms, but since the *difference* between cross-sex and same-sex ratings was not statistically examined, no conclusion can be offered with regard to the effect of any of these interventions on reducing classroom sex segregation.

A nonexperimental study that sheds light on the effects of the opportunity to interact on cross-sex interaction is Berk and Lewis' (1977) investigation of organizational context effects on differences in cross-sex interaction. In this study, cross-sex social contacts or interchanges were observed in four preschools, one of which was described as "progressive." The ratio of same-sex to cross-sex interchanges was lower in the progressive school than in the other three schools (Berk & Lewis, 1977). Although the authors do not describe what was meant by progressive, schools described as "progressive" in the 1970s characteristically provided many environmental opportunities that encouraged student interaction.

TEACHER REINFORCEMENT

A second factor thought to be of importance in determining the extent of cross-sex interaction is the teacher's reinforcement of cross-sex cooperation. For example, in one experimental study (Serbin, Tonick, & Sternglanz, 1977), higher levels of cross-sex interaction were observed after nursery school teachers began reinforcing cross-sex collaborative play. When the intervention was concluded, however, the children's behavior returned to the baseline levels of single-sex play.

STUDENT ATTITUDES

Several other related factors thought to be of importance in determining cross-sex interaction are student attitudes towards such interaction (Lockheed & Harris, 1984), specific student likes and dislikes for particular other classmates (Best, 1983), and general sex-role stereotypes (Allport, 1954).

Consequences of Cross-Sex Interaction

The consequences of cross-sex interaction are also largely unexamined; where experimenters have claimed to examine effects of increased interaction, the results have been far from conclusive. For example, in the studies of collaborative learning mentioned previously, the effect of the presumed increase in interaction on subsequent reduction of sex segregation as indicated by sociometric ratings was not examined. Instead the researchers investigated overall affect in the classrooms. All ratings—both same-sex and cross-sex—in the experimental classrooms were more positive than those in the control classrooms. It cannot be concluded, however, that this was due to increased interaction, because the interaction was not observed.

Purpose of Present Study

The present study was designed to examine some of the determinants and consequences of cross-sex interaction in the classroom. This chapter focuses on whether and under what conditions cross-sex interaction leads to less cross-sex segregation, which is operationalized as the difference between the mean sociometric ratings given by students to their same-sex and cross-sex classmates. As noted previously, sociometric ratings of this type have been used widely to determine the clique structure of the classroom (Hallinan & Tuma, 1978) and to assess the effectiveness of specific desegregation interventions (Hansell, 1983). It is hypothesized that cross-sex interaction will be determined in part by student cross-sex affect and attitudes and by the opportunities that the teacher provides for interaction, and that the extent of cross-sex interaction in the classroom will—in combination with a positive teacher reaction to interaction—determine the degree to which the classroom is subsequently sex-integrated. Four specific questions are addressed: What is the extent of sex segregation in the classes under investigation; What are the opportunities for and the extent of cross-sex interaction in these classes; What are the determinants of observed cross-sex interaction; and What are the consequences of cross-sex interaction for subsequent sex integration?

METHODS

Sample

Data cited in this chapter are drawn from the classrooms of 29 fourth- and fifth-grade teachers. Half of the classrooms were located in schools in California and half were located in schools in Connecticut. Nine teachers and their students were observed multiple times over the course of two years, students in these classrooms were surveyed both at the beginning and the end of each school year. The remaining 20 teachers were observed multiple times during one year; the students in these classrooms were similarly surveyed at the beginning and the end of the year. Each year represents a discrete study, since individual students were not followed over the two years.

Observation

Observations were conducted eight times during the first year of the study in all 29 classrooms and six times during the second year of the study in 9 classrooms. For each observation, different randomly selected target students (three boys and three girls per classroom) were observed for the academic portion of an entire school day. Observations were conducted by trained observers using a low-inference recording procedure (Lambert, Hartsough, Caffrey, & Urbansky, 1976) specifically adapted for this study (Lockheed et al., 1981). For each observation day, trained observers sampled and recorded the behavior of the target student, noted the instructional context in which the student was working, and recorded with whom the student was speaking, if anyone. Interobserver reliability was established during training at .85 or better, was periodically reassessed through double observations, and was found to remain at this level throughout the study. Observations were coded for the following variables:

1. *Recipient of a bid.* If the behavior of the target student was preceeded by behavior on the part of another student that precipitated the target student's behavior, the student was coded as the recipient of a bid. If the child initiating this bid was the same sex as the target child, the bid was categorized as a same-sex bid; if not, the bid was categorized as a cross-sex bid.

2. *Initiator of a bid.* If the behavior of the target student was followed by the response of another student, the target student was coded as the initiator of a bid. If the child receiving this bid was the same sex as the target

child, the bid was categorized as a same-sex bid; if not, the bid was categorized as a cross-sex bid.

3. *Working in a group.* To be coded as working in a group, the target
student had to be working cooperatively with classmates, sharing information, and/or giving and receiving help. This code was used when the teacher
was leading the group, when the teacher stated that children could work
together, or when there was evidence that groups were an accepted classroom structure. Two or more students constituted a group, and separate
codings were used to indicate an all-boy group, an all-girl group, or a cross-
sex group.

4. *Teacher response.* Five major categories of teacher response to target
student behavior were coded: instructing responses (such as correcting,
explaining, or helping), managing responses (such as redirecting or inter-
vening), positive responses, negative responses, and neutral responses.

Student Rating

As in the study by Hallinan and Tuma (1978), students were provided
with a computer-generated list of all the students in their homeroom; they
were asked to indicate, for each one, how they would feel about working
with him or her on a science task. Three rating categories were developed
for this instrument: "Would really like to work with," "Wouldn't mind working with," and "Would mind working with." For each child, the mean rating
that he or she gave to the boys and the girls in his or her class was calculated; cross-sex ratings were characterized as the mean ratings given to girls
by boys and the mean ratings given to boys by girls. Since the ratings ranged
from 1–3, the difference in ratings had a possible range of 0–2, with 0
representing perfect integration, that is, on average the ratings given male
and female classmates were the same, and 2 representing perfect segregation. Within each class the mean same- and cross-sex ratings were computed for boys and girls separately; these measures served as the classroom
indicators.

Student Report

Students were administered an 80-item survey containing questions related to several domains of sex stereotypes. Included in the survey were six
items related to student-stated preference for same-sex or cross-sex work
partners that were adapted from the Attitude Toward Cross-Sex Interaction
subscale of the Lockheed–Harris Sex Role, Cross-Sex Interaction, and Fe-

male Leadership Scale (Parks, Bogart, Reynolds, Hamilton, & Findley, 1979).
The items are of the type, "Think of three people in your class that you
would choose to do school work with. Are they all boys, all girls, or both
boys and girls?" For this measure, cross-sex and mixed-sex responses were
combined, according to the sex of the respondent, into a scale having a
possible range of 0–6, with the higher value representing greater preference for cross-sex interaction.

Measures

All measures were aggregated by sex at the classroom level. Observed
cross-sex interaction was operationalized as the sum of cross-sex bid initiations and cross-sex bid receptions and expressed as a proportion of all bid
initiations and receptions observed in the classroom. Opportunities for interaction were operationalized as the observed amount of cross-sex groupings used by the teacher in organizing instructional contexts in the classroom. Sex segregation was operationalized as the difference between the
mean ratings given to cross-sex classmates and the mean ratings given to
same-sex classmates on the sociometric instrument.

Attitudes towards cross-sex interaction were measured by the six-item
scale described in the previous section. Affect towards male and female
classmates was measured by the mean sociometric rating given to boys and
girls by other boys and girls in their class.

RESULTS

The results of this study show that (1) sex segregation was characteristic
of the classes under observation, (2) teachers rarely organized their classrooms to promote cross-sex contact, (3) student attitudes about cross-sex
interaction and about the other children in their classes were strong predictors of cross-sex interaction, and (4) higher levels of cross-sex interaction
were associated with declines in sex segregation over the course of the
year. The variables used in the following analyses are defined in Table 8.2
and summary statistics are presented in Table 8.3.

Extent of Sex Segregation

Analysis of the student rating instrument, which compared the mean
ratings given to cross-sex classmates with the mean ratings given to same-
sex classmates, showed pervasive sex segregation. In the aggregate, for both

Table 8.2

List of Variables and Definitions

Variable	Definition
Sex segregation	Difference between mean same-sex rating and mean cross-sex rating given by students within the classroom; 0–2
Cross-sex interaction	Sum of cross-sex bid initiations and cross-sex bid receptions, as percent of all bid initiations and receptions; 0–100
Opportunity for cross-sex interaction	Observed cross-sex instructional contexts as percentage of all instructional contexts
Girls' rating of boys	Mean rating given by girls to boys in their classroom; 3 = would like to work with, 2 = wouldn't mind working with, 1 = would mind working with
Boys' rating of girls	Mean rating given by boys to girls in their classroom; 1–3
Girls' attitudes	Mean score of girls in classroom on 6-item survey of attitudes toward cross-sex groups; 0–6
Boys' attitudes	Mean score of boys in classroom on 6-item survey of attitudes toward cross-sex groups; 0–6
Teacher's positive response to girls	Positive teacher responses to female target student behavior, as a percentage of all teacher responses to target students within class
Teacher's positive response to boys	Positive teacher responses to male target student behavior as a percentage of all teacher responses to target students within class

years, same-sex classmates were rated approximately 0.63 points higher than cross-sex classmates on the 0–2 continuum representing total integration to total segregation (Table 8.3). The range in differences between same- and cross-sex ratings was 0.14 to 1.11, with only 7% of the classrooms showing difference less than 0.40; in 17% of the classrooms, same-sex ratings were fully 1.00 higher than cross-sex ratings. Sex segregation was essentially uniform across all classes and was consistent over time, changing little between Year 1 and Year 2 or between the fall and the spring.

Opportunities for and Extent of Cross-Sex Interaction

Opportunities for cross-sex interaction were defined as the percentage of observed instructional contexts in which the target students were working

Table 8.3

Summary Statistics

	Year 1		Year 2	
Variable	$\bar{X}$	SD	$\bar{X}$	SD
Sex segregation, pre	0.64	0.18	0.63	0.22
Sex segregation, post	0.63	0.17	0.63	0.20
Cross-sex interaction (%)	37.70	7.80	47.60	7.30
Opportunity for cross-sex interaction (%)	7.90	5.40	11.00	7.10
Girls' rating of boys, pre	1.60	0.16	1.64	0.16
Boys' rating of girls, pre	1.69	0.22	1.65	0.19
Girls' attitudes, pre	2.85	0.84	2.96	0.78
Boys' attitudes, pre	2.70	0.85	2.57	0.85
Teacher's positive response to girls (%)	3.20	1.60	3.50	2.10
Teacher's positive response to boys (%)	3.50	1.50	4.00	2.30

cooperatively with other students. These opportunities were, on the average, extremely rare. Only approximately 8% of all instructional contexts recorded in Year 1 and 11% of all instructional contexts recorded in Year 2 indicated that students were expected to be working together. Despite this absence of opportunities for interaction, cross-sex interaction was relatively frequent in these classrooms; during Year 1, nearly 38% of all interactions were cross-sex interactions, and in Year 2, nearly half of all interactions were cross-sex interactions. The frequency of cross-sex interactions in these classrooms was substantially higher than would have been predicted from the literature.

Determinants of Cross-Sex Interaction

To investigate some determinants of cross-sex interaction, multiple regression analyses of classroom means for both years were conducted; the results are presented in Table 8.4. Three types of predictors were considered: (1) the opportunity for interaction presented formally in the classroom, (2) students' expressed attitudes toward interacting with cross-sex peers in general, and (3) the students' willingness to interact with the specific students in their class. Opportunity for cross-sex interaction was not a significant factor in determining the amount of cross-sex interaction. In fact, the simple correlation between group instructional contexts and cross-sex interaction was $-.04, p = .42$, for Year 1 and $.28, p = .24$, for Year 2. Students' general attitudes towards cross-sex interaction, holding constant opportunities to interact, were significantly related to subsequent

Table 8.4

Some Determinants of Cross-Sex Interaction[a]

	Alternative Specifications									
	(1)		(2)		(3)		(4)		(5)	
Independent variables	Year 1	Year 2	Year 1	Year 2	Year 1	Year 2	Year 1	Year 2	Year 1	Year 2
1. Opportunity for CSI	-.04 (0.19)	.27 (0.76)	.02 (0.10)	.22 (0.60)	-.02 (0.11)	.18 (0.50)	.00 (0.00)	.29 (0.76)	.13 (0.68)	.27 (0.68)
2. Girls' ratings of boys			.33* (1.78)	.33 (0.87)						
3. Boys' ratings of girls					.14 (0.70)	.43 (1.38)				
4. Girls' attitudes							.35* (1.91)	.22 (0.59)		
5. Boys' attitudes									.43* (2.20)	-.06 (0.15)
r^2	.00	.08	.11	.18	.02	.25	.12	.08	.16	.12
$\bar{r}^2$	-.04	-.06	.04	-.09	-.05	-.00	-.06	-.23	.09	-.16

[a] The figures in this table are standardized regression coefficients (β) with the associated t statistic in parentheses.

* $p < .05$.

cross-sex interaction; the effects were less pronounced in Year 2 than in Year 1. Boys' attitudes toward cooperating with girls accounted for 16% of the unadjusted variance in cross-sex interaction in Year 1 and 5% of the unadjusted variance in Year 2. Girls' attitudes toward cooperating with boys accounted for 12% of the unadjusted variance in cross-sex interaction in Year 1 and 0.4% of the unadjusted variance in Year 2. Girls' and boys' attitudes were highly correlated ($r = .62, p < .001$ for Year 1 and $r = .58, p < .01$ for Year 2), and hence were not independent predictors of cross-sex interaction.

Student willingness to interact with other classmates, holding constant opportunities to interact, was also generally a significant predictor of interaction. Girls' rating of boys accounted for 11% of the unadjusted variance in Year 1 and 10% in Year 2. Boys' ratings of girls accounted for 2% of the unadjusted variance in Year 1 and 17% in Year 2. These factors were highly correlated with each other ($r = .77, p < .001$ for Year 1 and $r = .46, p < .03$ for Year 2) and with general attitudes for cooperation, and were not independent predictors.

Determinants of Sex Segregation

We hypothesized that sex segregation will be influenced by the extent of cross-sex interaction in the class and the response of students and teachers to that interaction. The anticipated sign of that effect is hypothesized to be negative, to reflect the reduction of the difference between same-sex and cross-sex ratings. In this study, student responses were not examined. Teacher reward contingencies were directly assessed through a record of teacher positive and negative reaction to the behavior of the target student who was the recipient or initiator of the interaction bid. Webster and Entwistle (1976) argued persuasively that a major role of the teacher is that of a high-status evaluator; we reasoned that students' interest in receiving positive teacher evaluations may have an effect on their decision to initiate a cross-sex interaction. To assess these effects, multiple regression analyses were conducted; these analyses were conducted for Year 1 data only, since the sample size for Year 2 was too small.

Although the effects were not statistically significant, the signs of the effects were generally in the direction predicted. Sex segregation at the pretest was strongly associated with sex segregation at the posttest ($\beta = .67; t = 4.37, p < .01$) and accounted for 55% of the unadjusted variance of posttest sex segregation. However, the more cross-sex interaction that was observed, the less sex segregation in student ratings was found ($\beta = -.16; t = 1.10, p < .10$); cross-sex interaction accounted for 2% of the unadjusted

Table 8.5

Correlations of Student Behavior and Teacher Response Variables
with Sex Segregation Posttest Measure

Variables	Year 1	Year 2
Sex segregation, pre	0.71***	0.60**
Cross-sex interaction	−0.21	−0.48
Teacher's positive response to girls	−0.02	0.65*
Teacher's positive response to boys	−0.09	0.31

* $p < .05$.
** $p < .01$.
*** $p < .001$.

variance in sex segregation at the end of the school year. The positive reaction of teachers to girls ($\beta = -.33$; $t = 1.11$, $p < .10$) but not to boys ($\beta = -.14$; $t = .51$) was also associated with a reduction in sex segregation.

In Table 8.5 the simple correlations between cross-sex interaction and teacher response, on the one hand, and sex segregation, on the other, are presented. The effects for Year 2 are much stronger, despite the small sample size, than for Year 1. Similar to the regression results for Year 1, greater cross-sex interaction and teacher positive response were associated with less sex segregation.

DISCUSSION

The classrooms in this study were typical of many elementary school classrooms, particularly insofar as they demonstrated few opportunities for the students to engage in cooperative activities. Nevertheless, a great deal of cross-sex interaction was observed. Boys were initiating contacts with and responding to contacts initiated by girls and vice versa. The student sociometric choices did not, overall, indicate this level of interaction. By and large the sociometric choices reflected a preference for same-sex over cross-sex work partner. The inconsistency between the two indicators of segregation, that is, one behavioral and one self-reported, raises some interesting questions regarding the use of sociometric instruments in studying segregation. Teachers, in particular, may be overly influenced by the stated preferences of children and may be relatively unaware of the rich world of cross-sex interaction going on in the class.

Of course, that world may not be a positive one. Webb (1982) demonstrated that in small learning groups, cross-sex contact is less positive for girls than for boys. In her study of math groups, she found that girls responded to requests for information from both boys and other girls, whereas boys responded only to other boys. In a review of 29 studies containing analyses of 64 data sets that examined cross-sex interaction in small groups of males and females of all ages, Lockheed (1985) reported that in 45 of the data sets, males were more influential over the group decision than were females. This difference was related to the nature of the task, with males more influential than females over "male" tasks and "neutral" tasks and females equally influential as males over "female" tasks. The sex difference in influence was argued to be a function of societally held beliefs regarding greater male competence, operating through performance expectations (Lockheed & Hall, 1976; Berger, Connor, & Fisek, 1974). Lockheed and Harris (1984) reported that greater opportunities for cross-sex interaction in the classroom are associated with an increase in cross-sex stereotypes, suggesting that the dynamics of small-group interaction in classrooms may indeed lead to negative experiences for girls.

In the classes in this study, however, greater cross-sex interaction was associated with a reduction, albeit modest, of sex segregation. This may have been due in part to the positive reactions of the teachers to the girls. If, as Webb (1982) suggests, cross-sex interaction is limited by the *boys'* reluctance to respond to the girls, then teacher behavior that leads the boys to consider girls a valuable resource may encourage boys to initiate cross-sex contacts.

The remarkable stability and cross-sex negativity of the student ratings on the sociometric instruments suggests that the act of stating a cross-sex choice for a work partner may imply something different to the student than simply talking to a cross-sex classmate. Best (1983) reported that fourth- and fifth-grade students are unwilling to identify cross-sex classmates as friends out of fear of having that designation interpreted in a romantic context. Children of this age actually lack a word that indicates cross-sex friendship as contrasted to romantic attraction. Often the expression "just a friend" is used to distinguish a person of the other sex from those about whom a child may have romantic inclinations. Studies that utilize sociometric rating instruments, particularly those that use the term "friend" as part of the rating category, may be artificially exaggerating the cross-sex distances in the class. Although many studies report more frequent same-sex than cross-sex interactions in class, on the order of two to one, this difference is not nearly what one would anticipate from the ratings, in which cross-sex classmates are rarely chosen as work partners or friends.

In deciding whether or not to utilize cross-sex groupings in class, teachers may be well advised not to be unduly influenced by the stated preferences of the children concerning cross-sex grouping. As with many other human behaviors, children's performances may speak louder than their preferences.

REFERENCES

Allport, G. W. (1954). *The nature of prejudice.* New York: Addison-Wesley Publishing Co. Inc.
Berger, J., Conner, T. L., & Fisek, M. H. (1974). *Expectation state theory: A theoretical research program.* Cambridge, MA: Winthrop Publishers.
Berk, L. E., & Lewis, N. G. (1977). Sex role and social behavior in four school environments. *Elementary School Journal, 3,* 205–217.
Best, R. (1983). *We've all got scars: What boys and girls learn in elementary schools.* Bloomington: Indiana University Press.
Day, B., & Hunt, G. (1974). *Verbal interaction across age, race, and sex in a variety of learning centers in an open classroom setting* (Final Report). Chapel Hill: North Carolina University, Frank Porter Graham Center.
DeVries, D. L., & Edwards, K. J. (1974). Student teams and learning games: Their effects on cross-race and cross-sex interaction. *Journal of Educational Psychology, 66*(5),741–749.
Grant, L. (1982). *Sex roles and statuses in peer interactions in elementary schools.* Paper presented at the annual meeting of the American Educational Research Association, New York.
Hallinan, M. T. (1977). *The evolution of children's friendship cliques.* University of Wisconsin, Madison. (ERIC Document Reproduction Service No. ED 161 556).
Hallinan, M. T., & Tuma, N. B. (1978). Classroom effects on change in children's friendships. *Sociology of Education, 51,* 170–282.
Hansell, S. (1983). *Cooperative groups, weak ties, and the racial and sexual integration of peer friendships.* Manuscript submitted for publication.
Lambert, N. M., Hartsough, C. S., Caffrey, C., & Urbanski, C. (1976). *APPLE: Lexicon for APPLE observations.* Berkeley: University of California.
Lockheed, M. E. (1985). Sex and social influence: A meta-analysis guided by theory. In J. Berger & M. Zelditch (Eds.), *Status, rewards and influence* (pp. 406–429). San Francisco: Jossey-Bass.
Lockheed, M. E., Amarel, M., Finkelstein, K. J., Harris, A. M., Flores, V., Holland, P., McDonald, F., Nemceff, W., & Stone, M. (1981). *Year one report: Classroom interaction, student cooperation, and leadership.* Princeton, NJ: Educational Testing Service.
Lockheed, M. E., Finkelstein, K. J., & Harris, A. M. (1979). *Curriculum and research for equity: Model data package.* Princeton, NJ: Educational Testing Service.
Lockheed, M. E., & Hall, K. P. (1976). Conceptualizing sex as a status characteristic: Application to leadership training strategies. *Journal of Social Issues, 32,* 111–124.
Lockheed, M. E., & Harris, A. M. (1984). Cross-sex collaborative learning in elementary classrooms. *American Educational Research Journal, 21,* 275–294.
Oishi, S., Slavin, R. E., & Madden, N. A. (1983). *Effects of student teams and individualized instruction on cross-race and cross-sex friendships.* Paper presented at the meeting of the American Educational Research Association, Montreal, Canada.
Parks, B. J., Bogart, K., Reynolds, D. F., Hamilton, M., & Finley, C. J. (1979). *Sourcebook of measures of women's educational equity.* Palo Alto, CA: American Institutes for Research.
Raviv, S. (1982). *The effects of three teaching methods on the cross-sex cooperative and*

competitive behaviors of students in ethnically mixed seventh-grade classes. Paper presented at the Second International Conference on Cooperation in Education, Provo, Utah.

Schofield, J. W., & Sagar, H. A. (1977). Peer interaction patterns in an integrated middle school.
Sociometry, 40(2), 130–138.

Serbin, L. A., Tonick, I. J., & Sternglanz, S. H. (1977). Shaping cooperative cross-sex play. *Child
Development, 48,* 924–929.

Sharan, S. (1980). Cooperative learning in small groups: Recent methods and effects on
achievement, attitudes, and ethnic relations. *Review of Educational Research, 50*(2),
241–271.

Webb, M. M. (1982). *Interaction patterns: Powerful predictors of achievement in cooperative
small groups.* Paper presented at the annual meeting of the American Educational Research Association, New York.

Webster, M., & Entwisle, D. R. (1976). Expectation effects on performance evaluations. *Social
Forces, 55,* 493–502.

Wilkinson, L. C., & Subkoviak, M. (1981, December). *Sex differences in classroom communication.* Paper presented at the International Interdisciplinary Congress on Women, Haifa,
Israel.

Sex Differences and Sex Segregation in Students' Small-Group Communication*

LOUISE CHERRY WILKINSON, JANET LINDOW, AND CHI-PANG CHIANG

INTRODUCTION

We are concerned with sex differences in communication in peer-directed instructional groups. Mixed-sex instructional groups not led by the teacher are common throughout elementary school in curriculum areas such as reading and mathematics; however, little is known about the interactional and communicative processes that operate in these groups and how these processes are related to achievement. We are specifically interested in (1) whether there are sex differences in communicative processes

---

* The research reported in this paper was funded by a grant from the National Institute of Education (NIE-G-81-0009) as part of the program of research of the University of Wisconsin, Center for Education Research. The opinions expressed in this chapter do not necessarily reflect the position, policy, or endorsement of the National Institute of Education.

GENDER INFLUENCES
IN CLASSROOM INTERACTION
ISBN: 0-12-752075-9

185

in these groups (e.g., Do males dominate the interaction?), and (2) whether there are sex differences in communication patterns as a function of interactants' gender (i.e., same- vs. cross-sex interaction).

Abundant research on small groups in noneducational settings has documented sex differences in some aspects of interaction. For example, Lockheed and Hall (1976) found that when decision making involved material unfamiliar to all group members, boys exerted more influence in determining the outcome. Lockheed's (in press) meta-analysis of studies that examined mixed-sex groups engaged in collaborative tasks showed that boys dominated the activity. From a developmental perspective, some evidence suggests that with increasing age (between kindergarten and third grade), girls become more active in attempting to influence both male and female members through producing "assertive bids" (Sgan & Pickert, 1980).

Lakoff's (1973) model postulates gender differences in adult females' and males' speech, specifically that women use more polite and indirect forms (e.g., "I'm thirsty." instead of "Get me a drink."). Goodwin's (1981) study of urban black children's directives in a recreational context revealed a pattern consistent with Lakoff's theory only with same-sex partners. For example, during boys' group activities, their directives were more likely to be phrased as imperatives for action to be completed immediately; they reflected asymmetrical status relationships between speaker and target of the directive (e.g., "Give me your hanger Tokay."). On the other hand, girls phrased their directives using "let's" and mitigated forms to propose actions to be carried out in the future; they reflected symmetrical status relationships (e.g., "Hey let's go in there and ask do they have some cases."). Goodwin explained boys' and girls' differential use of aggravated and direct forms in terms of the differential social organization of same-sex play groups. When these children interacted in a mixed-sex group, girls used aggravated and direct forms as often as boys did, especially during argumentation. Although Goodwin studied a sample culturally different from the sample in our study, and the interaction occurred in a nonschool setting, her findings imply the need for further investigation into boys' and girls' same- and cross-sex language in instructional, small-group contexts.

It is difficult to consider sex differences in communication without considering the listener as well as the speaker, since how an individual communicates is influenced by the cocommunicator. Several researchers have found a tendency for sex segregation, that is, greater frequency of interaction between same-sex compared with cross-sex children, in verbal exchanges among school-age children (Grant, see Chapter 4, this volume); Lockheed & Harris, 1984; Wilkinson & Subkoviak, 1981). However, other research suggests that choice of interactional partners during academic activities may be influenced more by proximity than by gender (Goetz,

1981). Classroom structure (e.g., open vs. traditional) has also been shown to influence the frequency of cross-sex interaction (Berk & Lewis, 1977).

A sociolinguistic perspective guided the present research, with a focus on language as it is used naturally by students in classrooms (Wilkinson, 1982). Specifically, we examined two ways in which language is typically used in classrooms: to request and receive information and action and to engage in verbal disagreements. Both of these uses of language are central to the teaching and learning processes that occur in small instructional groups. Request and response sequences allow students to exchange information and to manage group functioning; through dissension episodes, students with conflicting answers are likely to arrive at agreement on a single answer. Previous research has found that requests are common in all elementary school classroom situations. For example, they account for two thirds of teachers' speech to students (e.g., Mehan, 1979); and request–response sequences constitute approximately half of students' interactional exchanges in peer-led small instructional groups (Wilkinson & Calculator, 1982a, 1982b; Wilkinson & Spinelli, 1983).

No previous research has examined in detail sex differences in students' use of requests and responses in peer-directed instructional groups. However, we proposed a model of the effective speaker that characterizes requests and responses by school-age children; this model has received support from data collected on first-, second-, and third-grade students in their groups (Wilkinson & Calculator, 1982a, 1982b; Wilkinson & Spinelli, 1983). We introduced a model of the effective speaker (Wilkinson & Calculator, 1982a) that characterizes requests and responses by students in groups. The model identifies the following characteristics of requests that predict obtaining appropriate responses from listeners in this context. First, speakers express themselves clearly and directly in an attempt to minimize misinterpretations of their requests. For example, speakers may use direct forms and specifically designate them to one particular listener when making a request. Second, in the classroom, requests that are on-task, that is, those that refer to the shared activities in the teaching–learning situation, are most likely to be understood by listeners and thus are most likely to be successful in obtaining compliance from listeners. Third, requests that are understood by listeners as sincere are most likely to result in obtaining appropriate responses. Finally, effective speakers are flexible in producing their requests; for example, speakers revise their initial request when appropriate responses from listeners are not obtained.

Other research has shown that responses to requests, particularly explanations, are positively related to achievement. Several "process–product" studies have shown that providing explanations and, in some cases, receiving explanations is positively related to achievement (Peterson & Janicki,

1979; Peterson, Janicki, & Swing, 1981; Swing & Peterson, 1982; Webb, 1980, 1982a; Webb & Kenderski (see Chapter 10, this volume). In contrast, receiving inadequate responses or no responses to requests for explanations of academic procedures (e.g., receiving the answer to a problem instead of an explanation of how to do the problem) have been shown to be negatively related to achievement (Webb, 1980, 1982b, 1982c; Webb & Cullan, 1983; Webb & Kenderski, 1984).

The second focus of our study is on dissension episodes, verbal conflicts that occur in peer-directed instructional groups. A *dissension episode* is defined as the interaction following a verbal assertion of disagreement about an answer to a problem during small-group seatwork. Verbal conflict or controversy has been postulated as a cognitive process that affects academic performance in learning groups. Johnson and Johnson (1979) hypothesized a process in which incompatible opinions generate conceptual conflict among students, lead the adversaries to seek more information in order to clarify their positions, and consequently result in increased learning. Smith, Johnson, and Johnson (1981) provide supportive evidence for their contention that small-group learning involving controversy facilitates higher achievement than small-group learning involving concurrence-seeking goals.

Piaget (1932) maintained that children's involvement in interpersonal conflicts, such as arguments, enhances their cognitive development. He hypothesized that interpersonal conflicts force children to take another's perspective and thereby contribute to the decline of egocentric thought. Although there is some empirical support for Piaget's notion in the area of conservation acquisition (cf. Botvin & Murray, 1979; Miller & Brownell, 1975), the mechanisms through which interaction leads to the acquisition of conservation skills need further study. Most of the studies that have examined conflict in relation to achievement, conservation acquisition, or some other outcome have focused on the presence of conflicting positions rather than the verbal exchanges through which the conflicting positions are expressed. In the present study, we focus on verbal controversy by examining the initiation and resolution of dissension episodes.

From a sociolinguistic perspective, speech events, such as request and response sequences and dissension episodes that occur within a small group, are influenced by the social characteristics of the group members, such as sex and other members' speech. A speech event initiated by any group member, such as a request or a dissension episode, in turn, influences other group members' speech. Each group, then, creates its own sociolinguistic context so that the observations of an individual group member's speech are dependent on the observations of the other group member's speech. Consequently, we believe it is appropriate to use the group as the unit of analysis, or in some other statistically valid way to recognize the dependencies among observations when using the individual as the unit of analysis (e.g., Wilkinson & Calculator, 1982a, 1982b). Therefore, we analyzed the data in two ways: (1) using the individual as the unit of analysis and addressing the problem of dependencies among observations, and (2) using the group as the unit of analysis.

In this study we analyzed sex differences in communicative processes and sex segregation in choice of interactional partners in peer-led elementary mathematics groups. The research questions were (1) Are there sex differences in communication in mixed-sex instructional groups, specifically in requests and dissension episodes? (2) If there are sex differences in communication, are they associated with same-sex interaction or cross-sex interaction?

METHODS

The data for this study were gathered from 20 videotapes of six peer-directed mathematics work groups (24 students total). The tapes were collected in October 1981 as part of a study on students' requests for information and action and on small-group process behaviors in relation to achievement (Peterson, Wilkinson, Spinelli, & Swing, 1984).

Subjects and Small-Group Composition

The subjects were second- and third-grade students in two mixed-grade math classes. There were four students per group with equal numbers of boys and girls in each group. The school was located in a middle-class, predominantly white neighborhood in a Midwestern university community. All subjects spoke English as their first language.

We formed stratified ability groups within each classroom, that is, one high-ability student, two medium-ability students, and one low-ability student, based on scores from standardized mathematics tests. At the beginning of the study, students completed the following aptitude measures: Mathematics Concept Level C/Form 1 subtest of the SRA Achievement Test (Science Research Associates, 1978); and the Mathematics Computation Level C/Form 1 subtest of the SRA Achievement Test (Science Research Associates, 1978). The sex and ability composition of the 6 groups is described in Table 9.1. At the completion of the 10-day unit on money and time, student achievement was assessed using a 38-item achievement test constructed by the experimenters that was designed to measure comprehension and appli-

Table 9.1

Group Compositional Characteristics Including Gender, Ability Test
Scores, Ability Designation, and Achievement Scores

Group	Gender	Ability level	Ability test score[a]	Achievement[b]
A	Female	High	1.302	.941
	Male	Medium	−0.461	.667
	Female	Medium	−2.106	.440
	Male	Low	−3.337	.000
			$\bar{X} = -1.505$	.512
			$SD = (2.02)$	(0.40)
B	Female	High	0.738	.447
	Male	Medium	−1.738	.553
	Female	Medium	−1.848	.538
	Male	Low	−3.039	.457
			$\bar{X} = -1.4718$	.499
			$SD = (1.59)$	(0.06)
C	Male	High	−0.743	.368
	Male	Medium	−1.056	.579
	Female	Medium	−1.558	.500
	Female	Low	−3.611	.241
			$\bar{X} = -1.742$	.422
			$SD = (1.2904)$	(0.15)
D	Male	High	2.274	.842
	Female	Medium	1.318	.605
	Female	Medium	1.028	.789
	Male	Low	−0.476	.568
			$\bar{X} = 1.0360$	.701
			$SD = (1.14)$	(0.14)
E	Female	High	2.822	.921
	Male	Medium	2.289	.838
	Female	Medium	1.043	.595
	Male	Low	−1.543	.762
			$\bar{X} = 1.1528$	.780
			$SD = (1.95)$	(0.14)
F	Male	High	2.681	.868
	Female	Medium	1.882	.686
	Female	Medium	1.020	.868
	Male	Low	−0.202	.658
			$\bar{X} = 1.3453$	.770
			$SD = (1.24)$	(0.11)

[a] Ability test scores are standard z scores.
[b] Achievement test scores are the proportion of correct answers out of
the total number of problems attempted.

cation of the major concepts taught in the unit. This test was composed of problems taken from daily seatwork assignments and included an approximately equal number of problems from each seatwork lesson. Each student's raw score on the achievement test was computed as well as the percentage of correct answers of the total number of problems attempted by the student.

Recording Small-Group Interaction

Each group was videotaped three or four times over the course of a 2-week unit on time and money. The videotaped segments of small-group work, which averaged 20 minutes per day, followed a period of teacher-led, whole-group instruction that also lasted about 20 minutes. During whole-group instruction, each teacher reviewed the previous day's lesson, presented new material, and gave students a chance to work on practice problems. Before small-group work started each teacher passed out booklets of seatwork problems and went over the instructions for each set of problems; sometimes she had everyone work a few problems together. Teachers instructed the children to ask other group members for help before consulting them; however, students were responsible for turning in their own seatwork assignments. The teachers also instructed the groups to check their answers with each other after everyone had finished three or four problems. During seatwork the teachers monitored the groups to ensure their compliance with these instructions.

Transcription and Coding of Small-Group Interaction

The segments of small-group interaction, from the time that the teacher gave the signal to begin working until the end of math class, were fully transcribed according to conventions established and described by Wilkinson and Calculator (1982a, 1982b). Complete and accurate transcriptions of the language used by each of the students in the videotaped groups were transcribed in print. Subsequent analysis and coding focused on discrete categories of language behavior.

REQUEST–RESPONSE SEQUENCES

Following Wilkinson and Spinelli (1983), a request was coded when a student asked for information from another student. The request could occur as a wh–question, a yes–no question, a tag question, a statement issued as a question by the use of rising pitch, a declarative statement issued with the intention of eliciting information, an imperative, or a nonlexical request in which vocal or gestural displays indicated a request for information. The type of request was coded into one of two categories:

1. Requests for action (i.e., directives) were attempts by speakers to elicit actions from listeners (e.g., "Give me a pencil.").
2. Requests for information (i.e., questions) were attempts by speakers to elicit information from listeners (e.g., "What is the answer to number 7?").

All responses to requests were coded as *appropriate* if the requested action or information was provided or if the individual indicated she or he did not know the answer. *Inappropriate* responses included responses where the listener explicitly refused to comply ("No, I won't tell you"), nonresponses, postponements ("I'll tell you later"), and irrelevant responses ("Doo-de-doo-de doo").

DISSENSION EPISODES

A dissension episode was defined as the interaction following a verbal assertion of disagreement about an answer or step in arriving at an answer to a mathematics problem during the seatwork. Speech events similar to dissension episodes have been described as having a characteristic structure (Eisenberg & Garvey, 1981). The episodic structure was operationalized in the present investigation as follows: The initiation of dissension was preceded by an antecedent position, that is, the assertion of an answer or step in arriving at the answer to a mathematics problem (e.g., "Number 4 is two thirty."). The antecedent position could be verbally expressed, as in the preceding utterance, or nonverbally expressed, as a written answer on somebody's worksheet. The second component, or the dissension move, expressed an opposition to or contradiction of the antecedent position, that is, a verbal display of dissent (e.g., "Un-unh, number 4 is three thirty."). The verbal interaction that followed the dissension move, or resolution move, was related to the dissented issue and reflected the participants' attempts to convince each other of the correctness of their positions. The episode ended when the participants reached consensus or when the interaction shifted to a new topic. Consensus was signaled verbally (e.g., "I guess you're right.") or nonverbally (e.g., changing one's written answer). Similarly, lack of consensus was signaled either verbally (e.g., "You can keep your answer if you want to get it wrong.") or nonverbally (e.g., dissension move ignored; students resumed working independently).

Episodes were coded along the following dimensions:

1. *Initiator:* Person who issued the dissension move.
2. *Participants:* Persons who made at least one verbal move that was related to the dissented issue.
3. *Number of resolution moves:* A resolution move consisted of all utterances during a speaker's turn at talk that addressed the dissented issue and occurred after the dissension move. A resolution move could overlap another's speech or receive no response. Examples include restating one's position, asking for clarification, and providing justification.
4. *Type of demonstration move:* A demonstration move was a specific type of resolution move that provided justification, evidence, or a reason for one's position; it went beyond merely restating one's position or countering another's. Demonstration moves were coded as (1) appeals to authority (e.g., "It's right because the teacher told me."); (2) pointing out evidence on the worksheet (e.g., "Dimes are these."); (3) reading part of the problem aloud ("The party started one-half hour ago."); (4) counting aloud (e.g., "One, two, three, four, five."); or (5) asserting arithmetic procedures/processes (e.g., "But it's takeaway, the third one is.").
5. *Prevailing answer:* An answer proposed by the initiator or other episode participant(s) that was eventually accepted as the correct answer by the participants.

Measures

Several measures were computed for each student and all measures were adjusted to account for the different lengths of time and/or the different opportunities for producing the speech events under investigation. The frequencies of requests for action and information were adjusted for all students to represent frequency of requests per 20 minutes of seatwork. The frequency of each student's dissension moves was adjusted to represent frequency of moves per 20 minutes of task-related verbal interaction. Time in task-related interaction was chosen for this measure rather than time in seatwork because dissension occurred more often during ongoing interaction, whereas request–response sequences occurred at all times during seatwork.

In addition, the proportion of appropriate responses was computed for all requests. These scores were adjusted for individuals' frequencies of requests. For example, the proportion of appropriate responses to requests for action was the percentage of responses to requests for action that were appropriate out of all coded requests for action. The proportions of requests for action and information directed to same- or cross-sex listeners were adjusted for the individual frequencies of designated requests and the number of possible same- or cross-sex listeners within the group. Due to the relatively small speech sample, requests for action and information were combined when computing the proportions of the preceding characteristics (only requests designated to specific students were included) to same and cross-sex listeners. Each measure was adjusted for the proportion of requests addressed to either same- or cross-sex listeners. Finally, the proportions of providing appropriate responses to either same- or cross-sex speakers was computed (adjusted for the frequency of requests received from the respective sex).

The measure of participation in dissension episodes was the proportion of episodes in which individuals participated, adjusted for the number of episodes that occurred in the group. The proportion of demonstration moves was adjusted for the number of resolution moves produced by individuals. The proportion of episodes in which individuals' answers prevailed was adjusted for each individual according to the number of episodes in which that individual participated.

Analyses

Two methods of analysis were used. In the first analysis, individual scores were pooled for all boys and all girls across groups; in the second analysis, boys' and girls' scores were compared within their groups. In the analyses of between-gender differences, the variables of interest were (1) adjusted frequencies of making requests for action and information, and of initiating dissension episodes; and (2) proportions of using direct forms, getting appropriate responses, providing appropriate responses, participating in dissension episodes, providing demonstrations, and having the prevailing answers when consensus was reached. In the analyses of same- versus cross-sex interaction, the variables of interest were the proportions of making requests for action and information, using direct forms, and getting and providing appropriate responses.

Given the necessary restrictions on group composition, the small number of groups used in these analyses led to limited power to detect significant differences. Therefore each comparison was tested individually at the .05 alpha level; we recognize the increased likelihood of committing a Type I error with this individual rather than experimentwise alpha level.

In the individual analysis, the differences between boys' and girls' (pooling all the boys' and girls' scores across groups) were examined using the Kruskal–Wallis Test, whereas the differences between same- and cross-sex interaction variables were examined with the Wilcoxon Matched-Pair Test. Because the observations within the same group were dependent, these analyses yielded questionable results. One solution to this problem was to select a statistic that measures an effect of interest and to jackknife that statistic by groups (Mosteller & Tukey, 1977). Jackknifing is a method for assessing the degree to which an effect estimated from the data for all subjects persists when a group of subjects is deleted from the analysis. The jackknifing procedure was used when the initial test was significant at .05. The .05 alpha was also used to determine significance with the jackknifing analysis.

The second analysis based on groups used the Wilcoxon Matched-Pair Test. To test for sex differences in request–response sequences and dissension episodes, averages of the measures computed for boys were paired with those of the girls in each group. The differences between the pairs were then tested across all six groups. To test for differences in request–response sequences to the same or opposite sex, the averaged proportions to the same sex were paired with the averaged proportions to the opposite sex within the group for both boys and girls. The differences between the pairs were then tested across the six groups. Given the small number of groups, only those differences having the same direction in all six groups were statistically significant.

QUANTITATIVE RESULTS

The data base contained 959 requests: 403 requests for action and 556 requests for information. A total of 756 requests were directed to a specific listener. The ranges of individual frequencies of making requests were from 2 to 57 for requests for action and from 5 to 77 for requests for information. A total of 92 dissension episodes occurred within the six groups; the range of group frequencies was from 10 to 21.

The results were separated into two subsets: differences between boys and girls, and differences between same- and cross-sex interaction. The two types of analyses (individual jackknifing by groups and group analysis) yielded consistent results.

Differences between Boys and Girls

There was a statistically significant sex difference in the frequency of one's answer prevailing, with boys' answers prevailing more often than girls' as can be seen in Figure 9.1: for the individual analysis, $\chi^2(1) = 4.952, p \leq$

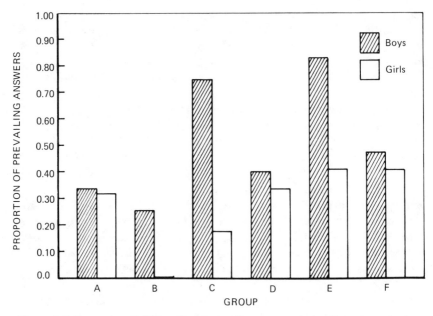

Figure 9.1. Proportion of girls' and boys' prevailing answers during dissension episodes.

.05; for the jackknife analysis, $t(5) = 3.707, p \leq .05$; for the group analysis, $T_{(+)} = 21, p \leq .05$.

No significant differences between boys and girls were found in the adjusted frequencies of producing requests for action and information across the groups, the frequency of initiating dissension episodes, the average proportion of receiving and providing appropriate responses, and the proportion of dissension episodes in which students participated.

Differences between Same- and Cross-Sex Interaction

The data show that boys made many more requests for both action and information to boys than to girls: for the individual request for action analysis, $z = -2.353, p < .05$; for the jackknife analysis, $t(5) = -7.279, p \leq .05$; for the group analysis, $T_{(+)} = 21, p \leq .05$; for the individual request for information analysis, $z = -2.312, p \leq .05$; for the jackknife analysis, $t(5) = -7.652, p \leq .05$; for the group analysis, $T_{(+)} = 21, p \leq .05$. Figure 9.2 and Figure 9.3 represent the boys' averaged proportions of same- and cross-sex interactions for each group. With respect to direct form and providing appropriate responses, however, boys did not differentiate between the

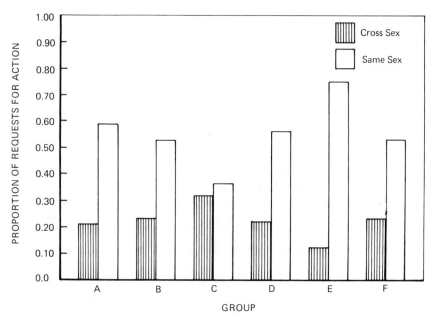

Figure 9.2. Boy's proportions of requests for action to same- and cross-sex listeners.

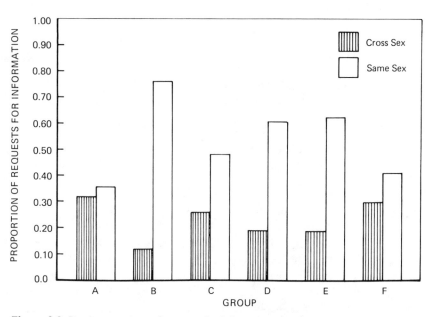

Figure 9.3. Boys' proportions of requests for information to same- and cross-sex listeners.

same and opposite sex. They received neither more nor fewer appropriate responses from either sex.

There were no significant differences in girls' and boys' production of requests for action and information or in their providing and receiving appropriate responses.

QUALITATIVE RESULTS AND DISCUSSION

There are several interpretations for the finding that boys' answers prevailed more often than girls'. One possibility is that boys' answers prevailed because their higher status allowed them greater influence over the outcome of dissension. However, it is apparent from close scrutiny of the data that the prevailing answer was correct in 61 of the 66 episodes in which consensus was reached. As Examples 1 and 2 illustrate, consensus was reached in more than one way and not through boys' exerting higher status.

Example 1 (Group A, Jamie and Amy are working the same problem aloud)
1. Jamie: (counting aloud while working addition problem)
2.   Zero, one, eight nine ten eleven, twelve.
3. Amy: Twelve?
4. Jamie: Yup, two down, and one up here, it's
5.   two.
6. Amy: Ne-unh.
7. Jamie: Yes, one up here, two.
8. Amy: Oh.
9. Jamie: Eh kay, two dollars, 'n twenty-one cents.

Example 2 (Group B, Ryan and Andrea are working independently)
1. Ryan: Andrea you're wrong.
2. Andrea: What, (in a challenging voice)
3. Ryan: Um, turn back, that's wrong.
4.   it's twelve-thirty.
5. Andrea: (erases her former answer)

Examples 1 and 2 both involved one boy and one girl. In the first example Amy initiated the episode (lines 3 and 6), whereas a boy initiated the episode in Example 2 (line 1). The boys' correct answers prevailed in both episodes although the interaction that led to consensus was different. Specifically, in the first example Amy signaled her acceptance of Jamie's position (line 8) after first questioning (line 3) and then denying (line 6) Jamie's proposed answer. Jamie's repeated demonstrations (lines 4–5 and 7) may have facilitated mutual agreement about the answer. On the other hand, Andrea accepted the answer that Ryan proposed in line 4 immediately, without asking for or receiving justification for Ryan's answer. This example suggests that in some instances a status characteristic may have influenced acceptance of the correct (thus prevailing) answer.

Another interpretation that would account for the sex differences in the correct-prevailing answers is boys' superiority in math. Although it is generally acknowledged that girls are superior in reading and boys are superior in math (Aiken, 1973; Gates, 1961), the ability test scores of the students in the present study revealed no significant differences between the girls and boys in these two classes; in fact, the girls' average was slightly higher than the boys' ($\bar{X} = 0.169$ and $\bar{X} = -0.449$, respectively). It is doubtful that boys had more extant knowledge about time and money because there was essentially no difference in boys' and girls' average scores on the test items that concerned initial ability for knowledge of time and money. There was a similar lack of significant difference between girls' and boys' mean achievement scores that were adjusted for initial level of students' ability ($\bar{X} = 0.6309$ and $\bar{X} = 0.5967$, respectively).

Given the similarity between girls' and boys' ability and achievement scores, it is difficult to determine whether the outcome of dissension (i.e., consensus on the correct answer) was any more beneficial to the girls than working alone would have been. In other words, would girls eventually have arrived at the correct answers without having engaged in dissension episodes? This question cannot be answered by any statistical analysis of the data collected in the present study. However, observation of several dissension episodes provides some anecdotal information on the interpersonal dynamics that may have accompanied the resolution of dissension. Examples 3 and 4 suggest that some dissension episodes may have served a primarily social function.

Example 3 (Group B, Ryan, Kirsten, and Michael)
1. Ryan: (to Kirsten) Do you need some help?
2. Kirsten: That one's wrong (pointing to Ryan's paper).
3. Ryan: No it isn't.
4. Kirsten: Yes it is.
5. Ryan: This is four thirty (goes to side of Kirsten's desk).
6. You're nuts.
7. Kirsten: No I'm not.
8. Ryan: Yes you are, see, it's not on the five, 's still on the—it doesn't matter.
9. Michael: See, ya have to in between, this one's first before five,

10.   I think you learned that last year if you were in Mrs., if you were in Mrs. um.

11. Ryan: Bertha Petrovsky's.

12. Kirsten: (inaudible).

13. Michael: You were? Did you learn that?

14.   Kirsten: I had to.

15. Michael: So you should remember.

             (During the next five turns, Michael asks Ryan a question that he answers); then Kirsten initiates the same topic in Example 4.

Example 4 (Group B, Kirsten, Ryan, and Michael)

1. Kirsten: Ryan it's not thirty (to Ryan, who is returning from
2.   helping Michael), it's four thirty-five (said softly while
3.   looking at camera), it's four thirty-five Ryan.
4. Ryan: No it isn't.
5. Kirsten: Yes it is (nodding head "yes").
6. Michael: Where? (sarcastically).
7. Ryan: It's look, it's not five after.
8. Kirsten: Five, ten, fifteen, twenty, twenty-five, thirty (pointing on her paper while counting).
9. Michael: It is not thirty-five, the six is thirty you're dumb.
10. Ryan: (points to Kirsten's paper) Five ten, fifteen twenty,
11.   twenty-five thirty, you're dumb (returns to own desk).
12. Michael: Stupid, girlie.
13. Michael: Are you all finished? Is everybody finished?
14. Andrea: Yes.
15. Kirsten: (to Ryan) It's thirty-five.
16. Ryan: It is not.
17. Michael: No it isn't you did it wrong.
18. Ryan: C'mon, let's go ask. (Ryan leaves group to find teacher)
19. Michael: I know, we a'ready know (stands up at desk). What? (to Ryan, who turns around to look for teacher in other direction).
20. Kirsten: Is this thir- four thirty-five? (to teacher).
21. Ryan: That's four thirty.
22. Kirsten: This one right there (points out problem to teacher).
23. Ryan: Four thirty.
24. Teacher: No it's four thirty, cuz lookit, five ten, fifteen twenty,
25.   twenty-five thirty. (to Ryan) You could have explained it to her that way, by counting.
26. Ryan: We I-, did I showed her like that but she.
27. Michael: She said it was still.

28. Teacher: Well now she knows (teacher leaves group).
29. Michael: (turning toward Kirsten) See.
30. Ryan: Ok, let's check em.
31. Michael: You're dumb (to Kirsten).

There are several notable features of these two sequential episodes. In Example 3, Kirsten initiated the dissension episode (line 2) in response to Ryan's offer to help her. Kirsten asserted that Ryan's answer was wrong; however, she did not provide an alternative answer or give a reason why his was wrong. Ryan defended his answer by providing justification (line 8) after participating in two assertion–denial exchanges (lines 3–5; lines 6–8), the latter of which was an insult ("you're nuts"). Michael supported Ryan's position (line 9) by offering another justification for the answer four-thirty. The topic then shifted to whether Kirsten had prior experience with telling time in the previous year's math class (lines 10–14). Once it was established that she indeed had prior exposure to similar problems, Kirsten became the recipient of a "scolding" (line 15).

In Example 4, after a question–answer interchange between Ryan and Michael, Kirsten reinitiated dissension about the same problem by asserting that the answer was four thirty-five instead of four-thirty. Although Kirsten designated Ryan as the listener (line 3), Michael became an early third participant in the interaction (line 6). Kirsten attempted to defend the answer four thirty-five by providing a counting demonstration (line 8); however, she stopped counting at "thirty" instead of "thirty-five." Both Ryan and Michael denied Kirsten's proposed answer (lines 7 and 9); Michael insulted Kirsten's intelligence as well (lines 9 and 12). Ryan also demonstrated by counting (lines 10–11) in the same way that Kirsten had; he repeated Michael's earlier insult ("you're dumb"). Kirsten remained unconvinced and reasserted her position (line 15) despite having received several insults. Rather than engage in another round of demonstrations and insults, Ryan sought the teacher's counsel (line 18). Ironically, the teacher settled the dispute with the same counting demonstration that both Kirsten and Ryan had provided to defend their answers. The episode ended with one last insult (line 31).

Within these two episodes, Ryan and Michael provided six demonstration moves compared with Kirsten's one. The two boys also insulted Kirsten five times. The teacher intervened to confirm the correct answer, and Ryan's and Michael's answers prevailed. Several interpretations of the interaction are suggested. Lack of understanding in the first episode may have been due to the ineffectiveness of the demonstrations; that is, Ryan and Michael defended the answer "four thirty" instead of helping Kirsten to see her error (although she had not informed them of her answer). The demonstration moves in the second episode, however, were more specific refutations of Kirsten's proposed answer. At the episode's termination, Kirsten may or may not have understood why the answer was four-thirty even though she accepted it as the answer. Perhaps because of the teacher's authority, Kirsten did not persist in defending her position as she had with Ryan; or perhaps she felt too "dumb" to admit to the teacher that she still did not understand. Given that Kirsten's demonstration move actually supported the opponent's answer, another possibility is that the interaction was not necessarily maintained to resolve dissension between two discrepant answers, but rather the interaction may have reflected Kirsten's social goals, that is, to engage in cross-sex social interaction.

Another example of a dissension episode that may have served as a vehicle for cross-sex social interaction occurred between one girl and two boys in Group C. This episode was over 30 moves in length. It involved Erica, who insisted that her answer was correct, and Chuck and Steven, who advocated a different and correct answer. Similar to the previous example, Chuck and Steven provided a series of demonstration moves that failed to convince Erica that her answer was wrong. Unlike the insulting atmosphere that accompanied dissension in the previous example, all three students in this group seemed to enjoy the dissension, evidenced by frequent giggling, touching, and joking (at one point in the episode Chuck remarked while laughing, "Our table's drunk"). The teacher also intervened in this episode to show Erica that her position was wrong, again using the demonstration move that Steven and Chuck had provided earlier. Although both of these triadic interchanges were initiated by a girl and depicted a two-against-one situation, it seems that the social goal was a mutually shared feature of the interaction in the latter episode.

The data do not show any evidence of sex segregation in dissension episodes. We examined the sex composition of the 92 episodes, that is, the number of boys and girls involved in each. Of the 38 dyadic episodes, 9 involved both boys, 2 involved both girls, and 27 involved one boy and one girl. Of the 59 three- or four-person episodes 10 involved two girls and one boy, 24 involved two boys and one girl, and 20 involved two girls and two boys, that is, the whole group. In other words, only 12% of the episodes involved students of the same sex.

Contrary to this apparent absence of sex segregation in participation in dissension episodes, the data show that boys made more requests for action and information to other boys than to girls, whereas girls made equal numbers of requests to boys and girls. This finding only partially supports previous evidence of sex segregation in communication, but it provides support for Charlesworth and Hartup's (1967) finding of greater exclusivity in boys than in girls, that is, boys direct more of their interactions to boys, whereas girls direct their interactions equally to boys and girls. Boys' preference for same-sex interaction may result in the patterns of sex segregation we see in school-age children. Boys may prefer to interact with other boys because they believe them to be more competent and/or more likely to provide the action–information requested.

Both of the following examples (5 and 6) from Group E illustrate Bobby's preference to request help from the other boy in the group, even though his initial request was unsuccessful.

Example 5 (Group E, Bobby, Gerry, Heidi)
1. Bobby: (looking at Gerry) What's the last one?
2. Gerry: I'm not on your same page (Gerry turns toward Heidi and looks over her shoulder as she works problem).
3. Bobby: Well turn it to the, to the other page
4.   well then turn it to the other page (Gerry writes something on his paper).
5.   Please? (Gerry starts reading problem to himself)
6. Bobby: No, this page. No this page (to Gerry; who ignores him).
7.   (Heidi reaches across in front of Gerry and turns his workbook back to the previous page; as Heidi does this Gerry utters: "Oh well.")
8. Gerry: Three fifteen. Easy enough (to Bobby).
9. Bobby: Three. Fifteen (writing).

Example 6 (Group E, Bobby, Gerry, Heidi)
(Bobby is still working on worksheet; Gerry and Heidi have finished and are making up problems for each other to work)
1. Bobby: I don't get it. I don't get this. I don't get this
2.   Gerry I don't get this.
3. Heidi: (stands up at desk to see Bobby's page) What?
4. Bobby: I don't get this (Heidi gets out of desk and goes to Bobby's desk to help him)
(Heidi explains problem to Bobby)

Example 5 illustrates Bobby's refusal to take "no" for an answer. Following his initial request for information, Gerry gave a reason for his noncompliance (line 2). Bobby's second attempt, a directive to "turn it to the other page," was ignored. Bobby's third mitigated request ("please?"), was also futile. He persisted (line 6) by clarifying the page on which he wanted help. Bobby may have persisted longer in his bids for help from Gerry had Heidi not intervened (line 7). Rather than helping Bobby herself, Heidi facilitated Gerry's helping him by turning Gerry's page. Example 6 occurred a few minutes after Example 5. Although Bobby's requests for help were more indirect this time (line 1), he again designated Gerry as the recipient (line 2). Heidi responded, however, by first asking for clarification and then helping him.

Both instances illustrate Bobby's failure to get the requested help from Gerry and his success at getting help through Heidi's unsolicited intervention. In addition to illustrating sex segregation in the designated recipient of the request, these two examples suggest that girls may be more tuned-in to other students' needs for help. This explanation may also account for the similar findings of Webb and Kenderski (see Chapter 10, this volume).

CONCLUSION

We examined various aspects of sex differences in communication in peer-instructional groups. The results of this study suggest that boys and girls may differ in their small groups. Specifically, boys' answers prevailed more often than girls' in dissension episodes, and in request–response sequences boys and girls differed in their choice of interactional partners. We also suggested that social and personality differences may have caused these observed differences. Although there were no differences in the girls' and boys' achievement in this study, the differences in their interactional experiences may influence later differential achievement patterns. For example, Kirsten's self-esteem and interest in math may suffer as a result of repeated insults to her competence and intelligence.

We found that the sociolinguistic perspective is useful for studying sex differences in communication in the classroom. Information about both instructional and social goals can be gleaned from studying peer groups as they naturally occur in classrooms. Sampling particular speech events reflects children's interactional experiences in these groups and thus allows description of differences as they occur in context. It is important to address the methodological problem of violating the assumption of statistical independence of observations when analyzing students' behavior in groups or dyads. We demonstrated two acceptable approaches here: (1) using the group as the unit of analysis, and (2) jackknifing by groups. Both quantitative and qualitative analyses are useful in understanding the differences that exist between the sexes and their communicative processes. The theoretical and practical implications of these results follow.

The issue of equity in the classroom is an enduring concern to educational practitioners. Documenting patterns of inequity that exist, such as those found through this research, is a first step in understanding classroom life as it occurs for both boys and girls. Gender alone should not be the primary determinant of who interacts with whom, the kind of information that is exchanged, and the interactional experiences that are available to boys and girls. Girls should have as many opportunities as boys to respond to questions, to provide explanations, and to get the right answers.

Teachers need to become involved in effecting cross-sex interaction by deliberately structuring situations that enhance the likelihood of achieving goals of sex equity. Teachers might also consider using same-sex small work groups, if there is indeed a tendency for girls to prolong dissension episodes in order to engage in cross-sex social interaction. In addition, girls who work in same-sex groups would have more opportunities to demonstrate their competence without risking insults. Further research is needed to clarify the differences in boys' and girls' academic performance during the seatwork activity. Teachers might also encourage the expression of controversy and dissension when it is appropriate in the service of promoting and stimulating cognitive growth. Several techniques are available to teachers that might provide individuals flexibility in experiencing a variety of roles, such as taking on the role of both teacher and student in peer-tutoring exchanges. They might also teach students to be aware of their communicative processes (both positive and negative) through the use of stimulated recall techniques (Peterson et al., 1984).

Ultimately, sex equity in the classroom can be enhanced if there is equity in the communicative and interactional processes that operate in classrooms. The self-assignment of boys and girls to one specific role during communicative interaction limits all children in that classroom, because it does not give individuals a chance to learn different roles. By varying their use of language, children can develop their ability to be flexible and to respond to the situational demands as they occur. Our hope is that teachers will be sensitive to the processes that create and sustain inequities in classrooms, and that they will intervene in order to increase the likelihood of interactional equity.

ACKNOWLEDGMENTS

We express our appreciation to Penelope Peterson, coprincipal investigator on this research project. The data reported in this chapter are a reanalysis of data collected by Peterson, Wilkinson, Spinelli, and Swing (1984). We thank Linda Milosky, Fran Spinelli, Susan Swing, Kevin Stark, and Greg Waas for their assistance with data collection; Alex Cherry Wilkinson, Joel Levin, and Ron Serlin for statistical consulting; Donna Eder, Cora Marrett, and Alex Cherry Wilkinson for constructive comments on an earlier version of this chapter; and Crescent Kringle for typing this manuscript. We also thank the teachers in the study, Sue Bohlman and Lois Narges; the principal, Joanne Yatvin; and the students for their cooperation in this research.

REFERENCES

Aiken, L. R., Jr. (1973). Ability and creativity in math. *Review of Educational Research, 43,* 405–432.

Berk, L. E., & Lewis, N. C. (1977). Sex role and social behavior in four school environments. *Elementary School Journal, 3,* 205–217.

Botvin, G. J., & Murray, F. B. (1975). The efficacy of peer modeling and social conflict in the acquisition of conservation. *Child Development, 46,* 796–799.

Charlesworth, R., & Hartup, W. W. (1967). Positive social reinforcement in the nursery school peer group. *Child Development, 38,* 993–1002.

Gates, A. (1961). Sex differences in reading ability. *Elementary School Journal, 61,* 431–434.

Goetz, J. P. (1981). Children's sex role knowledge and behavior: An ethnographic study of first graders in the rural south. *Theory and Research in Social Education, 8*(4), 31–54.

Goodwin, M. H. (1981). Directive-response speech sequences in girls' and boys' task activities. In S. McConnell-Ginet, R. Barker, & N. Furman (Eds.), *Women and language in literature and society.* New York: Praeger.

Eisenberg, A., & Garvey, C. (1981). Children's use of verbal strategies in resolving conflicts. *Discourse Processes, 4,* 149–170.

Johnson, D. W., & Johnson, R. T. (1979). Conflict in the classroom: Controversy and learning. *Review of Educational Research, 49,* 51–70.

Lakoff, R. (1973). Language and woman's place. *Language in Society, 2,* 45–79.

Lockheed, M. E. (in press). Sex and social influence: A meta-analysis guided by theory. In J. Berger & M. Zelditch (Eds.), *Status, rewards and influence.* San Francisco: Jossey-Bass.

Lockheed, M. E., & Hall, K. P. (1976). Conceptualizing sex as a status characteristic: Applications to leadership training strategies. *Journal of Social Issues, 32,* 111–124.

Lockheed, M. E., & Harris, A. M. (1984). Cross-sex collaborative learning in elementary school classrooms. *American Educational Research Journal, 21*(2), 275–294.

Mehan, H. (1979). *Learning lessons.* Cambridge, MA: Harvard University Press.

Miller, S. A., & Brownell, C. A. (1975). Peers, persuasion, and Piaget: Dyadic interaction between conservers and nonconservers. *Child Development, 46,* 992–997.

Mosteller, F., & Tukey, J. (1977). *Data analysis and regression.* Reading, MA: Addison Wesley.

Peterson, P., & Janicki, T. (1979). Individual characteristics and children's learning in large-group and small-group approaches. *Journal of Educational Psychology, 71,* 677–687.

Peterson, P. L., Janicki, T. C., & Swing, S. R. (1981). Ability × Treatment interaction effects on children's learning in large-group and small-group approaches. *American Educational Research Journal, 18,* 453–473.

Peterson, P. L., Wilkinson, L. C., Spinelli, F., & Swing, S. (1984). Merging the process-product and sociolinguistic paradigms: Research on small-group processes. In P. L. Peterson, L. C. Wilkinson, & M. Hallinan (Eds.), *The social context of instruction: Group organization and group processes.* New York: Academic Press.

Piaget, J. (1932). *The language and thought of the child* (2nd ed.). London: Routledge & Kegan Paul.

Science Research Associates (1978). *SRA achievement series level C/Form 1.* Chicago: Science Research Associates.

Sgan, M. L., & Pickert, S. M. (1980). Cross-sex and same-sex assertive bids in a cooperative group task. *Child Development, 51,* 928–931.

Smith, K., Johnson, D. W., & Johnson, R. T. (1981). Can conflict be constructive? Controversy versus concurrence-seeking in learning groups. *Journal of Educational Psychology, 73,* 651–663.

Swing, S., & Peterson, P. (1982). The relationship of student ability and small-group interaction to student achievement. *American Educational Research Journal, 19,* 259–274.

Webb, N. M. (1980). A process–outcome analysis of learning in group and individual settings. *Educational Psychologist, 15,* 69–83.

Webb, N. M. (1982a). Student interaction and learning in small groups. *Review of Educational Research, 52,* 421–445.

Webb, N. M. (1982b). Group composition, group interaction and achievement in cooperative small groups. *Journal of Educational Psychology, 74,* 475–484.

Webb, N. M. (1982c). Peer interaction and learning in small cooperative small groups. *Journal of Educational Psychology, 74,* 642–655.

Webb, N. M., & Cullan, L. K. (1983). Group interaction and achievement in small groups: Stability over time. *American Educational Research Journal, 20,* 411–424.

Webb, N. M., & Kenderski, C. M. (1984). Student interaction and learning in small group and whole class settings. In P. L. Peterson, L. C. Wilkinson, & M. Hallinan (Eds.), *The social context of learning: Group organization and group processes.* New York: Academic Press.

Wilkinson, L. C. (Ed.). (1982). A sociolinguistic approach to communicating in the classroom. In *Communicating in the classroom.* New York: Academic Press.

Wilkinson, L. C., & Calculator, S. (1982a). Effective speakers: Students' use of language to request and obtain information and action in the classroom. In L. C. Wilkinson (Ed.), *Communicating in the classroom.* New York: Academic Press.

Wilkinson, L. C., & Calculator, S. (1982b). Requests and responses in peer-directed reading groups. *American Educational Research Journal, 19,* 107–122.

Wilkinson, L. C., & Spinelli, F. (1983). Using requests effectively in peer-directed instructional groups. *American Educational Research Journal, 20,* 479–501.

Wilkinson, L. C., & Subkoviak, M. (1981, December). *Sex differences in classroom communication.* Paper presented at the International Interdisciplinary Congress on Women, Haifa, Israel.

Gender Differences in Small-Group Interaction and Achievement in High- and Low-Achieving Classes*

NOREEN M. WEBB AND CATHY M. KENDERSKI

INTRODUCTION

Although there is an abundance of literature on cooperative learning settings in the classroom, in which female and male students work together in small groups, little is known about the dynamics of interaction among females and males in such groups. Most of the research on interaction in mixed-gender groups has been conducted outside the classroom using non-

* The research reported here was supported in part by grants from the National Institute of Education (NIE-G-80-0068) and the Spencer Foundation (seed grant through the University of California). We are grateful to the teachers involved in this program of research, Beverly French, Marian Graves, Audrey Kopp, and Yasuko Morihara. We also thank Phyllis Blumenfeld for her comments and suggestions.

209

academic tasks (games, puzzles, nonacademic discussion, machine fixing, jury deliberations, and spatial-judgment decisions). In much of this work, the male has been shown to dominate group activity (e.g., Borgatta & Stimson, 1963; Heilbrun, 1968; Lockheed, in press; Strodtbeck & Mann, 1956; Strodtbeck, James, & Hawkins, 1957).

Two studies have shown, however, that gender interacts with other variables in its effects on group dynamics. Lockheed and Hall (1976) found that male high school students tended to dominate group activity only when group members had no previous experience with the material discussed in the groups; when students had previous experience with the material, female and male students were equally active. Further, Lockheed (1977) reported that gender interacted with cognitive style: Adolescent females and males were equally active in field-independent groups, but males were more active than females in field-dependent groups. However, the studies on gender differences in interaction took place outside the school setting or used nonacademic tasks and, consequently, may not generalize to the regular classroom setting.

In this chapter we investigate gender differences in small-group interaction and achievement in two studies of small-group work in regular classroom settings. The first study focuses on above-average mathematics classes in which students were predominantly white and from middle- to upper-middle class neighborhoods; the second study focuses on low-achieving mathematics classes in which students were predominantly minority (black and Hispanic) and from lower SES neighborhoods.[1] Except for the student population differences (achievement level, ethnic background, and socioeconomic status) and the math topic being taught, the setting and procedures of the two studies were identical. The two studies took place in the same school at nearly the same grade level (eighth grade vs. ninth grade), lasted for 2 to 3 weeks each, and used the same procedures for small-group work.

Although the setting and procedures in the two studies were the same, there were differences between the achievement of female and male students. In the high-achieving classes males outperformed females, but in the low-achieving classes males and females showed equal achievement. Gender differences in small-group interaction that may help explain the gender differences in achievement in one study and the lack of gender differences in the other study were explored.

This chapter focuses on verbal behavior that has been shown in previous research to be beneficial or detrimental to achievement: giving and receiving adequate help versus giving and receiving inadequate help. Many studies of learning in cooperative group settings examined help giving without distinguishing between different kinds of help, with mixed results. Some studies reported results consistent with a positive relationship between achievement and giving and receiving help (Johnson, 1979; DeVries & Mescon, 1975; DeVries, Mescon, & Shackman, 1975; Edwards & DeVries, 1975), while others reported no relationship (Hanelin, 1978; Slavin, 1978a, 1978b).

Not surprisingly, when different kinds of help were distinguished in later studies, the inconsistencies among the earlier studies started to resolve. A series of studies distinguishing between explanations (step-by-step descriptions of how to solve problems or detailed accounts of how to correct errors) and terminal responses to questions (help that did not include detailed descriptions, i.e., giving the correct answer to a problem without explaining how to obtain it) showed that the relationship between achievement and help was different for explanations than for terminal responses (Webb, 1980a, 1980b, 1982a, 1982b, 1982c, 1983; Webb & Cullian, 1983; Webb & Kenderski, 1984). Giving explanations was positively related to achievement, whereas giving terminal responses was not. Receiving explanations was generally positively related to achievement, whereas receiving terminal responses and receiving no responses were negatively related to achievement.

Distinguishing between explanations and other kinds of help finds support in research conducted by Peterson, Wilkinson, and colleagues and also helps to resolve some inconsistencies in that research. Swing and Peterson's (1982) conceptual-sequencing explanations correspond to explanations defined in this chapter, and their directions correspond to terminal responses. Giving and receiving explanations were positively related to achievement in the Swing–Peterson study, whereas giving and receiving terminal responses were uncorrelated or negatively correlated with achievement. And the lack of a significant relationship between receiving help and achievement in two of Peterson's studies (Peterson & Janicki, 1979; Peterson, Janicki, & Swing, 1981) may be explained by their "help" being a combination of explanations, answers, and procedural information.

It is important to note the similarity between the approach to coding responses to questions used in this chapter and that used by Wilkinson, Lindow, and Chiang, (see Chapter 10 this volume). Wilkinson et al. differentiate appropriate responses from inappropriate responses. Responses were considered appropriate if they included the information or action being requested. Inappropriate responses included any responses not providing the requested information as well as nonresponses. In this chapter, requests for explanations are coded separately from requests for procedural information and appropriate and inappropriate responses are coded for each. For requests for explanations, appropriate responses include explanations and inappropriate responses include terminal responses or no response. For requests for information, appropriate responses consist of the information requested and inappropriate responses consist of nonhelpful responses or no response.

Because the adequacy of the responses to questions seems so important for learning in small-group settings, this chapter presents data on gender differences in help giving and receiving (1) to help clarify the experiences that girls and boys had in the two studies reported here and (2) to shed light on the gender differences in achievement that appeared in the first study but not in the second study. The primary focus of this chapter is on the success of females and males in receiving adequate help. Not only are the interaction data presented for females and males, they are also presented for same-sex and cross-sex interaction to determine whether the experiences of students who asked students of their own gender for help differed from those who asked students of the opposite gender.

METHOD

Sample

Sixty-eight eighth-grade students in two above-average mathematics classes[2] and 57 ninth-grade students in two below-average mathematics classes participated in group work. In the high-achieving classes, there were 33 females and 35 males. In the low-achieving classes there were 29 females and 28 males, and approximately 75% of the students were minority (black or Hispanic) and 25% were white. One teacher taught both high-achieving classes; another teacher taught both low-achieving classes.

Measures

ABILITY AND ACHIEVEMENT

At the beginning of the school year, all students were administered an ability test. The high-achieving classes took a 40-item test of mathematical reasoning ability and the low-ability classes took the Comprehensive Test of Basic Skills (CTBS). The CTBS scores available for this study were percentile scores for the total test. At the end of group work, an achievement test was administered to all students. The test was similar in content and form to the problems that students had solved during group work. The test in the high-achieving classes covered exponents and scientific notation (internal consistency alpha reliability = .88). The test in the low-achieving classes measured students' ability to complete income tax forms from income tax tables and information about earnings, expenses, and deductions (internal consistency alpha = .79).

VERBAL INTERACTION

Data on verbal interaction among group members came from transcripts of audiotapes of group work. *Requests for explanations* included "how" questions and questions asking for extended descriptions of solutions to problems, for example, "How do you do number 14?" *Requests for information* included all questions about the correct answer to an exercise and procedures that did not pertain directly to determining the correct answer: "What did you get for number 16?," "What number are you on?," and "What page are we supposed to be working on?" *Explanations* included step-by-step or extended descriptions of the solution process:

Question: How do you do it?
Response: Look for 150 and 175. Then you go over here (points) and you're gonna say, um, $23. Then you go over here (points).
Question: How did you get ten to the second for $10^5/10^4 \times 10$?
Response: You substract one, and you multiply it [ten] by [ten to the] one, and you get ten to the second.

Information included the answer or other procedural information that was requested: "I got 95.1392 for that one," "I'm on number 4," and "The problems begin on the middle of page 17." *Receiving no explanation* in response to a request for one included receiving only a terminal response ("You guys know how to do these?" "No" and "Wait, how do you do number 20?" "It's 10 to the minus 7.") or no response. *Receiving no information* included receiving a noninformational response ("I'm busy, ask someone else.") or no response. Information was coded according to whether it was correct or incorrect; a response was coded as information or an explanation only if it was correct.

Reliability of the coding of the interaction categories from the audiotapes was assessed by two generalizability studies with two coders working on the same random sample of transcripts (for extensive discussion of generalizability theory and procedures, see Cronbach, Gleser, Nanda, & Rajaratnam, 1972). The estimated generalizability coefficients for one coder ranged from .82 to .97 for the above categories.

Procedure

Before the start of each study, students were assigned randomly to small groups with the constraints that all groups had equal mean ability, female and male students, and minority and white students. Most groups had four students; some had three. Students worked in small groups throughout each study. They were instructed to work together and not to divide the work; to help those having difficulty; and to ask for help when they needed it. The teacher began each class period with a short lecture on the material of the day and occasionally interrupted the class during group work to go over some aspect of the material if it appeared that all groups were having difficulty.

All groups were tape-recorded at least once during the unit for at least 15 minutes. Using clip-on microphones and a hand-held stereo tape recorder, it was possible to record all group conversation and to identify the speaker of each utterance. Group members' microphones were connected to one channel of the tape recorder and the observer's microphone was connected to the other channel. The observer identified each speaker by number and made comments about group interaction (e.g., describing the activity in the group when students were using nonverbal means to communicate, such as pointing, and to clarify who was helping whom when several group members were speaking simultaneously). The frequencies of interaction categories presented in this chapter have been adjusted to represent the frequency per 45-minute class period.

At the end of the unit, all students completed the achievement test. Students worked on the test individually.

Analysis of Gender Differences

Because an individual's experience in the group is not independent of the behavior of other group members, it was necessary to take into account the dependence among group members in analyses of gender differences in interaction. Similarly, because students learned in small groups, group members' learning was not independent. Hence it was necessary to take into account the dependence among group members in analysis of gender differences in achievement as well as in interaction. To take into account the indentifiable subgroups in the designs of the two studies, differences in interaction and achievement between females and males were tested using hierarchical analysis of variance with small groups nested within gender (see Myers, 1979). This analysis had the effect of treating the students of the same gender in a group as a subgroup. The error term for the gender effect in the statistical analyses was the variation among subgroups nested within gender rather than the variation among individual students.

An alternative solution to the problem of dependence among students in a group (used by Wilkinson et al., see Chapter 9, this volume) is to use subgroups as the unit of analysis and ignore variation among students in the statistical analyses. We did not choose this solution because the substantive issue underlying these studies is the relationship between interaction in the group and individual achievement. That is, does receiving adequate responses to questions help the student learn? The question of interest concerns the impact of an individual's experience on his or her learning, not the impact of the group mean experience on group achievement. By using hierarchical analysis of variance, it was possible to take into account the dependence among students within intact groups while preserving information about the variation among students within those groups.

RESULTS

High-Achieving Classes

INTERACTION AND ACHIEVEMENT

Table 10.1 presents the correlations between categories of interaction and achievement for all students and the means and standard deviations of achievement, ability, and interaction for females and males. Partial correlations are presented to show whether the relationships between interaction and achievement were sustained when ability was controlled. The upper part of Table 10.1 presents information on the frequencies of interaction. For some interaction variables, however, the frequencies present only part of the picture. For receiving explanations and information, it is also important to take into account the number of questions that were asked and examine the percentage of the questions that were answered. The data on percentages of requests for help that were granted appear in the lower part of Table 10.1. Only students who asked for explanations or information are included in the percentages.

Four categories of interaction were related to achievement when ability was controlled. Giving explanations and receiving explanations were positively related to achievement, and receiving no explanations and receiving no information were negatively related to achievement. Furthermore, as shown by the results in the bottom section of Table 10.1, students who received answers to the majority to their requests for explanations and information performed better on the achievement tests than students who received answers to a small percentage of their requests for help.

Table 10.1

Achievement, Ability, and Interaction by Gender for High-Achieving Classes

Measure	Females		Males		Partial r with achievement
	$\bar{X}$	SD	$\bar{X}$	SD	
Achievement	11.1	3.4	13.3	3.2	
Ability	30.9	3.0	31.1	3.5	
Frequencies[a]					
Asks for explanation	9.1	9.7	9.4	10.4	−.04
Receives explanation	3.2	4.2	5.6	8.7	.23**
Receives no explanation	6.0	8.3	3.9	5.3	−.28***
Asks for information	12.5	12.7	13.5	12.6	−.13
Receives information	7.6	7.5	10.9	10.0	.08
Receives no information	5.0	10.8	2.6	4.9	−.28***
Gives explanation	9.0	12.0	8.6	11.9	.17*
Gives information	12.1	10.4	10.2	10.6	−.06
Percentages for students who asked questions					
Asks for explanation[b]					
Receives explanation	42.1	37.4	51.5	40.3	.34***
Receives no explanation	57.9	37.4	48.5	40.3	−.34***
Asks for information[c]					
Receives information	70.4	25.2	81.9	27.4	.27**
Receives no information	29.6	25.2	18.1	27.4	−.27**

[a] $n = 33$ female, 35 male.
[b] $n = 25$ female, 25 male.
[c] $n = 24$ female, 28 male.
$*p < .10, **p < .05, ***p < .01$.

Although females and males had similar ability, males outperformed females on the achievement test, $F(1, 32) = 7.50, p < .01$. Tests of gender differences for individual interaction variables were not statistically significant, but a clear pattern emerges. (1) Males received more explanations and information than females did. When these two variables were combined, the test for the difference between females and males was significant, $F(1, 32) = 3.64, p < .07$. (2) Females were more likely than males to receive no answers to their requests for explanations and information. Although the above two findings suggest that males were more successful than females in obtaining answers to their questions, the direct evidence appears in the lower section of Table 10.1. Among the students who asked for explanations and information, males received answers to a higher percentage of their questions than females did, although the difference was only about 10%. The third effect shown in Table 10.1 is that females tended to give more help than males did.

SAME-SEX AND CROSS-SEX INTERACTION

Between-Gender Comparisons

Although the trends indicating different interaction patterns for females and males in Table 10.1 are suggestive, the dynamics of same-sex and cross-sex interaction that help clarify the gender differences in giving and receiving help are disguised. The findings in Table 10.2 reveal much more information about how females and males interacted with each other. Table 10.2 presents the frequencies of same-sex and cross-sex interaction for females and males and the percentages of requests for help that were answered. It should be noted that the data on same-sex and cross-sex interaction for females and males can be directly compared as can the data on cross-sex interaction for females and males. Groups differed in the ratio of female to male; some groups had equal numbers of females and males while other groups had more students of one gender than another. Five groups had two females and two males; six groups had one female and several males; and six groups had one male and several females. Since there were equal numbers of groups with majority females and with majority males, however, the opportunities for same-sex interaction were the same for females and males overall, and the opportunities for cross-sex interaction were the same for females and males overall. For same-sex interaction, on the average, each female had the opportunity to interact with 1.33 females and each male had the opportunity to interact with 1.37 males. For cross-sex interaction, each female had the opportunity to interact with 1.67 males and each male had the opportunity to interact with 1.63 females. Therefore, it is possible to examine gender differences in the incidence of same-sex interaction and in the incidence of cross-sex interaction. These tests are reported in Table 10.2.

As can be seen in Table 10.2, there were two consistent patterns of gender differences in same-sex and cross-sex interaction. When females asked other females for explanations, they were rarely ignored: Each female was ignored an average of 1.7 times. In contrast, when males asked other males for explanations, they were more often ignored: Each male was ignored an average of 2.4 times. For cross-sex interaction, the findings were the opposite. When females asked males for explanations, they were often ignored (an average of 5.3 times for each female). On the other hand, when males asked females for explanations, they were rarely ignored (an average of 1.4 times for each male). Similar findings appeared for information. Furthermore, the percentages in the lower section of Table 10.2 give a similar picture. In same-sex interaction, when females asked other females for explanations, about three-quarters of their requests were answered. When males asked other males for explanations, only half of their requests were

Table 10.2

Same-Sex and Cross-Sex Interaction for High-Achieving Classes

Measure	Same-sex interaction					Cross-sex interaction				
	Females		Males			Females		Males		
	$\bar{X}$	SD	$\bar{X}$	SD	F	$\bar{X}$	SD	$\bar{X}$	SD	F
Frequencies[a]										
Asks for explanation	2.8	4.2	5.3	8.2	1.97	6.3	8.9	4.2	6.5	0.99
Receives explanation	2.1	3.3	2.8	7.0	0.21	1.1	2.0	2.7	5.6	2.80
Receives no explanation	0.7	1.7	2.4	4.3	4.66**	5.3	8.2	1.4	2.6	5.68**
Asks for information	4.4	5.2	6.3	8.2	1.02	8.1	12.4	7.2	10.7	0.06
Receives information	4.0	4.9	4.8	6.1	0.23	3.5	5.1	6.1	9.5	1.16
Receives no information	0.4	1.0	1.6	3.8	3.42*	4.6	10.9	1.0	2.3	1.84
Gives explanation	2.4	3.6	5.2	11.3	1.89	6.6	11.5	3.4	5.3	1.25
Gives information	4.0	4.9	5.8	8.0	1.14	8.1	8.1	4.4	8.0	2.72
Percentages for students who asked questions										
Asks for explanation[b]										
Receives explanation	74.5	29.2	50.4	44.4	2.19	24.0	34.6	56.6	39.9	6.55**
Receives no explanation	25.6	29.2	49.6	44.4	2.19	76.0	34.6	43.4	39.0	6.55**
Asks for information[c]										
Receives information	92.5	12.6	82.2	22.4	3.50*	54.9	33.7	83.2	29.1	8.48***
Receives no information	7.5	12.6	17.8	22.4	3.50*	45.1	33.7	16.8	29.1	8.48***

[a] n = 33 female, 35 male.

[b] For same-sex interaction, n = 16 female, 17 male; for cross-sex interaction, n = 18 female, 18 male.

[c] For same-sex interaction, n = 19 female, 16 male; for cross-sex interaction, n = 21 female, 22 male.

* $p < .10$, ** $p < .05$, *** $p < .01$.

granted. In cross-sex interaction, when females asked males for explanations, fewer than a quarter of their requests were answered. When males
asked females for explanations, over half of their requests were answered. A
similar pattern occurred for the percentage of requests for information that
were answered. In summary, in both same-sex and cross-sex interaction,
females were more responsive than males to requests for help.

Differences between Same-Sex and Cross-Sex Interaction within Gender

The hierarchical analyses of variance presented in Table 10.2 and discussed previously show important differences between female and male in
same-sex interaction and in cross-sex interaction, but they do not reveal
whether students' experiences in the group were different when they interacted with students of their own gender from when they interacted with
students of the opposite gender. Further tests were conducted to answer
this question. Because the opportunities for same-sex and cross-sex interaction were *not* the same within gender (e.g., in a two female–two male
group, each student had twice as many opportunities for cross-sex interaction as for same-sex interaction; the opportunities for cross-sex interaction
over the entire sample were 22% greater than those for same-sex interaction), the data on the frequencies of same-sex interaction cannot be compared directly to those of cross-sex interaction. To test the difference between same-sex and cross-sex interaction within gender, the observed
proportion of interaction that was due to cross-sex interaction was compared to the expected proportion using a conventional z test for comparing
a sample mean to an expected mean. For females, the expected proportion
of cross-sex interaction was 0.56 of their total interaction [1.67/(1.33 +
1.67)]. For males, the expected proportion of cross-sex interaction was 0.54
[1.63/(1.37 + 1.63)]. Only students who asked questions or gave help were
included in these tests.

The choice of a statistical test for the difference between same-sex and
cross-sex *percentages* of questions that were answered was more problematic. The measures were so defined that they were already adjusted for the
different opportunities for same-sex and cross-interaction within the gender. Hence, the logical statistical test was a correlated t test (analogous to a
repeated measures F test). However, because, the students who asked for
help from students of the same gender were not always the same students
who asked for help from students of the opposite gender, it was not possible
to carry out correlated t tests without substantial loss of degrees of freedom.
Instead, conventional t tests for independent means were performed but
were tested using the number of students (minus 1) as the degrees of

freedom instead of the number of data points (approximately twice as large as the number of students). This test was more conservative than the correlated t test but was more accurate because it used all the data.

Unlike the analyses of variance of between-gender differences, the statistical tests used to compare same-sex and cross-sex interaction were not easily modified to take into account the dependence among students within a group. The only possible solution might be to use the mean of the gender subgroup in place of individual scores. However, because only students who asked questions were included in the analysis, not all students in the subgroup would be represented. In fact the footnotes to Tables 10.1 and 10.3 show that about 25% of students in the first study and over half of the students in the second study did not ask one of the two kinds of questions and, consequently, would not be included in the analyses. Therefore, an analysis of subgroup means would not capture the dependence among all students in many groups. In addition it would be necessary to introduce a weighted means procedure to take into account the different numbers of students included from each group. Because the necessary statistical tests would have been very complicated and not easily interpreted, the tests reported here are based on individual scores.

There were several differences between same-sex and cross-sex interaction for both females and males. For females, the differences between same-sex and cross-sex interaction were significant for receiving help and for giving help, but not for asking for help. Although the results shown in Table 10.2 suggest that females asked males for explanations and information more often than expected, the results were not statistically significant for the students who asked for help. Among the 25 females who asked for explanations, .59 of their requests were directed toward males compared to the expected proportion of .56. Among the 24 females who asked for information, .54 of their questions were directed toward males compared to the expected proportion of .56.

Since the proportions of requests for explanations and information that females directed to females and to males were close to the expected proportions, it is appropriate to compare the proportions of explanations and information that were *received* from females and males. These proportions were calculated by dividing the number of explanations that a student received from students of one gender by the total number of explanations that a student received. Among the 25 females who asked for explanations, fewer explanations came from males (and more came from females) than expected: .27 of the explanations that females received came from males compared to the expected proportion of .56 ($z = 3.94, p < .001$). The same picture emerges from the percentages of females' requests for explanations that were granted. Females were much more likely to receive explanations when they asked females than when they asked males (74% vs. 24%, $t(15)$ = 4.69, $p < .001$). The results for receiving information paralleled those for receiving explanations. Females received less information from males (and more from females) than expected. Among the 24 females who asked for information, .43 of the information they received came from males compared to the expected proportion of .56 ($z = 1.71, p < .09$). Similarly, the percentage of females' requests for information that were answered was much higher when they asked other females than when they asked males (92% vs. 55%, $t = 4.71, p < .001$).

The final significant result was that females gave more information to males than expected (.68 of the information that females gave was directed to males compared to the expected proportion of .56, $z = 2.26, p < .03$). The result for giving explanations was in the same direction but was not significant.

In summary, the major finding was that females were much more successful in obtaining help when they asked other females than when they asked males.

The findings for males were different from those for females. As was the case among females, the observed proportions of requests for explanations and information that males directed to females (.49 for explanations and .55 for information) were very close to the expected proportion of .54. Consequently, it is appropriate to compare the frequency of males' same-sex and cross-sex receiving of help. Two significant findings emerged: (1) Males were less likely to be ignored by females when they asked for explanations (and more likely to be ignored by males) than expected. For the 25 males who asked for explanations, .39 of their failures to elicit a response came from females compared to the expected proportion of .54 ($z = 2.28, p < .03$). (2) Males were less likely to be ignored by females when they asked for information (and more likely to be ignored by males) than expected. For the 28 males who asked for information, .23 of their failures to elicit a response came from females compared to the expected proportion of .54 from females ($z = 4.22, p < .001$).

Given the findings for same-sex and cross-sex interaction among females and males, it seems that *everyone* in the group was better off asking the females for help than asking the males for help. Furthermore, the beneficial effect of asking females for help was greater for females than for males. Stated conversely, females fared much worse than males when they asked males for help. These results also help to explain the gender differences found in Table 10.1. In particular, the finding that females were less likely than males to receive answers to their questions seems to have resulted from females' lack of success in obtaining answers from *males.* Females were much more successful in obtaining help from other females.

Table 10.3

Achievement, Ability, and Interaction by Gender for Low-Achieving Classes

Measure	Females $\bar{X}$	Females SD	Males $\bar{X}$	Males SD	Partial r with achievement
Achievement	9.3	3.1	8.3	3.2	
Ability	48.6	13.3	49.1	12.2	
Frequencies[a]					
Asks for explanation	1.9	3.3	2.2	4.3	−.03
Receives explanation	1.0	2.3	0.8	2.3	.03
Receives no explanation	0.9	2.8	1.4	2.7	−.08
Asks for information	6.9	13.6	8.5	13.2	.18*
Receives information	2.1	3.8	3.4	5.7	.25**
Receives no information	4.8	10.9	5.1	8.7	.08
Gives explanation	7.3	7.5	4.0	7.7	.24**
Gives information	17.2	18.5	17.6	24.2	.24**
Percentages for students who asked questions					
Asks for explanation[b]					
Receives explanation	55.6	52.7	32.8	39.4	.21
Receives no explanation	44.4	52.7	67.2	39.4	−.21
Asks for information[c]					
Receives information	33.0	32.1	44.3	36.0	.25*
Receives no information	67.0	32.1	55.7	36.0	−.25*

[a] n = 29 female, 28 male.
[b] n = 9 female, 8 male.
[c] n = 14 female, 15 male.
* $p < .10$, ** $p < .05$.

Low-Achieving Classes

INTERACTION AND ACHIEVEMENT

Table 10.3 presents the partial correlations between interaction and achievement and the means and standard deviations of achievement, ability, and interaction for females and males in low-achieving classes. The interaction categories that related to achievement were somewhat different for the low-achieving classes from those for the high-achieving classes (see Table 10.1). First, neither receiving explanations nor receiving no explanations related to achievement. Since the frequencies for those interaction categories were very small (students in these classes rarely asked for explanations), the near-zero correlations may have resulted from restriction of range. Second, giving and receiving information were both positively related to achievement, whereas neither variable related to achievement in the high-achieving classes. Third, receiving no information did not seem to be detrimental to achievement, in contrast to the findings in nearly all previous studies. The only finding that replicated the achievement relationships in the high-achieving classes was the positive correlation between giving explanations and achievement.

Not only were the patterns of relationships between interaction and achievement different in the low-achieving classes, but the frequencies of interaction were different as well. First, as previously mentioned, was the very low frequency of asking for explanations. Second, the frequencies of giving explanations and procedural information were much higher than those of *asking for* explanations and procedural information, showing that students in these classrooms gave a lot of unsolicited help. In the high-achieving classes, in contrast, students gave almost no unsolicited help.

The gender differences in achievement and interaction differed considerably from those for high-achieving classes. Females tended to outperform males on the achievement test, although the result was not statistically significant. Furthermore, females and males showed very similar verbal behavior patterns (no test of gender differences was statistically significant). The means show no tendency for males to receive more help than females, nor for females to be less successful in obtaining responses to their questions than males. The proportions of requests for explanations and information that were granted also show no consistent pattern.

SAME-SEX AND CROSS-SEX INTERACTION

Between-Gender Comparisons

As in the high-achieving classes, the ratio of females to males across groups was balanced in the low-achieving classes. Therefore, female and male students had the same opportunity for same-sex interaction (1.03 for each female and 1.07 for each male) and the same opportunity for cross-sex interaction (1.55 for each female and 1.61 for each male) and it was possible to examine gender differences in same-sex interaction and in cross-sex interaction. These tests are reported in Table 10.4.

The dynamics of same-sex and cross-sex interaction shown in Table 10.4 differ markedly from those in the high-achieving classes. In contrast to the findings for the high-achieving classes, none of the tests for gender differences in same-sex interaction was statistically significant. Females asked for as much help, received as much help, and gave as much help to females as males gave to males.

In cross-sex interaction, only two gender differences were statistically significant. The first difference was in the opposite direction from the result for high-achieving classes: Females were *less* likely than males to receive no

Table 10.4

Same-Sex and Cross-Sex Interaction for Low-Achieving Classes

Measure	Same-sex interaction					Cross-sex interaction				
	Females		Males			Females		Males		
	$\bar{X}$	SD	$\bar{X}$	SD	F	$\bar{X}$	SD	$\bar{X}$	SD	F
Frequencies[a]										
Asks for explanation	1.5	3.1	1.2	2.9	0.19	.4	1.7	1.0	2.1	0.96
Receives explanation	0.5	1.6	0.4	1.4	0.05	.4	1.8	.4	1.1	0.02
Receives no explanation	1.0	2.8	0.7	2.2	0.15	.0	.0	.7	1.6	3.06*
Asks for information	1.6	3.1	2.5	5.9	0.53	5.3	13.7	6.0	11.3	0.03
Receives information	0.5	1.6	0.9	2.7	0.56	1.6	3.7	2.6	4.9	0.38
Receives no information	1.2	2.1	1.6	3.7	0.37	3.7	11.0	3.5	7.1	0.01
Gives explanation	2.8	3.9	2.3	5.4	0.14	4.5	6.2	1.7	2.9	3.61*
Gives information	4.8	6.2	6.8	10.2	0.53	12.4	18.4	10.8	16.9	0.07
Percentages for students who asked questions										
Asks for explanation[b]										
Receives explanation	42.9	53.5	52.0	50.2	0.13	50.0	70.7	36.1	42.7	2.08
Receives no explanation	57.1	53.5	48.0	50.2	0.13	50.0	70.7	63.9	42.7	2.08
Asks for information[c]										
Receives information	26.2	38.9	30.6	24.5	0.09	37.8	35.0	45.2	37.8	0.31
Receives no information	73.8	38.9	69.4	24.5	0.09	62.2	35.0	54.8	37.8	0.31

[a] n = 29 female, 28 male.

[b] For same-sex interaction, n = 7 female, 5 male; for cross-sex interaction, n = 2 female, 6 male.

[c] For same-sex interaction, n = 8 female, 6 male; for cross-sex interaction, n = 8 female, 14 male.

* p < .10.

response to their requests for explanations. The second significant difference between females and males was consistent with that for high-achieving classes: Females gave more explanations than did males. None of the differences between males and females in the proportions of help received were significant.

Differences between Same-Sex and Cross-Sex Interaction within Gender

Although females and males seemed to have similar interaction experiences, the results in Table 10.4 do not indicate whether students interacted more (or less) with students of the opposite gender than with those of the same gender. To answer this question, the same statistical tests were carried out here as in the high-achieving classes. The observed proportions of cross-sex interaction were compared to the expected proportions of cross-sex interaction for females and males using a z test for the difference between a sample mean and an expected mean. The expected proportion of cross-sex interaction was .60 for females [1.55/(1.03 + 1.55)] and .60 for males [1.61/ (1.07 + 1.61)]. Also as before, the differences between proportions were tested using a t test for the difference between means with the size of the sample, rather than the number of data points, as the degrees of freedom.

Few differences between same-sex and cross-sex interaction appeared within gender, and the significant effects that emerged show a very different picture from that in high-achieving classes. Females directed fewer of the requests for explanations to males than expected; of their requests for explanations only .22 were directed to males in contrast to the expected proportion of .60 ($z = 2.57, p < .02$). Given that finding, it is not surprising that females received fewer explanations from males than expected (an observed proportion of .22 compared to the expected proportion of .60, $z = 2.57, p < .02$). Similarly, fewer of the females' failures to obtain explanations came from males than expected (an observed proportion of .11 compared to the expected proportion of .60, $z = 4.41, p < .001$). The latter two findings disappear when the fact that females asked females for help more than they asked males for help is taken into account. The percentages in the lower section of Table 10.4 show that females were about equally successful in obtaining explanations from females and males (43% vs. 50%).

For males, only one difference between same-sex and cross-sex interaction was statistically significant. Males received fewer explanations from females than was expected (an observed proportion of .24 compared to an expected proportion of .60, $z = 2.76, p < .01$). However, the difference in percentages was not significant, showing that when males asked females for explanations they were about as likely to receive responses as when they asked males (36% vs. 52%). It is interesting that, although the result is not significant, the trend is in the opposite direction from that in high-achieving classes. While in the high-achieving classes males were more likely to receive explanations when they asked females than when they asked males, males in the low-achieving classes were somewhat less likely to receive explanations from females than from males.

In summary, the picture in low-achieving classes was one of near equality in the interaction of females and males. The only significant differences were (1) a tendency for males to be less successful than females in obtaining explanations and (2) a tendency for females to ask for explanations from females rather than from males. Since these effects occurred for few variables and in few analyses, they are not considered major features of interaction in low-achieving classes.

Intensive Analyses of the Questions Asked

To help explain why females in high-achieving classes were less likely than males to receive help when they requested it (particularly when they asked males) and why females in low-achieving classes, in contrast, were equally successful as males in obtaining help, the questions that students asked were intensively analyzed. Particular attention was paid to the form of the questions asked because, according to Wilkinson's sociolinguistic model of the effective speaker, students who ask questions "clearly and directly, in attempt to minimize ambiguity and multiple interpretations of the same utterance" are likely to obtain responses (Peterson, Wilkinson, Spinelli, & Swing, 1984, p. 127).

A logical analysis of the transcripts produced 13 types of questions. These 13 types were further classified in five categories on the basis of their logical similarity and the frequencies with which they elicited responses. The five categories included general questions, general questions delivered as statements, commands for help, questions that asked for specific information, and questions that asked for a yes or no response. Five types of questions fell in the first category, *general questions:* Nonspecific how questions ("How do you do that?"), nonspecific what questions ("What do we do now?"), nonspecific why questions ("Why do I have to do that?"), questions that asked how to do an exercise or problem ("How do you do number 19?"), and nonspecific indications of confusion ("Huh?"). There were two kinds of *statements* that could be interpreted as requests for help: A statement indicating lack of understanding ("I can't figure this out."), and a statement asked like a question ("In these problems you do them differently, don't you?"). Some students *commanded* an explanation, either as a direct state-

Table 10.5

Questions and Responses in High-Achieving Classes

Type of question—whether response received	Females			Males			Total
	Received from			Received from			
	Female	Male	Total	Female	Male	Total	Total
General question	2	19	21	5	9	14	35
Yes	1	5	6	1	2	3	9
No	1	14	15	4	7	11	26
Statement	2	12	14	10	13	23	37
Yes	1	0	1	2	5	7	8
No	1	12	13	8	8	16	29
Command	0	0	0	1	3	4	4
Yes	0	0	0	1	2	3	3
No	0	0	0	0	1	1	1
Specific question	15	24	39	30	27	57	96
Yes	14	12	26	25	19	44	70
No	1	12	13	5	8	13	26
Yes–no question	8	14	22	15	16	31	53
Yes	7	9	16	15	14	29	45
No	1	5	6	0	2	2	8

ment ("Now explain it to me.") or as a request ("Would you just explain how to do it?"). Students asked three types of *specific questions:* Specific how questions ("How did you get 10^{14} on that?"), specific what questions ("What did you get for number 17?"), and specific why questions ("Why do you subtract them?"). Finally, students often asked *yes–no questions* ("Did you get 8 times 10^8 for number 2?"). For a somewhat different classification of requests according to grammatical forms, see Wilkinson et al. (Chapter 9, this vol.; see also Peterson et al., 1984; Wilkinson & Calculator, 1982a, 1982b).

Tables 10.5 and 10.6 present the breakdowns of questions for females and males in high-achieving and low-achieving classes, respectively. Each table shows the number of questions and answers for all students combined, for females and males, and for same-sex and cross-sex interaction.

HIGH-ACHIEVING CLASSES

In high-achieving classes, as shown in Table 10.5, general questions and statements tended not to be answered: Only 26% of general questions and 22% of statements received responses (last column in Table 10.5). Commands and questions soliciting specific information, in contrast, tended to

Table 10.6

Questions and Responses in Low-Achieving Classes

Type of question—whether response received	Females			Males			
	Received from			Received from			
	Female	Male	Total	Female	Male	Total	Total
General question	9	13	22	11	14	25	47
Yes	4	2	6	3	7	10	16
No	5	11	16	8	7	15	31
Statement	6	2	8	2	2	4	12
Yes	4	0	4	0	1	1	5
No	2	2	4	2	1	3	7
Command	0	0	0	0	1	1	1
Yes	0	0	0	0	0	0	0
No	0	0	0	0	1	1	1
Specific question	13	32	45	34	19	53	98
Yes	8	27	35	28	16	44	79
No	5	5	10	6	3	9	19
Yes—no question	14	8	22	24	8	32	54
Yes	8	4	12	18	6	24	36
No	6	4	10	6	2	8	18

be answered: 75% of commands, 73% of specific questions, and 83% of yes—no questions received responses. Therefore, the first two categories of questions were "unsuccessful" questions, whereas the last three categories were "successful" questions.

While it made no difference to whom unsuccessful questions were directed—females answered 26% of the questions they received (5 of 19) and males answered 23% (12 of 53)—it made a considerable difference to whom students directed *successful* questions. Females answered 90% of the commands, specific questions, and yes—no questions they received (62 of 69), whereas males answered only 67% (56 of 84). Consequently, the finding reported earlier in this chapter that females were more responsive than males to questions pertains only to questions with a specific intent, not to questions indicating only a lack of understanding.

The tendency for some kinds of questions to be more successful than others in producing responses, combined with the breakdown by gender of questions and answers, helps clarify why females received fewer answers to their questions than males did. First, females tended to ask somewhat fewer successful questions than males did: 64% of females' questions were commands, specific questions, or yes—no questions, compared to 71% of males' questions. Second, females directed more specific questions and yes—no questions to males than to females. Since males were less responsive to these questions than females were, as described above, females received fewer responses than they would have received had they directed more of their questions to females. Third, females directed nearly all their general questions and statements of confusion to males. Although the numbers are small, they indicate that females may have been more successful in obtaining responses to these unsuccessful questions had they asked females instead. Finally, females never commanded other students to give them help. Although males gave few commands, all but one produced responses.

LOW-ACHIEVING CLASSES

Table 10.6 presents the breakdown of questions and answers for the low-achieving classes. As in the high-achieving classes, general questions and statements tended not to be successful in eliciting responses (35% of general questions and 42% of statements elicited responses), whereas specific and yes–no questions were more successful (81% of specific questions and 67% of yes–no questions were answered). There the similarity ends. Females in low-achieving classes were *not* more responsive than males to *any* kind of question. The rate of responding to general questions and statements was 39% for females and 32% for males, and the rate of responding to specific questions and yes–no questions was 73% for females and 79% for males.

The near-equality of female and male interaction in low-achieving classes reported earlier is mirrored in the same-sex and cross-sex breakdowns in Table 10.6. The only effect of note in Table 10.6 is that students were more likely to receive responses to the unsuccessful kinds of questions when they asked students of their own gender than when they asked students of the opposite gender. When students asked students of their own gender, the response rate was 53% for females and 50% for males. When students asked students of the opposite gender, the response rate was 13% for females and 23% for males. This effect did not occur for successful kinds of questions nor did it appear in the high-achieving classes.

DISCUSSION

In summary, the analyses of gender differences in small-group interaction showed that the higher achievement of males than females in high-achieving classes may be explained by the tendency of males to be more successful than females in obtaining help when requested. This result was due to females being more responsive than males to requests for help and to males being particularly unresponsive to females. Closer examination of the questions that students asked showed that some questions were more successful than others in eliciting responses. Questions asking for specific information or focusing on a specific part of a problem were more likely to elicit responses than questions or statements indicating general confusion. And females were more likely than males to ask the general kinds of questions that usually elicited no response. Furthermore, males were particularly unresponsive to these kinds of questions.

The low-achieving classes showed none of the gender differences in achievement and interaction that appeared in high-achieving classes. Females were at least as successful as males in obtaining help, and they were not more responsive than males to requests for help. The lack of gender differences also extended to the different kinds of questions that students asked. Females and males showed similar frequencies of asking for and receiving answers to specific and general questions.

Previous literature on gender differences has advanced at least two mechanisms to explain differences in achievement between females and males and differences in their experiences in a variety of settings. The first is the hypothesis that gender may often operate as a status characteristic. Using the theory of diffuse status characteristics and expectation states (see Berger, Cohen, & Zelditch, 1972; Berger, Conner, & Fisek, 1974), males are expected to be more competent than females and consequently they are more likely than females to hold positions of power, prestige, and influence in the group (Lockheed, 1977, in press; Lockheed & Hall, 1976; Lockheed & Harris, 1984; Lockheed, Harris, & Nemceff, 1983; see also Broverman, Vogel, Broverman, Clarkson, & Rosenkrantz; Mischel, 1974). This hypothesis is particularly germane to mathematics learning. Fox (1977), Fennema and Sherman (1977, 1978), and Sherman and Fennema (1977) have shown that mathematics is often perceived as a male domain in which males are expected to be better than females, particularly in middle and late adolescence.

Although there is no direct evidence in the present study that gender operated as a status characteristic in high-achieving classes, it is possible to speculate how it may have operated. Perhaps males exhibited their dominant position in small groups by being very selective in whom they chose to help. In the low-achieving classes, both females and males may have perceived that no one was good in mathematics, resulting in a lack of differentiation between them and allowing the females a more prominent position in group interaction. An inoperative gender stereotype is consistent with Kagan's (1982) finding of a weak or nonexistent male performance stereotype in working-class samples and his suggestion that the stereotype may not operate in some minority groups. Since the student populations in the present study differed on three factors: achievement level, socioeconomic status, and proportion of minority students, it is important to identify which student characteristics are linked to the presence or absence of a gender stereotype.

A related mechanism is the perception among males, particularly in groups with only one female, that females are low on work orientation (see Frank & Katcher, 1977; Wolman & Frank, 1975). Males may have been unresponsive to females in the high-achieving classes because they perceived that giving help to females might not be beneficial. It is possible that this perception did not operate in low-achieving classes.

Although the mechanisms of gender as a status characteristic and the perceptions of females as low on work orientation may help to explain why females in high-achieving classes were less successful than males in obtaining help when they needed it, the most direct explanation lies in the kinds of questions that students asked. Unlike females in low-achieving classes, females in high-achieving classes asked questions that were so general that other students did not know how to answer them. Other students could either not determine from the question where the difficulty lay or the questions were not recognized as requests for help, as when students stated that they were having trouble. Such statements often seemed to be interpreted as seeking confirmation that other students in the group were also having difficulty (a typical response to such a statement was "I'm having trouble too") rather than as requests for help.

Although more data are needed to explain *why* females in high-achieving classes asked so many general questions and directed so many of them to males, these findings do have practical implications for small-group work in classrooms. In this study, students were instructed to ask other group members for help when they had difficulty understanding the material. Specific instruction on how to ask questions that are likely to elicit responses, perhaps in the form of role playing, behavior modification, or coaching, might be more helpful. Perhaps students should be encouraged to attempt to solve a problem before asking for help so that they can be more specific about the type of help they need. In the present study it is possible that girls' questions were more general and less effective than boys' questions because girls asked their questions soon after looking at the problem, whereas boys attempted a solution first. These speculations needed to be tested empirically. It may also be useful to encourage students to be alert for hidden meaning underlying group members' questions. The general questions that girls (and perhaps boys) asked may have signified group-facilitating behavior ("Let's work together as a group.") rather than only admissions of confusion.

Although the explanations considered thus far for the differences in achievement and interaction results between high-achieving and low-achieving classes have concentrated on the characteristics of the students, it is important to take into account the difficulty level and task demands of the mathematics topics being learned in the two studies. The literature on gender differences in achievement has shown that boys may outperform girls on tasks requiring higher level cognitive processes but not on lower level tasks involving routine computation (see Wilson, 1972). Therefore, the higher achievement of males than females in the high-achieving classes and the equal achievement of males and females in the low-achieving classes in the present study is consistent with the high-achieving classes having worked on high-level material and the low-achieving classes having worked on low-level material.

Although it is difficult to categorize precisely the curricula in the two sets of classes, a description of the material may help clarify the differences. The high-achieving classes learned exponents and scientific notation. Students in these classes learned how to express large numbers in scientific notation and solved word problems that involved performing computations of large numbers in scientific notation. Their exercises also included making up word problems involving large numbers ("If a fish aquarium holds 20 gallons of water, and each gallon contains 5,000,000 molecules of water, how many molecules does the whole aquarium contain?"). Although some of the material involved routine applications of algorithms, such as converting large numbers to scientific notation, and might be considered low-level material, other material, such as inventing and solving word problems, clearly involved higher level skills.

The low-achieving classes learned how to complete income tax forms using information about wages, deductions, and expenses. Students had to follow instructions given on the tax forms ("If you checked the box on line 2 or 5, enter the greater of $2,500 OR 18% of line 13a, but not more than $3100."), multiply numbers involving decimals and percentages (18% of $3275), and locate information on tax tables ("Find the tax for a single person earning $9430."). This material, then, seemed to involve low-level skills.

Looking only at the complexity of the skills involved in learning the material, the different task demands in the two studies may help to account for the different patterns of achievement. A qualification is in order, however, about difficulty level. The complexity of the skills does not necessarily correspond to difficulty level here because the two samples differed in ability level. While the high-achieving classes may have found the income tax unit easier than their unit on scientific notation, the income tax unit may have been as difficult for the low-achieving classes as scientific notation was for the high-achieving classes. Indeed, the data on achievement in the two studies show that the low-achieving classes obtained a lower proportion of items correct on the achievement test than the high-achieving classes.

To the extent that the high-achieving classes worked on high-level material and the low-achieving classes worked on low-level material, it is useful to determine whether the behavior of students in the two sets of classes conforms to predictions based on cognitive complexity. Fennema and Peterson (see Chapter 2, this volume, Autonomous Learning Behavior section) postulate that autonomous learning behaviors, including "working independently on high-level tasks, persisting at such tasks, choosing to do and achieving success in such tasks" (p. 20), may promote learning of high-level material. Although the present study did not collect data about these autonomous learning behaviors, some of the group interaction data may be relevant. In particular, the tendencies of males in the high-achieving classes not to ask general questions and not to respond to questions may indicate independent behavior. Furthermore, as suggested earlier, the lower frequencies of general questions among males than among females may indicate persistence at the task if males tried to solve the problem before asking for help and thus expressed their difficulties in specific questions. The similar interaction patterns for females and males in the low-achieving classes may reflect comparable independent behavior and perseverance at the task. In summary, while the data presented here cannot be used to confirm the Fennema–Peterson model, their model does provide possible explanations for the achievement and interaction gender differences in the high-achieving and low-achieving classes.

The previous discussion suggests several directions for further research on gender differences in classroom interaction. First, it is important to obtain introspective or retrospective accounts from students about the meanings of their own questions and the questions asked by others to determine when they were asking for help, when they were trying to stimulate group activity, when they were seeking confirmation of their difficulties, and when they were trying to demonstrate their competence. Such introspective accounts are particularly important for girls' general questions to determine whether they really did not know how to begin to solve a problem or knew the areas of their difficulty but did not verbalize them. Similarly, asking about their interpretation of the general questions asked by others might reveal whether such questions were interpreted as requests for help. These introspective accounts might also indicate when during problem-solving girls and boys tend to ask questions, before or after they have attempted to solve the problem.

Second, to determine whether cross-sex and same-sex interaction results are related to a male or female performance stereotype, students should be asked directly about their perceptions of males' and females' competence in the subject matter being learned and in verbal interaction. In addition, they should be asked how their perceptions of others guide their behavior.

Finally, it is important to isolate the student characteristics that relate to performance stereotypes and gender differences in behavior. As mentioned earlier, it is not clear whether the differences in interaction patterns across the two studies reported here are derived from the achievement level, socioeconomic status, or racial background of the students. Related to this point is the importance of disentangling the effects of student characteristics from the task difficulty and cognitive complexity of the material being learned. Future studies should examine a variety of task difficulties and levels of cognitive complexity for each student population to clarify the antecedents of gender differences in classroom interaction.

NOTES

[1] Although the data for high-achieving classes have been presented elsewhere (Webb, 1984), they are presented here to enable comparisons to be made with low-achieving classes. Furthermore, the analyses presented in this chapter are different from those presented previously; they are condensed, simplified, and based only on groups with both females and males.

[2] Although the original sample had 77 students, 9 students in all-male groups have been excluded from the analyses presented here.

REFERENCES

Berger, J., Cohen, B. P., & Zelditch, M., Jr. (1972). Status conceptions and social interaction. *American Sociological Review, 37,* 241–255.

Berger, J., Conner, T. L., & Fisek, M. H. (Eds.). (1974). *Expectation states theory: A theoretical research program.* Cambridge, MA: Winthrop.

Borgatta, E. F., & Stimson, J. (1963). Sex differences in interaction characteristics. *Journal of Social Psychology, 60,* 89–100.

Broverman, I. K., Vogel, S. R., Broverman, D. M., Clarkson, F. E., & Rosenkrantz, P. (1972). Sex-role stereotypes: A current appraisal. *Journal of Social Issues, 28,* 59–78.

Comprehensive Test of Basic Skills (1963). Monterey: CTB/McGraw-Hill.

Cronbach, L. J., Gleser, G. C., Nanda, H., & Rajaratnam, N. (1972). *The dependability of behavioral measurements.* New York: Wiley.

DeVries, D. L., & Mescon, I. T. (1975). *Teams-games-tournament: An effective task and reward structure in the elementary grades* (Rep. No. 189). Baltimore: Center for Social Organization of Schools, Johns Hopkins University.

DeVries, D. L., Mescon, I. T., & Shackman, S. L. (1975). *Teams–games–tournament in the elementary classroom: A replication* (Rep. No. 190). Baltimore: Center for the Social Organization of Schools, Johns Hopkins University.

Edwards, K. J., & DeVries, D. L. (1974). *The effects of teams–games–tournament and two instructional variations on classroom process student attitudes, and student achievement* (Rep. No. 172). Baltimore: Center for Social Organization of Schools, Johns Hopkins University.

Fennema, E., & Sherman, J. (1977). Sex-related differences in mathematics achievement, spatial visualization, and sociocultural factors. *American Educational Research Journal, 14,* 51–71.

Fennema, E., & Sherman, J. (1978). Sex-related differences in mathematics achievement and related factors: A further study. *Journal for Research in Mathematics Education, 9,* 189–203.

Fox, L. H. (1977). The effects of sex role socialization on mathematics participation and achievement. In L. H. Fox, E. Fennema, & J. Sherman, (Eds.), *Women and mathematics: Research perspectives for change.* Washington: DC: National Institute of Education.

Frank, H. H., & Katcher, A. H. (1977). The qualities of leadership: How male medical students evaluate their female peers. *Human Relations, 30,* 403–416.

Hanelin, S. J. (1978). *Learning, behavior, and attitudes under individual and group contingencies.* Unpublished doctoral dissertation, University of California, Los Angeles.

Heilbrun, A., Jr. (1968). Influence of observer and target sex in judgments of sex typed attributes. *Perceptual and Motor Skills, 27,* 1194.

Johnson, J. A. (1979). *Learning in peer tutoring interactions: The influence of status, role change, tim-on-task, feedback, and verbalization. Dissertation Abstracts International, 38,* 5469A–5470A. (University Microfilms No. 79-06,175).

Kagan, S. (1982). *The impact of cooperative teams and competitive tournaments on social relations among primary grade pupils.* Paper presented at the Second International Conference on Cooperation in Education, International Association for the Study of Cooperation in Education, Brigham Young University, Provo, Utah.

Lockheed, M. E. (1977). Cognitive style effects on sex status in student work groups. *Journal of Educational Psychology, 69,* 158–165.

Lockheed, M. E. (in press). Sex and social influence: A meta-analysis guided by theory. In J. Berger & M. Zelditch (Ed.), *Status, attributions and rewards.* San Francisco: Jossey-Bass.

Lockheed, M. E., & Hall, K. P. (1976). Conceptualizing sex as a status characteristic: Applications to leadership training strategies. *Journal of Social Issues, 32,* 111–124.

Lockheed, M. E., & Harris, A. M. (1984). Cross-sex collaborative learning in elementary classrooms. *American Educational Research Journal, 21,* 275–294.

Lockheed, M. E., Harris, A. M., & Nemceff, W. P. (1983). Sex and social influence: Does sex function as a status characteristic in mixed-sex groups of children? *Journal of Educational Psychology, 75,* 877–888.

Mischel, H. M. (1974). Sex bias in the evaluation of professional achievements. *Journal of Educational Psychology, 66,* 157–166.

Myers, J. M. (1979). *Fundamentals of experimental design.* (Third Ed.) Boston: Allyn and Bacon, Inc.

Peterson, P. L., & Janicki, T. C. (1979). Individual characteristics and children's learning in large-group and small-group approaches. *Journal of Educational Psychology, 71,* 677–687.

Peterson, P. L., Janicki, T. C., & Swing, S. R. (1981). Ability × Treatment interaction effects on children's learning in large-group and small-group approaches. *American Educational Research Journal, 18,* 453–473.

Peterson, P. L., Wilkinson, L. C., Spinelli, F., & Swing, S. R. (1984). Merging the process-product and the sociolinguistic paradigms: Research on small group processes. In P. L. Peterson, L. C. Wilkinson, & M. T. Hallinan (Eds.), *Instructional groups in the classroom: Organization and processes.* New York: Academic Press.

Sherman, H., & Fennema, E. (1977). The study of mathematics by high school girls and boys: Related variables. *American Educational Research Journal, 14,* 159–168.

Slavin, R. E. (1978a). Effects of student teams and peer tutoring on academic achievement and time on-task. *Journal of Experimental Education, 48,* 252–257.

Slavin, R. E. (1978b). Student teams and achievement divisions. *Journal of Research and Development in Education, 12,* 39–49.

Strodtbeck, F. L., James, R. M., & Hawkins, C. (1957). Social status in jury deliberations. *American Sociological Review, 22,* 713–719.

Strodtbeck, F. L., & Mann, R. D. (1956). Sex role differentiation in jury deliberations. *Sociometry, 19,* 3–11.

Swing, S. R., & Peterson, P. L. (1982). The relationship of student ability and small-group interaction to student achievement. *American Educational Research Journal, 19,* 259–274.

Webb, N. M. (1980a). Group process: The key to learning in groups. *New Directions for Methodology of Social and Behavioral Science: Issues in Aggregation, 6,* 77–87.

Webb, N. M. (1980b). A process-outcome analysis of learning of group and individual settings. *Educational Psychologist, 15,* 69–83.

Webb, N. M. (1980c). An analysis of group interaction and mathematical errors in heterogeneous ability groups. *British Journal of Educational Psychology, 50,* 1–11.

Webb, N. M. (1982a). Group composition, group interaction and achievement in cooperative small groups. *Journal of Educational Psychology, 74,* 475–484.

Webb, N. M. (1982b). Peer interaction and learning in cooperative small groups. *Journal of Educational Psychology, 74,* 642–655.

Webb, N. M. (1982c). Student interaction and learning in small groups. *Review of Educational Research, 52,* 421–445.

Webb, N. M. (1983). Predicting learning from student interaction: Defining the interaction variables. *Educational Psychologist, 18,* 33–41.

Webb, N. M. (1984). Sex differences in interaction and achievement in cooperative small groups. *Journal of Educational Psychology, 76,* 33–34.

Webb, N. M., & Cullian, L. K. (1983). Group interaction and achievement in small groups: Stability over time. *American Educational Research Journal, 20,* 411–424.

Webb, N. M., & Kenderski, C. M. (1984). Student interaction and learning in small group and whole class settings. In P. L. Peterson, L. C. Wilkinson, & M. T. Hallinan (Eds.), *Instructional groups in the classroom: Organization and processes.* New York: Academic Press.

Wilkinson, L. C., & Calculator, S. (1982a). Effective speakers: Students' use of language to request and obtain information and action in the classroom. In L. C. Wilkinson, (Ed.), *Communicating in the classroom.* New York: Academic Press.

Wilkinson, L., & Calculator, S. (1982b). Requests and responses in peer-directed reading groups. *American Educational Research Journal, 19,* 107–120.

Wilson, J. W. (1972). *Patterns in mathematics achievement in grade 11: Z population.* National Longitudinal Study of Mathematical Abilities, No. 17. Stanford: Stanford University Press.

Wolman, C., & Frank, H. (1975). The solo woman in a professional peer group. *American Journal of Orthopsychiatry, 45,* 164–171.

Gender, Classroom Organization, and Grade Level as Factors in Pupil Perceptions of Peer Interaction

GRETA MORINE-DERSHIMER

INTRODUCTION

The growing interest in research on pupil perceptions has been carefully detailed by Weinstein (1983), who notes that this research, as indeed most recent research on teaching, has tended to focus on academic rather than social aspects of classrooms and on pupil–teacher interactions rather than pupil–pupil interactions. What little systematic research has been done on pupil perceptions of peers has focused on peer ability (e.g., Stipek, 1981; Filby & Barnett, 1982) and on peer behavior (e.g., Rohrkemper, 1981). In much of this research, attention has been paid to the influence of factors such as grade level, classroom organization, and gender. These studies suggest that accurate assessment of the ability of peers is accomplished earlier

GENDER INFLUENCES
IN CLASSROOM INTERACTION
ISBN: 0-12-752075-9

than accurate assessment of self (Stipek, 1981; Blumenfeld, Pintrich, Meece, & Wessels, 1982); there is greater consensus about the comparative ability of peers in classrooms in which there is more public performance, for instance, in whole class instruction versus group instruction or group instruction versus individualized instruction (Rosenholtz & Wilson, 1980; Filby & Barnett, 1982); and both boys and girls in the early grades see girls as better behaved, more successful, and better liked by the teacher (Brophy & Good, 1974; Maccoby & Jacklin, 1974).

Several studies examined relationships between ability grouping and formation of friendship groups, indicating that friendships tend to be formed within ability groups (Rosenbaum, 1980). In one sociolinguistic study of pupil perceptions of classroom interaction, there were strong relationships between pupil ability in reading and pupil status with peers, as measured by a sociometric device (Morine-Dershimer & Tenenberg, 1981).

An important gap exists in the research on pupil perceptions of peers. Almost without exception, studies of pupil perceptions have used data collection procedures that ask pupils to report about characteristics of peers that are identified by the researchers as important. Thus, while we are accumulating more and more information about pupil perceptions of the ability and classroom behavior of peers, we have little evidence to suggest that these are characteristics that are particularly pertinent to pupils.

A somewhat different gap exists in the classroom interaction research. Studies of both pupil perceptions of classroom interaction and gender-related differences in classroom interaction have tended to focus on teacher–pupil interaction rather than on pupil–pupil interaction. Bossert (1983) argued that at upper elementary levels more attention must be paid to peer group influences on pupil perceptions of sex-appropriate behavior, because of the effects these groups may have on both attitudes and interactive behavior. Since stable peer relationships begin to emerge between fourth and sixth grades, the intermediate grades appear to be a particularly critical point at which to examine other aspects of pupil–pupil interaction as well.

This chapter reports on an exploratory study designed to address these two gaps in the literature. First, the study focuses on pupil perceptions of interactive characteristics of peers that were identified as important by pupils, rather than by researchers. Second, the study focuses on pupil–pupil interaction by examining friendship group patterns, as perceived by pupils. Because of prior research (Rosenbaum, 1980) noting the importance of classroom ability grouping procedures in formation of friendship groups, special attention was paid to relationships between friendship groups and ability groups as well as relationships between friendship groups and the interactive characteristics of peers as perceived by pupils.

This study addressed the following questions:

1. What do pupils identify as important interactive characteristics of their peers?
   (a) Do these vary by grade level or gender?
   (b) Are these related to classroom management systems?
2. Is membership in friendship groups more closely associated with reading group assignment or with the interactive characteristics of peers identified as important by pupils?

METHOD

This was a 2-year descriptive study using a structured interview technique to examine interactive characteristics of peers that were considered important by intermediate grade pupils, and the relationship that these characteristics might have to friendship groupings. Grade level, classroom management patterns, and gender were also studied as variables that might provide insight into these pupil perceptions of social interaction in classrooms.

Setting

The setting for the study was an elementary school located in a white, middle-class suburban community in central New York. The school community was remarkably stable, and most of the pupils involved in the study had attended the school for several years. Achievement in the school as a whole tended to be at or above national norms in basic skill areas.

Instructional grouping was a school-wide practice and was highly structured in the intermediate grades. There were three classrooms at each grade level. Each classroom had three reading groups, and at the end of the year a whole reading group was moved into a new classroom so that reading group membership was maintained virtually unchanged over several years. In addition, in the intermediate grades, pupils were grouped across classrooms, within each grade level, for instruction in spelling and mathematics. There were also three groups in each of these subjects, with one teacher taking the higher achievers, another the average achievers, and a third the low achievers. Children moved out of their "home" classroom into their assigned ability group for one period a day for each of these two subjects. As a result of this instructional grouping system, pupils knew which of their peers had achievement levels similar to their own in reading, math, and spelling within each classroom and across the grade level, but they had little information about performance of pupils in other ability groups.

Subjects

Subjects were 73 pupils in three classrooms. Pupils were interviewed in fourth grade and again in fifth grade in order to examine possible grade level changes in perceptions. Not all pupils in all classrooms agreed to be interviewed. In Classroom A, 12 girls and 11 boys participated out of a class of 15 girls and 13 boys. In Classroom B, 12 of 15 girls participated and 11 of 16 boys. In Classroom C, all 11 girls and 16 of 18 boys participated. Nonparticipants were quite evenly distributed across ability groups in reading within each classroom.

Data Collection

During the spring semester of each of the two school years, pupils were individually interviewed for a period of 20 to 30 minutes. Each pupil was presented with a randomly organized array of photographs of all his/her classmates, and a structured interview protocol was followed:

Interviewer: I know that there are a lot of things that you are taught in school, but I think that you probably learn a lot of things without being taught, too. I'm interested in finding out what you've learned about your classmates. Suppose I were a new kid coming into your class. What would be a good thing for me to know about the other kids? What would you want to tell me?

Pupil responds: (Typical responses were "They're nice," or "who they hang around with," or "who gets in trouble.")

Interviewer: Can you show me the kids who are nice (or who hang around together, or who get in trouble)? (Pupil points out photographs, and these are removed from the array. Each photograph has a subject identification number on the back.) Okay, these are the kids who are nice. What about these others (remaining photographs)? Are they all alike as far as being nice, or would you divide them up somehow? (Process is continued until no more groups are formed. Pupil description of the characteristic of each group is recorded, in addition to the subject identification number of each group member. Photographs are returned to the random array.)

Interviewer: All right, you've told me one thing about the kids in your class. What else would be good for me to know if I were a new kid coming into your class? (Entire process is repeated until the pupil has formed groups based on three different types of characteristics.)

Interviews were conducted outside the classroom during the school day. All pupils in a given class were interviewed over a 2-day period.

Interaction in each classroom was observed informally on three separate occasions within a month's span to identify general management procedures, and teachers were asked to explain their grouping, seating, and discipline practices. Observations and interview data were recorded in written notations immediately following each classroom visit.

Data Analysis

The descriptions of their classmates generated by pupils were analyzed to identify the general types of interactive characteristics attended to, and seven general categories were identified, based on the "labels" used by pupils to explain differences among the groups they formed. Overall patterns of emphasis on various types of characteristics were identified, and comparisons of category emphasis were made by grade level, classroom, and gender.

Whenever more than a third of the pupils interviewed in a given classroom identified a particular type of characteristic as important, a detailed analysis was made of the rankings or pairings[1] of individual pupils, as reported by every pupil responding. A composite rating[2] or pairing[3] was developed to arrive at overall groupings that seemed to reflect the general class perception of the ranking or pairing of individual pupils with regard to that characteristic. Similarly, whenever more than half of the boys or girls interviewed in a given classroom identified a particular characteristic as important, a composite rating or pairing was developed to arrive at groupings that seemed to reflect the girls' (or boys') perceptions of individual pupils.[4]

In each of the three fifth-grade classrooms more than two-thirds of the pupils interviewed reported friendship patterns.[5] Comparisons were made of friendship patterns reported by boys versus girls to identify similarities and differences. Friendship patterns identified by each group were compared to reading group membership, and to composite ratings based on other interactive characteristics identified as important by the same group of pupils, to identify the peer characteristics that might contribute to friendship patterns within each classroom, for each gender.[6] Comparisons were made within classrooms of boys' versus girls' perceptions of the friendliness of both boys and girls, to identify similarities and differences in perceptions of same-sex and opposite-sex peers.

Descriptive statistics and graphics have been used to summarize the data. Interpretations are based on findings from prior classroom research (e.g., Brophy & Good, 1974; Stipek, 1981) and from child development theory. The findings of this small-scale exploratory study should be viewed as possibilities to be examined in greater depth in more extensive research. This chapter concentrates on the findings associated with classroom and gender-related differences in the interactive characteristics of pupils associated with friendship groupings.

FINDINGS

The basic findings of this study were that (1) the interactive characteristics of peers identified as important by pupils varied by grade level, by gender, and by classroom management system; (2) the interactive characteristics of peers identified by these pupils were somewhat different than those most frequently identified by researchers in other studies; (3) reading group assignment was not a more important component of friendship groups than the important interactive characteristics of peers identified by pupils; and (4) the most important components of friendship groups varied by gender, and for boys the important components varied by classroom management system.

General Patterns

ACHIEVEMENT AND CLASSROOM MANAGEMENT

The three classrooms in this study were rather different with regard to both reading achievement and classroom management procedures. Table 11.1 shows pupil distribution across the fifth-grade classrooms by reading achievement levels. In Mrs. Avery's class (fictitious names are used throughout) high-achieving pupils clearly predominated. In Mr. Bentley's class there was a more evenly distributed range from high average to low average, with a low-achieving group consisting only of boys. In Mr. Crouse's class pupils were predominantly low in achievement, and there were more boys than girls at each reading level (18 boys to 11 girls overall). These class configurations were essentially unchanged from the fourth grade. In fact, from fourth to fifth grade, only three pupils changed in classroom assignment.[7]

Table 11.1

Pupil Distribution by Gender within Reading Achievement Levels

Class		High	High average	Average	Low average	Low
				Reading level		
Mrs. Avery's	Boys	6	6	0	2	0
	Girls	6	5	0	3	0
	Total	12 (43%)	11 (39%)	0	5 (18%)	0
	($n = 28$)					
Mr. Bentley's	Boys		4	0	5	7
	Girls		8	0	7	0
	Total		12 (39%)	0	12 (39%)	7 (23%)
	($n = 31$)					
Mr. Crouse's	Boys	0	0	8	6	4
	Girls	0	0	5	3	3
	Total	0	0	13 (45%)	9 (31%)	7 (24%)
	($n = 29$)					

In addition, these three classrooms varied in task orientation, in the amount of social interaction with peers permitted by the teacher, and in the degree to which teachers engaged in disciplinary action with pupils. The higher achieving class was more task-oriented, was permitted and engaged in less social interaction (e.g., reading instruction was individualized), and required little or no disciplinary action. The middle-achieving class was also task-oriented and required little disciplinary action but was permitted much more social interaction with peers. Pupils were encouraged to help each other with their work. The lower achieving class was not highly task-oriented, social interaction was discouraged by the teacher, though it clearly occurred, and the teacher spent a good deal of class time in disciplinary action, frequently recording names of transgressors on the chalkborad. This pattern of variation over the three classes was consistent over 2 years in both the fourth and the fifth grades, and this was at least partially due to the fact that the principal selected a teacher with a "suitable style" to work with each class.

PUPIL INTERACTIVE CHARACTERISTICS
IDENTIFIED

In total, 217 "important things to know" about classmates were identified by the 73 pupils interviewed at the fifth-grade level. These characteristics were rather readily organizable into seven general categories. In order of frequency of use, these categories were friends, nice–friendly versus un-friendly–mean, classroom behavior, talent–interest, smart–achievement, personality, and enemies. Examples of pupil language associated with identi-fication of these characteristics follow:

1. *Friends.* Who they hang around with, who sticks together, they stick around together and sit together at lunch, go to lunch together and play together;

2. *Nice–friendly versus unfriendly–mean.* Kids that pick on us and tease, nice (don't holler at you for things you do), who calls me names, don't say things that hurt others, don't like others, good to borrow things from, would help you get acquainted, hang around in own group and wouldn't want to be bothered, helpful (if you have a problem, they'll help you out, school work or not);

3. *Classroom behavior.* Kids that get their work done, kids who get in trouble for fooling around, always get in trouble, talk a lot and get in trouble, talk a little and get away with it, usually get their names on the board, get their work done on time;

4. *Talent–interest.* All have sticker collections, all like sports, make up their own video games, all like rock music, like wrestling, play football on the same team, do kung fu and karate, like electronic games, like to draw pictures, collect baseball and football cards, play instruments (clarinet, trumpet, drums, flute);

5. *Smart–achievement.* Do good work in class, real intelligent, all in the same reading group, slower than other kids so don't make fun of them, smart and tell you things, talk a lot when the teacher's asking questions, not very smart, who goes to "Delphi" (the special program for gifted children);

6. *Personality.* Tell jokes all the time, brag a lot about what they got and how much it cost, bossy and like to tell others what to do, leaders and like to organize clubs and plays, kids who are selfish, think they're great at every-thing, giggle all the time; and

7. *Enemies.* The worst enemies, don't like each other and fight a lot, get into fights with each other, who dislike each other.

Figure 11.1 shows the proportions of fifth-grade pupils interviewed who identified each of these seven types of interactive characteristics as impor-tant things to know about their peers. It is worth noting that social charac-teristics (e.g., nice vs. mean) are mentioned much more frequently than academic characteristics (smart–achievement), and that attention to inter-action with peers (e.g., friends) is much stronger than attention to interac-tion with the teacher (classroom behavior). Apparently these pupils consid-ered that the important things to know were how their classmates fit into

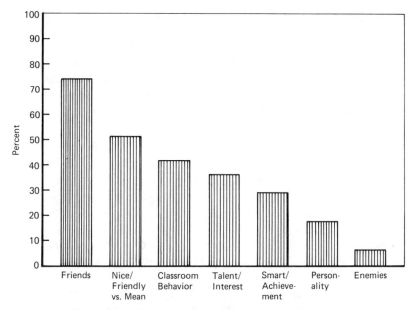

Figure 11.1 Types of categories formed overall ($n = 73$).

the classroom social structure, and primarily the peer group structure, rather than the instructional–management structure.

GRADE LEVEL DIFFERENCES

Only one major change in the frequency of mention of the seven types of pupil characteristics was observed from fourth grade to fifth grade for the 67 pupils who were interviewed in both years. The emphasis on friendship patterns increased drastically from fourth to fifth grade (44% of pupils responding to 73%). There was an 8% decrease in pupils mentioning nice–friendly versus unfriendly–mean. All other categories showed shifts of only 5% or less between the 2 years.

GENDER DIFFERENCES

At the fifth-grade level there were clear differences between boys and girls with regard to emphasis on particular types of categories. Friendliness and classroom behavior as important characteristics were mentioned much more frequently by girls than by boys (60 to 42%, 49 to 37%, respectively). Talents and interests and academic ability as important characteristics were mentioned much more frequently by boys than by girls (47 to 23%, 37 to 20%, respectively). Friendship patterns were of greatest importance for both groups, and personality and enemies were both mentioned with relatively low frequency by both groups. Thus, while social relationships with peers were important for both groups, patterns of social interaction with both peers and teacher were emphasized more by girls, while special interest–ability and achievement were emphasized more by boys.

CLASSROOM DIFFERENCES

There were also clear classroom differences at the fifth-grade level in emphasis on particular characteristics as important things to know about peers. In all three classrooms, friendship patterns were the most frequently mentioned item (A = 74%, B = 78%, C = 70%), and enemies were the least frequently mentioned (A = 1%, B = 4%, C = 0%). In Mrs. Avery's class, secondary emphasis was placed about equally on who was nice versus mean (48%) and who was smart or achieved well (43%). In Mr. Bentley's class, secondary emphasis was strongly focused on who was nice–friendly (65%). Meanness was rarely mentioned. In Mr. Crouse's class, secondary emphasis focused strongly on classroom behavior (67%), and there was also a reasonably strong third level of emphasis on talents and interest (48%) and who was nice–friendly (41%).

It is worth noting that pupil mention of who was smart or achieving well was most heavily emphasized in the highest achieving class and least heavily emphasized in the lowest achieving class (A = 43%, B = 30%, C = 17%). Instead of achievement, the lowest achieving class emphasized the talents and interests of peers. Furthermore, classroom behavior was least emphasized in the class which was quietest and most highly task-oriented, and most heavily emphasized in the class which was the least task-oriented and the most frequent recipient of teacher disciplinary action (A = 22%, B = 35%, C = 57%). Finally, the class in which the teacher permitted and encouraged the most social interaction among peers was the one which most strongly emphasized who was nice and friendly. It appears that pupil patterns of emphasis on interactive characteristics of peers were associated with classroom differences in instructional–management systems.

GENDER DIFFERENCES WITHIN CLASSROOMS

When gender differences are examined within classrooms, the classroom differences are even more striking (see Figure 11.2). Within each of the three classrooms, boys and girls placed about equal emphasis on friendship

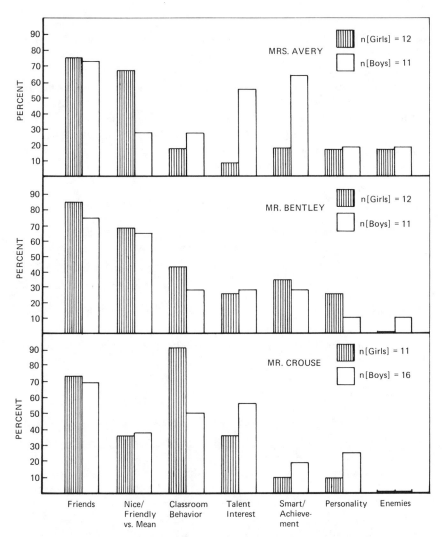

Figure 11.2   Categories formed: Gender differences within classrooms.

patterns, but there the similarities ended. Mr. Bentley's middle-achieving, socially interactive class was notable in that there were almost no differences in the patterns of emphasis of boys as compared to girls. In Mrs. Avery's high-achieving class, where little social interaction was permitted during work periods, girls put heavy emphasis on who was nice–friendly versus mean, while boys mentioned it only occasionally (67 to 27%). Boys placed heavy emphasis on who was smart and achieving as well as on the talents and interests of peers, while girls almost ignored these characteristics (64 to 17%, and 55 to 8%, respectively). In Mr. Crouse's low-achieving class, where teacher disciplinary action was commonplace, girls placed much stronger emphasis on classroom behavior than did boys (91 to 50%), while boys placed much stronger emphasis on talents and interests than did girls (56 to 36%). Thus the tendency for girls to focus more on social characteristics and for boys to focus more on achievement and interest–ability characteristics was enacted differently in these three classrooms that differed in patterns of academic ability, social interaction among peers, and teacher–pupil interaction related to discipline.

SUMMARY

The general patterns of pupil perceptions of important interactive characteristics of their peers in these three classrooms showed grade level differences, gender differences, and classroom differences. Within classrooms, gender differences followed a variety of forms that seem to reflect classroom differences in instructional–management systems. The remaining sections of this report explore classroom differences, particularly gender differences within classrooms, in more detail, focusing on relationships between interactive characteristics of pupils and friendship groupings.

Friendship Patterns

The patterns of friendship groupings identified by pupils in this study differed both by classroom and by gender. In general, the classroom that permitted the least social interaction exhibited the largest and most closed friendship groups, while the two classrooms where more peer interaction occurred (with or without teacher approval) exhibited smaller and more open friendship groups. In each of the three classrooms girls identified more friendship linkages for girls than boys did, while boys identified more friendship linkages for boys than girls did. It was not uncommon for boys to place all girls together in a group and say "they all hang around together." Girls were more apt to identify two or three friendship pairs for boys, then say, "I'm not sure about the others." Because of these differences in awareness, girls' responses have been used as the most accurate indicator of girls' friendship groups, while boys' responses have been used as the most accurate indicator of boys' friendship groups.

Although prior research has tended to indicate strong relationships between friendship groups and reading group membership, there was strong evidence that reading group membership was not the most important com-

Table 11.2

Proportional Distribution of Friendship Pairs within and across Reading Groups

Friendship pairs	Mrs. Avery's class		Mr. Bentley's class		Mr. Crouse's class	
	Girls	Boys	Girls	Boys	Girls	Boys
Within-group	.49	.36	.43	.26	.28	.41
Across-group	.51	.64	.57	.74	.72	.59

ponent of friendship groups for these pupils. Table 11.2 presents findings on the proportionate number of identified friendship pairs that were members of the same reading group (within-group pairs) compared to the proportionate number of identified friendship pairs that were members of different reading groups (across-group pairs), as identified by boys and girls in each classroom. In *no instance* were half of the identified friendship pairs members of the same reading group. Thus, these pupils consistently identified friendship pairs that were formed across reading groups. Accordingly, friendship groupings within each classroom were analyzed carefully to determine what interactive characteristics might be considered more important components of friendship patterns.

MRS. AVERY'S CLASS

Mrs. Avery's class was the highest achieving of the three classes, and social interaction among peers during the course of instruction was clearly not encouraged in this classroom. Pupils in this class reported rather large, closed friendship groups as the norm, and these friendship groups were more closely tied to reading group membership than in the other classrooms, particularly for girls. Figure 11.3 shows the friendship groups of boys (as perceived by boys) and girls (as perceived by girls) and illustrates the distribution of these perceived friendship groups over reading groups.[8] In this classroom, reading group membership appeared to be a more important component of girls' friendship groups than of boys' friendship groups (i.e., friendship groups were more completely composed of members of a single reading group), but it was clearly not the only important component for either. To identify other possible important components, we turn to the peer characteristics identified as important by pupils in this classroom.

Eight of the 11 boys interviewed (73%) identified friendship patterns as an important interactive characteristic of peers. After friendship patterns, the second most frequently identified pupil characteristic for boys in this class was smart–helpful. Seven of 11 boys (64%) mentioned this character-

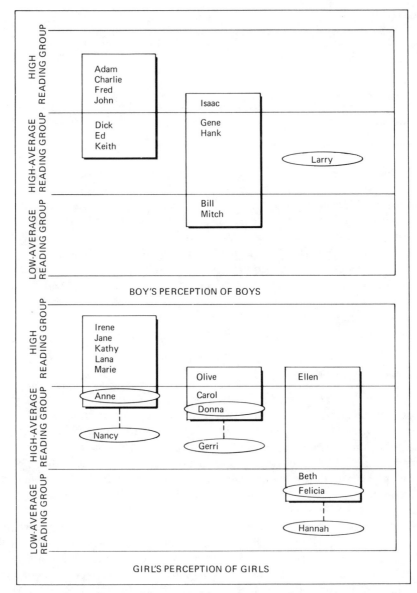

Figure 11.3 Distribution of friendship groups over reading groups: Mrs. Avery's class.

istic. Based on composite rankings by boys, four groups of boys were formed, ranging from very smart–helpful to not smart–helpful. Friendship pairs were analyzed according to this division, and .49 of the identified friendship pairs ($n = 158$) were within-group pairs (i.e., were perceived as belonging in the same category on this interactive characteristic of smart–helpful) compared with .36 within-group pairs based on reading group membership.

The next most frequently identified characteristic for boys in Mrs. Avery's class was special talents–interests (identified by 55% of boys). The only two types of talents–interests specified were sports and music. Pupils were identified as participating in a variety of sports and playing a variety of instruments. Where two or more pupils were mentioned as sharing a common interest in a particular sport, they were noted as paired on this characteristic. Friendship pairs were analyzed according to this characteristic, and .77 of the identified friendship pairs were within-group pairs.

Clearly, the most important component of friendship groups for boys in this class was a shared interest in sports. It is worth noting that the only pupil-perceived isolate in this class, Larry, was a boy in the middle reading group who exhibited no interest in sports, while Isaac, the only member of the top reading group who was not included in the largest (and presumably most prestigious) boys' friendship group, also exhibited no interest in sports.

Nine of the 11 girls (75%) interviewed in Mrs. Avery's class identified friendship patterns as an important interactive characteristic of peers. The second most frequently mentioned characteristic was nice–friendly versus mean (identified by 67% of girls). Based on composite rankings by girls on this characteristic, three groups of girls were formed, ranging from very nice to okay. Friendship pairs were analyzed according to this characteristic, and .62 of the identified friendship pairs ($n = 204$) were within-group pairs compared to .49 within-group pairs based on reading group membership.

Anne and Nancy, the only two girls from the middle reading group associated with the largest (and presumably most prestigious) girls' friendship group, were rated as very nice. Only two of the top reading group, Irene and Ellen, did not receive this high rating. Nonetheless, Irene was included in the large friendship group but Ellen was not. It is worth noting that Ellen and Gerri were the only two girls identified by boys as having interest and ability in sports. Ellen was excluded from the large girls' friendship group and was associated instead with the three lowest achievers among the girls, even though she was a high achiever. Gerri was perceived as linked in friendship with Donna but was not included as a full member of Donna's small friendship group. Thus, for girls in this classroom, friendliness was a more important component of friendship group membership than reading group membership, while interest and ability in sports may have led to exclusion from the more prestigious friendship groups.

MR. BENTLEY'S CLASS

Mr. Bentley's class was mainly composed of average achievers, students were generally task-oriented, and social interaction among peers was encouraged by the teacher. Friendship groups identified by pupils in this classroom tended to be small (only two or three pupils), with many pupils seen as linked in friendship rather than tightly bonded. Boys' friendship groups cut across reading groups. This was also true for girls' friendship groups, although the possibilities for wide distribution were limited since there were no girls in the lowest reading group in this class.

Ten of the 12 girls interviewed (83%) and 8 of 11 boys interviewed (73%) identified friendship patterns as an important interactive characteristic of peers. For both boys and girls in this class, the second most frequently mentioned pupil characteristic was nice–friendly (67% of girls and 64% of boys identified this as an important characteristic). Based on composite ratings, four groups of pupils were identified, ranging from very nice to not always friendly. Friendship pairs were analyzed according to this division, and .40 of the identified friendship pairs for boys ($n = 143$) were within-group pairs compared with .26 within-group pairs based on reading group membership. For girls, .56 of the identified friendship pairs ($n = 126$) were within-group pairs based on friendliness compared with .43 within-group pairs based on reading group membership.

It is interesting to note that a member of the middle reading group, who appeared to be the only class isolate, was rated as a very nice–friendly boy, suggesting that his status was more that of a pupil who interacted with everyone about equally than that of a pupil shunned by all. Also, a boy from the top reading group who was linked in friendship with three other boys, including two from the low reading group, was rated as very nice–friendly. The three boys who constituted the most closed friendship group were all rated as okay, that is, not particularly friendly. Also, the two girls who constituted the only girls' friendship pair without friendship linkages were both rated as not so friendly. Thus, for both boys and girls in this class, the pupil-perceived characteristic of nice–friendly appeared to be a more important component of friendship groups than membership in reading groups.

MR. CROUSE'S CLASS

Mr. Crouse's class was the lowest achieving of the three classes and the least task-oriented. Peer interaction was rarely task-directed and was clearly discouraged by the teacher, who regularly recorded on the chalkboard the names of pupils who were talking out of turn. Friendship groups in this classroom were small (two to three pupils) and fairly open (i.e., there were a number of friendship linkages to tight friendship groups), particularly for girls. The girls' friendship groups were more widely distributed across reading groups than the boys' friendship groups, but in neither case were friendship groups tightly defined by reading group membership.

Eleven of the 16 boys (69%) interviewed in this class identified friendship patterns as an important interactive characteristic of peers. After friendship patterns, the second most frequently mentioned pupil characteristic for boys in this class was special talents–interests (56% of boys responding identified this characteristic). Boys in Mr. Crouse's class specified a much wider variety of special interests than did boys in Mrs. Avery's class. Activities mentioned for boys included drawing, playing video games, listening to rock music, playing football, and doing kung fu and judo. The only activity mentioned for girls was collecting stickers. In almost all instances, boys identified as close friends shared a common interest. This was not as true for boys seen as more loosely linked in friendship. Friendship pairs were analyzed according to these shared interests, and .32 of the identified friendship pairs for boys ($n = 190$) were within-group pairs compared with .41 within-group pairs based on reading group membership. Thus, for boys in this class, in contrast to boys in Mrs. Avery's high-achieving class, shared abilities and interests were apparently a less important component of friendship groups than reading group membership.

Classroom behavior was also a frequently mentioned pupil characteristic for boys in this classroom (50% of boys identified this characteristic). Based on composite ratings, there were four groups of boys ranging from seldom in trouble to always in trouble. Friendship pairs were analyzed according to this division, and .41 of the identified friendship pairs were with-group pairs. The largest boys' friendship group comprised mostly boys rated as always in trouble or often in trouble. Clearly, staying out of trouble did not guarantee a boy a place in the social circle in this class, for three of the four isolates were reported as seldom in trouble or only sometimes in trouble.

Neither classroom behavior nor special interests defined boys' friendship groups in this classroom any more completely than reading group membership, although classroom behavior was as strong an indicator as reading group placement.

For girls in Mr. Crouse's classroom, classroom behavior was the most frequently mentioned pupil characteristic, looming even larger than friendship groups (91% of girls identified classroom behavior as important, while only 73% mentioned friendship groups). Friendship pairs were analyzed across four categories (from never in trouble to often in trouble), and .30 of the identified friendship pairs ($n = 115$) were within-group pairs compared with .28 within-group pairs based on reading group membership.

The third most frequently mentioned pupil characteristic for girls in Mr. Crouse's class was nice–friendly (36% of girls interviewed identified this as an important characteristic). Based on composite ratings, four groups of girls were identified ranging from very friendly to sometimes friendly. Friendship pairs were analyzed according to this characteristic because it was such an important characteristic for girls in general, although it was less emphasized by girls in this classroom, and .37 of the identified friendship pairs were within-group pairs.

All of the friendship linkages and "extra" friendship pairs that were reported involved girls rated as very friendly. Girls as a whole were rated high on the nice–friendly scale, a fact which seems to corroborate the picture of social cohesiveness suggested by the numberous friendship linkages. Thus, though the nice–friendly characteristic was not a frequently mentioned pupil characteristic for girls in this class, it may have been a somewhat more important component of friendship groups than reading group membership.

SUMMARY

In each of the three classrooms reading group placement was an important component of friendship group membership for boys and girls, but in no instance was it the only important component or the most important component. Table 11.3 summarizes the data on proportions of within-group pairs for all three classrooms. For girls in each of the three classrooms, peer ratings on the nice–friendly characteristic was an important component of membership in friendship groups, and this was also true for boys in Mr. Bentley's classroom, the middle-achieving, socially interactive class, where boys' and girls' perceptions were very similar. For boys in Mrs. Avery's class (high-achieving), academic achievement and shared interests in sports were important components of membership in friendship groups. For boys in Mr. Crouse's class (low-achieving, frequent disciplinary action) ratings on classroom behavior were just as important as reading group membership, while shared interests were less important.

In all instances, the important components of friendship groups were the second or third most frequently mentioned pupil characteristic. Friendship groups themselves were the most frequently mentioned by all pupils except

Table 11.3

Within-Group Proportions of Identified Friendship Pairs

Class	Reading group membership	Nice– friendly	Classroom behavior	Talent– interest	Smart– achievement
Mrs. Avery's					
Boys	.36			.77	.49
Girls	.49	.62			
Mr. Bentley's					
Boys	.26	.40			
Girls	.43	.56			
Mr. Crouse's					
Boys	.41		.41	.32	
Girls	.28	.37	.30		

the girls in Mr. Crouse's class, who mentioned classroom behavior most frequently. Thus, the interactive characteristics of peers most frequently reported as important to know were characteristics which apparently contributed to membership in particular friendship groups. This underscores the general finding that information on patterns of interaction with peers was typically regarded as more important knowledge than information on patterns of interaction with the teacher.

Friendliness within and across Gender

The segregation of genders within these three classrooms was apparent in a variety of ways. First, no cross-gender friendship pairs were identified in any of the three classrooms, though in some cases boys who teased girls or girls who liked boys were identified. This is not surprising at either the fourth- or fifth-grade level, given normal patterns of child development. In addition to this, however, boys consistently began their selection of pupils to be categorized by picking other boys, and many ended by lumping all or most girls together in a single, undifferentiated mass of "others." Girls also typically began by categorizing other girls, then moving on to form groups of boys, or add boys to the groups already formed.

Given this gender split, we might expect to find differences in the perceptions of boys and girls with regard to rating of the same and the opposite sex as well as with regard to pupil characteristics deemed important. This was indeed the case for pupils in this study. Table 11.4 presents comparative mean ratings for nice–friendly, for each of the three classes, organized by the gender doing the rating and being rated. Without exception, girls rated

Table 11.4

Comparative Mean Ratings for Nice–Friendly:
within Gender and across Gender[a]

	Rated	
Raters	Girls	Boys
Mrs. Avery's class	($n = 12$)	($n = 11$)
Girls	1.44	1.87
($n = 8$)		
Boys	1.80	1.46
($n = 3$)		
Mr. Bentley's class	($n = 12$)	($n = 11$)
Girls	1.59	1.99
($n = 8$)		
Boys	1.69	1.63
($n = 7$)		
Mr. Crouse's class	($n = 11$)	($n = 16$)
Girls	1.32	1.81
($n = 4$)		
Boys	1.89	1.56
($n = 6$)		

[a] Ratings ranged from 1 (very friendly) to 3 (not so
friendly). Higher ratings denote more *un*friendliness.

boys as less friendly than girls, and boys rated girls as less friendly than boys.
These differences in mean ratings were strong except for the boys in Mr.
Bentley's class, who rated girls as only slightly less friendly than boys. Thus,
for most pupils in these classes, the absence of cross-gender friendship pairs
was accompanied by perceptions that members of the opposite gender
were not as friendly as members of the same sex. Boys in the middle-
achieving class, where the teacher permitted social interaction during instructional periods, were the only exception to this general rule.

DISCUSSION

The developing importance of friendship groups from fourth to fifth
grade, denoted by the large increase in pupils reporting this as an important
characteristic, as well as the fact that it was the first characteristic mentioned by 30 of the 73 pupils interviewed, was to be expected, given the
strong evidence from child development studies that more stable friendship
patterns begin to emerge in the early intermediate grades. For pupils in this

study, it was important to know which peers belonged to which friendship group and what might help you find a place in the friendship system, that is, the interactive characteristics that were associated with membership in friendship groups. These characteristics differed by gender, and for boys they differed by classroom. The girls' emphasis on being nice–friendly could be interpreted as reflective of sex-role stereotypes that girls are more cooperative. The emphasis of Mrs. Avery's boys on shared interest in sports, and of Mr. Crouse's boys on classroom behavior, could be interpreted as reflective of sex-role stereotypes that boys are more competitive and more resistant to authority. It is therefore particularly interesting to note that the class which showed the least gender difference in pupil perceptions, the class that might be considered the most integrated, the class in which being nice–friendly was an important component of boys' friendship groups, was Mr. Bentley's middle-achieving and socially interactive class.

The peer characteristics usually emphasized by researchers were not those that were most frequently mentioned as important by pupils in this study, except where these characteristics were a distinguishing feature of the classroom as a whole. Thus, pupil ability (smart–helpful) was emphasized by pupils in Mrs. Avery's high-achieving class, and classroom behavior was emphasized in Mr. Crouse's non-task-oriented, frequently disciplined class. These were particularly important interactive characteristics for boys in Mrs. Avery's class and for girls in Mr.Crouse's class, but in neither case were they the most important components of friendship groups as perceived by these pupils. One interpretation of this may be that these characteristics of peers only stand out as particularly important when they are heavily emphasized by the teacher in interaction with pupils (this was the case for both Mrs. Avery and Mr. Crouse).

As suggested by prior research, ability grouping in reading within the class (as distinguished from pupil categories of who was especially smart or not so smart) was a component of friendship group formations. This was most apparent for girls in Mrs. Avery's high-achieving class. However, in no case was ability grouping the most important component of friendship groups. Thus, the possible effects of instructional grouping systems on friendship patterns in these classrooms could be seen as mitigated to some degree by nonacademic qualities of the individual pupils as perceived by their peers.

Given the highly sex-segregated friendship groups, both boys and girls were quite probably "accurate" in their perceptions of peers, that is, boys rated boys as more friendly than girls, while girls rated girls as more friendly than boys. With regard to openness and inclusiveness of peer interaction, it is especially interesting to note that the more open friendship groups were found in the two classrooms where most peer interaction occurred. Mrs.

Avery's high-achieving class, where peer interaction during work time was not encouraged, was typified by large, closed friendship groups. Although there were boys who were isolates in each of the three classrooms, in Mr. Bentley's class, where pupil interaction over schoolwork was actively encouraged, the only "isolate" was viewed as a very nice–friendly boy, so that his lack of specific linkages to other boys appeared to be a result of his general friendliness with all. In Mr. Crouse's class, on the other hand, where pupil interaction during work time was negatively sanctioned or actively discouraged by the teacher, there were four isolates among 18 boys, and three of these were viewed as isolates even though they shared special interests with other boys in the class. There were no girls viewed as total isolates by girls in any of the three classrooms, thus the friendship patterns of girls were more inclusive than those of boys.

These patterns of openness and inclusiveness could be interpreted to suggest that the most difficult class for girls socially was Mrs. Avery's high-achieving class, while the most difficult class for boys socially was Mr. Crouse's low-achieving, heavily disciplined class. In Mrs. Avery's class, the girls' friendship groups were both most closed and most highly bound by reading group membership. In Mr. Crouse's class, while boys' friendship groups were more open and less closely associated with reading group membership, four boys were seen as isolated from the friendship formation. Is it merely coincidence that the class that might be expected to be the most academically competitive was most difficult for girls socially, while the class that might be expected to be least academically competitive was the most difficult for boys socially? Perhaps the most important finding of this study is the importance that pupils, even academically able pupils, place on the social aspects of classroom interaction, and the possible relationships between classroom management systems and gender-related differences in peer interaction.

The results of this study suggest that we may learn much from investigations of pupil perceptions of pupil–pupil interaction that utilize pupil-identified characteristics rather than researcher-identified characteristics of pupils. In these three classrooms, pupils did differ from researchers in their selection of important interactive characteristics of peers. Furthermore, the characteristics identified as important by pupils were generally more important components of friendship group membership than reading group placement, which has been so frequently cited in the literature as a highly influential factor in formation of friendship groups.

It is inappropriate to recommend implications for classroom practice based on an exploratory study of this nature, but the results suggest some important considerations with regard to practice. The problem of identifying productive learning environments is a serious one, according to the evidence presented in several other studies reported in this volume. Fennema and Peterson (see Chapter 2) note that when instruction was provided in sex-integrated learning groups, girls performed better on high-level mathematics problems and further, that low-achieving girls learned more in cooperative groups, while high-achieving boys learned less. Wilkinson, Lindow, and Chiang (see Chapter 9) indicate that in peer-directed study groups girls requesting information were frequently insulted by boys. Webb and Kenderski (see Chapter 10) report that males were more successful than females in obtaining help from peers in small-group interaction in high-achieving classes, because females were responsive to males' requests for help, while males were unresponsive to females' requests. In each of these cases the social aspects of the instructional management system employed seem to be affecting the cognitive outcomes. Further, the indications are that what is a productive learning environment for females may be unproductive for males and vice versa.

In this study it seems clear that students have a social agenda that may supersede the teacher's academic agenda in the classroom. Until we understand more about how this social agenda may be related to various instructional management systems, and how it may in turn relate to cognitive outcomes, we need to be very careful about recommending changes in classroom settings or interactive procedures. Further studies of pupil perceptions of pupil–pupil interaction, undertaken in a wider variety of classroom management systems, are essential in the development of a deeper understanding of these phenomena.

As a descriptive study of pupils in three classrooms in one school, this study can only provide us with information on the patterns of gender-related differences in pupil perceptions of classroom interaction that are possible and that have occurred in a given setting. To determine the probability that similar patterns occur in other settings, we need more extensive research. The exploratory findings reported here suggest that such research might be potentially productive of interesting and useful information.

NOTES

[1] Characteristics involving ranking of some students as better than others were used to develop pupil ratings. These included such categories as smart, gets in trouble, and nice–friendly. Characteristics not involving ranking included friendship groups and groups of students sharing similar interests or talents (sports participants, musicians, etc.). These reports were used to develop pupil pairings.

[2] Based on language used by the individual pupil in describing characteristics of pupil groups formed, each such group was labeled as high, average, or low on a given characteristic, and this was recorded as a 1 (high), 2, or 3 (low) rating. All ratings for each individual pupil on that

characteristic were combined to obtain a mean rating for that pupil as perceived by the class in general (all pupils reporting on that particular characteristic). Similarly, mean ratings were obtained to reflect the perceptions of girls in general (all girls reporting) or boys in general (all boys reporting).

[3] When friendship groups or special interest groups were reported, each group member was recorded as having been "paired" with every other group member (thus a four-member group yielded six pairs). When half of the pupils reporting identified a particular pair of pupils as friends or as sharing similar interests, this was counted as a generally perceived pairing. Where several pupils were generally perceived to be paired, each with all or most of the others, they were counted as a generally perceived group. In some instances, a pupil was perceived as paired in friendship with another pupil by over a third of the pupils responding, but less than half. In these cases, the pupil was counted as "linked" in friendship to the second pupil, rather than tightly "tied" in friendship.

[4] Final category placement for each pupil was determined by use of means and standard deviations of ratings for each characteristic, separately for each gender in each classroom. For example, for girls in Classroom B the mean rating for friendliness, on a 3-point scale, with 1 being high, was 1.74, and the standard deviation was 0.216. Four categories were formed. "Very nice–friendly" included all girls whose ratings were more than one standard deviation below the mean, i.e., closer to a 1 rating. "Nice–friendly" included those whose ratings fell less than 1 standard deviation below the mean. "Okay" included those whose ratings fell less than 1 standard deviation above the mean. "Not always friendly" included those whose ratings fell more than 1 standard deviation above the mean.

[5] These friendship patterns differed from those typically reported in sociometric studies, for here pupils were reporting on who they perceived to be the friends of other pupils in the classroom, whereas typically they only report on who are their own friends.

[6] A limitation of this study results from the use of pupil-identified characteristics of peers. Since not all pupils identified the same characteristics of peers, no two characteristics were rated by exactly the same set of pupils. However, for each of the characteristics identified here as important components of friendship groups, well over half of the pupils who rated peers on the characteristic also were involved in the identification of friendship patterns.

[7] From fourth to fifth grade, one pupil was moved from the high-achieving to the middle-achieving class and two were moved from the low-achieving to the middle-achieving class. In addition, one student in the middle-achieving class and three students in the low-achieving class were repeating fifth grade. Three students in the low-achieving class were new to the school in fifth grade.

[8] Closed friendship groups are denoted graphically by a closed box in Figure 11.3. A broken line between two individuals indicates that they were "linked" in friendship pair.

REFERENCES

Blumenfeld, P., Pintrich, P., Meece, J., & Wessels, K. (1982). The formation and role of self-perceptions of ability in elementary classrooms. *Elementary School Journal, 82,* 401–420.

Bossert, S. (1983). Understanding sex differences in children's classroom experiences. In W. Doyle & T. Good (Eds.), *Focus on teaching.* Chicago: University of Chicago Press.

Brophy, J., & Good, T. (1974). *Teacher–student relationships: Causes and consequences.* New York: Holt, Rinehart & Winston.

Filby, N., & Barnett, B. (1982). Student perceptions of better readers in elementary classrooms. *Elementary School Journal, 82,* 435–449.

Maccoby, E., & Jacklin, C. (1974). *The psychology of sex differences.* Palo Alto, CA: Stanford University Press.

Morine-Dershimer, G., & Tenenberg, M. (1981). *Participant perspectives of classroom discourse. Executive summary.* Syracuse University, Division for the Study of Teaching. (Mimeograph)

Rohrkemper, M. (1981). *Classroom perspectives study: An investigation of differential perceptions of classroom events.* Unpublished doctoral dissertation, Michigan State University.

Rosenbaum, J. (1980). Social implications of educational grouping. In D. Berliner (Ed.), *Review of research in education* (No. 8). American Educational Research Association.

Rosenholtz, S., & Wilson, B. (1980). The effect of classroom structure on shared perceptions of ability. *American Educational Research Journal, 17,* 75–82.

Stipek, D. (1981). Children's perceptions of their own and their classmates' ability. *Journal of Educational Psychology, 73,* 404–410.

Weinstein, R. (1983). Student perceptions of schooling. *Elementary School Journal, 83,* 287–312.

Author Index

Numbers in italic show the page on which the complete reference is cited.

A

Abrams, P., 73, *75*
Acland, H., 73, *76*
Adler, T., 27, *33,* 102–103, 111, *114,* 134, 135, *142*
Aiken, L. R., 19, *32,* 199, *206*
Alexander, K., 58, *77*
Allport, G. W., 173, *183*
Amarel, M., 174, *183*
Amidon, E., 136, *141*
Anderson, K. E., 40, *54*
Anderson, L., 126, 127, *141*
Anyon, J., 58, *75*
Apple, M., 58, 73, *75*
Armstrong, J. M., 38, *54*
Astin, H. S., 38, *55*
Auer, C., 131, *142*
Austin, D., 115, *141*
Ayres, L., 115, *141*

B

Bailey, M. M., 79, *114*
Baird, J. E., 39, 40, *55*
Bane, M., 73, *76*
Bank, B., 131, *141*
Bardwick, J. M., 21, *32*

Barker, R. G., 145, *164*
Barnett, B., 237, 238, *261*
Bar-Tal, D., 24, *32*
Baum, M., 126, 127, *141*
Bean, J. P., 39, *55*
Becker, A., 20, 24, 33, *35*
Becker, H., 59, 62, *75*
Becker, J., 26, *32,* 116, 133, 135, 141, *141*
Begle, E. G., 22, *32*
Benbow, C., 20, *32,* 38, *55*
Berger, J., 59, *75,* 182, *183,* 230, *234*
Berk, L. E., 3, 8, *14,* 168, 169, 172, *183,* 187, *206*
Best, R., 173, 182, *183*
Biber, H., 3, *14*
Biddle, B., 131, *141*
Bidwell, C., 59, *75*
Blakey, S., 127, *141*
Bledsoe, J. C., 40, *55*
Block, J. H., 6, *14*
Blumenfeld, P., 3, *14,* 82, 88, 90, *113, 114,* 238, *260*
Bogart, K., 176, *183*
Boocock, S., 59, *75*
Borgatta, E. F., 210, *234*
Bossert, S., 3, *14,* 62, 64, 76, 82, *113,* 238, *260*
Boswell, S., 112, *113*

263

Subject Index

A

EDUCATIONAL PSYCHOLOGY

continued from page ii

Phillip S. Strain and Mary Margaret Kerr. Mainstreaming of Children in Schools: Research and Programmatic Issues

Maureen L. Pope and Terence R. Keen. Personal Construct Psychology and Education

Ronald W. Henderson (ed.). Parent–Child Interaction: Theory, Research, and Prospects

W. Ray Rhine (ed.). Making Schools More Effective: New Directions from Follow Through

Herbert J. Klausmeier and Thomas S. Sipple. Learning and Teaching Concepts: A Strategy for Testing Applications of Theory

James H. McMillan (ed.). The Social Psychology of School Learning

M. C. Wittrock (ed.). The Brain and Psychology

Marvin J. Fine (ed.). Handbook on Parent Education

Dale G. Range, James R. Layton, and Darrell L. Roubinek (eds.). Aspects of Early Childhood Education: Theory to Research to Practice

Jean Stockard, Patricia A. Schmuck, Ken Kempner, Peg Williams, Sakre K. Edson, and Mary Ann Smith. Sex Equity in Education

James R. Layton. The Psychology of Learning to Read

Thomas E. Jordan. Development in the Preschool Years: Birth to Age Five

Gary D. Phye and Daniel J. Reschly (eds.). School Psychology: Perspectives and Issues

Norman Steinaker and M. Robert Bell. The Experiential Taxonomy: A New Approach to Teaching and Learning

J. P. Das, John R. Kirby, and Ronald F. Jarman. Simultaneous and Successive Cognitive Processes

Herbert J. Klausmeier and Patricia S. Allen. Cognitive Development of Children and Youth: A Longitudinal Study

Victor M. Agruso, Jr. Learning in the Later Years: Principles of Educational Gerontology

Thomas R. Kratochwill (ed.). Single Subject Research: Strategies for Evaluating Change

Kay Pomerance Torshen. The Mastery Approach to Competency-Based Education

Harvey Lesser. Television and the Preschool Child: A Psychological Theory of Instruction and Curriculum Development

Donald J. Treffinger, J. Kent Davis, and Richard E. Ripple (eds.). Handbook on Teaching Educational Psychology

Harry L. Hom, Jr., and Paul A. Robinson (eds.). Psychological Processes in Early Education

Educational Psychology Series